INTERNATIONAL SOCIETY FOR COMPARATIVE PHYSICAL
EDUCATION AND SPORT (ISCPES)

Ken Hardman/Joy Standeven (eds.)

Cultural Diversity and Congruence in Physical Education and Sport

Proceedings of the 10th ISCPES Biennial Conference 1996
in Hachi-ohji, Japan

Meyer & Meyer Sport

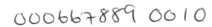

Die Deutsche Bibliothek – CIP-Einheitsaufnahme

Cultural diversity and congruence in physical education and sport :
1996 in Hachi-ohji, Japan / International Society for Comparative Physical
Education and Sport (ISCPES).
Ken Hardman / Joy Standeven (ed.).
– Aachen : Meyer und Meyer, 1998
(The proceedings of ... biennial conference of International Society for
Comparative Physical Education and Sport ... ; 10.1996)
ISBN 3-89124-557-2

© 1998 by Meyer & Meyer Sport, Aachen
Olten (CH), Vienna, Oxford,
Québec, Lansing/ Michigan, Adelaide, Auckland, Johannesburg
e-mail: verlag@meyer-meyer-sports.com • http://www.meyer-meyer-sports.com
Typesetting: Jonathan D. Hardman, Glossopdale Community College
Cover design: Walter J. Neumann, N&N Design-Studio, Aachen
Cover exposure: frw, Reiner Wahlen, Aachen
Printed and bound in Germany by
Firma Mennicken, Aachen
ISBN 3-89124-557-2

Contents

Acknowledgements

This collection of studies by contributors from the northern and southern hemispheres and representing occidental and oriental cultures and societies has been compiled from selected papers presented at the 10th Biennial Conference of the International Society for Comparative Physical Education and Sport (ISCPES). The Conference was held at the Inter-University Seminar House, Hachi-ohji, Tokyo, Japan 26 August-1 September 1996. I would like to take this opportunity to express gratitude to the delegates for their participation in the Conference and to the invited speakers George Sage, Hiromitsu Muta and Hebert Haag. Without their respective scholarly contributions, this compilation could not have happened. Special mention should also be made here of the joint recipients of the C. Lynn Vendien Scholarshp Award, Michael Letters (Australia) and Scott Martyn (Canada), both of whom gave outstanding presentations based on their investigative research.

Deep appreciation is extended to a hard-working Conference Organising Committee. Sadly, the preparatory planning phase of the Conference was marred by the unexpected death of Conference Committee Co-ordinator Mikio Maeda, a committed proponent of international activities and a kind and generous friend of, and mentor to, many. Despite this tragic setback, the Committee, under Chair, Yoshiro Hatano, and guided by Conference Secretary, Soichi Ichimura, strove enthusiastically to organise a successful meeting. It is rather invidious to single out other individuals who made distinctive contributions, however, amongst those who worked unselfishly to enhance the Conference administration, academic and social programmes were Noboro Ishikawa, Akihiko Kondo, Hiromi Miki and Masayuki Abo.

Appreciation is also extended to the International Council of Sport Science and Physical Education (ICSSPE) as well as to the ISCPES Executive Board for their subvention support for the publication of the Proceedings. The financial support from ISCPES is directly linked to a previous generous donation, by Sheikh Ahmad al-Fahad al-Sabah, President, Olympic Council of Asia and Kuwait Olympic Committee, in commemoration of his father, the late Sheikh Fahad al-Ahmad al-Sabah.

Sincere thanks are also due to Joy Standeven, whose assistance as co-editor of this book has been invaluable. Finally, I wish to acknowledge the support from my wife, Margaret, whose patience has known no bounds during the preparation of this manuscript and the inestimable contribution of my younger son, Jonathan, in preparing tables, figures and the final layout format of the text.

Ken Hardman,
Manchester, 1998

Contributors

Anna Barnett, University of Wales, U.K.

Alan M. Blum, Baylor College of Medicine, U.S.A.

Bob Carroll, University of Manchester, Manchester, U.K.

Robert Chappell, Brunel University College, Isleworth, U.K.

Mohammed Ehsani, Esfahan University, Esfahan, Iran

Adel Elnashar, El-Minia University, Egypt

Geir Espnes, University of Trondheim, Trondheim, Norway

Frank Fu, Hong Kong Baptist University, Kowloon, Hong Kong

Richard J. Fisher, St. Mary's University College, Twickenham, U.K.

Keith Gilbert, Queensland Technological University, Brisbane, Australia

Herbert Haag, University of Kiel, Kiel, Germany

Tadayuki Hanai, Gifu University of Education, Japan

Munehiko Harada, Osaka University of Health and Sport Sciences, Japan

Ken Hardman, University of Manchester, Manchester, U.K.

Ilse Hartmann-Tews, German Sport University, Cologne, Germany

Yoshiro Hatano, Tokyo Gakugei University, Tokyo, Japan

Sheila E. Henderson, University of London, London, U.K.

Jan Hoff, University of Trondheim, Trondheim, Norway

Miwako Hori, Nagoya University, Nagoya, Japan

Zou Da Hua, Shanghai Research Institute of Sports Science, Shanghai, People's Republic of China

Soichi Ichimura, University of Tsukuba, Tsukuba, Japan

Lu Da Jiang, University of Tokyo, Tokyo, Japan

Robyn L. Jones, Brunel University College, Isleworth, U.K.

Marian Jongmans, University of London, London, U.K.

Hidenori Kageyama, Nagoya University, Japan

Daniel Kerry, Brunel University College, Isleworth, U.K.

Koichi Kiku, Nara Women's University, Nara, Japan

Akihiko Kondo, Keio University, Japan

March L. Krotee, University of Minnesota, U.S.A.

Supranee Kuanboonchen, Srinakarinwirot University, Bangkok, Thailand.

Nicole M. LaVoi, Wellesley College, U.S.A.

Michael Letters, University of Queensland, Brisbane Australia

Scott G. Martyn, The University of Western Ontario, London, Canada

Mitsuhiro Matsumoto, University of Tsukuba, Tsukuba, Japan

Motohide Miyahara, University of Otago, Dunedin, New Zealand

Hiromitsu Muta, Tokyo Institute of Technology, Tokyo, Japan

Kosuke Nagaki, Hyogo University of Teacher Education, Japan

Kazuori Nakanishi, Nagoya University, Nagoya, Japan

Tamotsu Nishida, Nagoya University, Nagoya, Japan

Catherine O'Brien, University of Sydney, Sydney, Australia

Jennifer O'Dea, University of Sydney, Sydney, Australia

Gertrud Pfister, Free University of Berlin, Berlin, Germany

Paul A. Potrac, Brunel University College, Isleworth, U.K.

Tetsuya Sagawa, Kanazawa University, Japan

George H. Sage, University of Northern Colorado, Greeley, U.S.A.

Darwin M. Semotiuk, The University of Western Ontario, London, Canada

Eric J. Solberg, Baylor College of Medicine, U.S.A.

Joy Standeven, Poole, Dorset, U.K.

Yoshiro Sugiyama, National Institute of Fitness and Sports, Japan

Dieter Teipel, University of Jena, Jena, Germany

Masatsugu Tsujii, Gifu University of Education, Japan

Kanshi Uemukai, Keio University, Japan

Shi De Wei, Macao Polytechnic Institute, Macao

Chen Ji Zhi, Shanghai Institute of Physical Education, Shanghai, People's Republic of China

Preface

Ken Hardman

Unlike the intrepid and curious pioneer explorers and travellers of the ancient world, who sought to learn about other societies and cultures in the pursuit of enlightenment (and later commercial interest), academics and professionals in the present day so-called 'globalised village', demonstrate a revived interest in societal and cultural customs and practices. This interest is grounded in critical appraisal and evaluation rather than in curiosity of the strange and the exotic. Whilst, however, there is evidence of globalisation of some general principles, plans and implemented measures, it is also clear that policies and practices are often specifically 'localised' rather than generically 'globalised'.

The combination of historical and traditional legacies of the 'oriental' physical and spiritual arts and imported 'occidental' forms of sporting activity served to make Japan an eminently suitable country location for the 10th ISCPES Biennial Conference. Additionally, the specific site of the Conference was appropriately juxtaposed in the rural setting of the Hachi-ohji and in the near vicinity of metropolitan Tokyo. Tokyo's admixture of ancient and modern is the epitome of cultural divergence and congruence and hence, was a particularly apposite venue for national, international and cross-cultural comparisons related to an over-riding theme centrally concerned with divergence and congruence in physical education and sport. This theme was underpinned by five main topic areas:

1. Issues and theoretical and methodological considerations in comparative research;
2. Cross-cultural studies in sport;
3. Physical education and sport pedagogy;
4. Sport for all;
5. Sport-business and management

The topics facilitated opportunities to inform and discuss pertinent issues in the globalisation/localisation debate. They also provided ample scope for a true meeting of minds from different countries in four continental regions, societies and cultural backgrounds as well as with different languages.

The quality of scholarly presentations at the Conference was generally high. The task of selecting papers for inclusion in this book was made more difficult by financial constraints, which imposed strict limitations on the amount of papers to be published. Hence, regrettably, publication of all relevant papers was impossible. The 25 chapters in the book comprise edited papers presented by scholars from both the northern and southern hemispheres and representing occidental and oriental cultures and societies. Each contribution in the collection draws from quantitative and/or qualitative based research conducted by individuals or by groups of researchers to establish correlations or causal relationships. In essence, what has emerged is an amalgam of globally generic and locally specific factors and features. **Cultural Diversity and Congruence in Physical Education and Sport** provides invaluable source material for students and scholars alike within the domain of comparative, international and cross-cultural studies.

Presidential Address

Physical and Sporting Activity in International and Cross-cultural Context: Diversity or Congruence?

Ken Hardman

Introduction

The original over-riding theme of the 1996 ISCPES Biennial Conference offered an opportunity to raise a number of issues and express some concerns. Notably, the conference theme alluded generally to cultures in notional regional geographical entities. In doing so, it overlooked the diverse cultures **within** these entities. The theme, with its emphasis on "diversity **and** congruence" also inferred that these two features of cultural activity occur simultaneously and in tandem. The intention here is to address the linked themes by focusing on four inter-related aspects: (i) cultural transmission agencies, patterns and diversity; (ii) factors and features in congruence and diversity in historical and contemporary international and cross-cultural contexts; (iii) global crisis in school physical education: congruence?; and (iv) comparative physical education and sport research and methodological issues.

Cultural Transmission Agencies, Patterns and Diversity

Throughout history, physical activity has been in diverse ways a significant element in all cultures. In both formal and informal institutional settings, it has been considered an important component of the educational process as well as an end in itself. Its continued presence within various and different ideological and socio-cultural environments suggests that socialisation into physical activity engagement has also had a sustained presence from origins either directly or indirectly inspired and extrinsically or intrinsically motivated. Hence, physical and sporting activity can be conceptualised as a global phenomenon, testimony to which are world festivals of sporting events such as the Olympic Games and ubiquitous individual sports such as Soccer. However, at the same time, it is also subject to culturally specific 'local' interpretations. Implicit in the 'global'/'local' tenet is both a degree of international congruence and cross-cultural diversity.

The process of socialisation into physical and sports activity involves transmission of cultural patterns - norms, values, ideas and practices - from generation to generation, from group to group, from one individual to another. The transitions, which are effected during the lifetime, vary from society to society and the nature and scope of human activity has to be seen in the context and historical period in which it is set. Relevant here is the potential for socialisation to be subject to ideological and political manipulation. There are numerous examples of such manipulation in history and none more so than in recent times.

The main agencies responsible for the transmission of cultural patterns are the social groups to which a person belongs and is exposed, and these extend differentially throughout the life span. Some of the norms, values and practices will refer to positions or roles in society, thus, there will be expectations and prescriptions of behaviour appropriate to various and different roles. The efficacy of socialisation will depend on the nature of, and amount of conflicts between, the agents (some of which may be competing agencies) to which the individual is exposed.

Notwithstanding the almost unique, powerful **family**, **school**, and **peer group** agents' roles in influencing attitudes and behaviours and the respective ideological, political, socio-economic, and cultural and sub-cultural settings of each of these agents, the focus here is on broader issues in the congruence/diversity debate. It is also the intention to show that whilst congruence of physical and sporting activity is clearly evident, especially in the commercialised sport commodity global world, diversity is not merely only to be seen in an 'East-West' context but is apparent cross-, inter- and intra-culturally.

Different societies have different social structures. For example, the 'closed' social structure in the Indian caste system fixes position for life; and the 'open' social structure in N. America/Europe is more achievement orientated. Different **social groups** have different cultures, and each time a new culture is joined, learning occurs to act within it. Therefore, there are behavioural differences in different **cultural groups**. HARDMAN, KROTEE and CHRISSANTHOPOULOS (1988), HARDMAN (1989) and HARDMAN and NAUL (1994) have reported cultural differences amongst students' and teachers' attitudes towards competitive sport. ICHIMURA and NAUL (1991) found that differences in West German and Japanese females' socialisation into soccer (when and where it occurred, and perpetrators of introduction), were accounted for by cultural and sub-cultural differences. The differences were manifested in playing the game itself, sports socialisation of females and general attitudes to the role of women in society. A comparative research study (GAMBETTA and DEPAUW, 1995) focusing on elderly American and German people's attitudes toward physical activity showed differences in choices of activity, the age at which individuals were initiated into activity and agencies of socialisation. American senior citizens were disposed toward choice of activities, which had high 'visible presence' and had 'organised programmes'; German seniors tended towards activities associated with 'clubs' of their affiliation. Both sample populations cited 'self-motivation' as a primary factor in decisions to participate and identified 'friend/spouse' as the initiator(s) of participation. American males ranked 'wives' as a main reason for initiating activity significantly higher than German males, and German females ranked 'husbands' significantly higher than their American counterparts as the reason. The American sample subjects were more likely to identify the 'doctor' as a reason for initiation into activity and cited 'health and fitness' and 'relaxation' - herein possibly lies the link with medical practitioner initiation - as motivators; the German subjects rated 'pleasure/enjoyment' as important reasons for activity engagement. It was also noted that active life-styles commenced at a later age amongst the American subjects. Possible causal explanations may be found both in differences in school physical education and sport programmes and in socio-cultural differences in terms of sports club affiliation.

Different and various cultural influences on physical activities and activity behaviours have also been highlighted in several articles in the ISCPES Journal of Comparative Physical Education and Sport. YAN and THOMAS (1995), after investigating American and Chinese children's physical activity patterns, suggested that socio-cultural environment and ethnicity were influential both in physical activities in general and on children's exercise behaviours in particular. REES and BRANDL-BREDENBECK's (1995) research into body capital and importance of sport amongst German and American adolescents led them to record that whilst there are trans-Atlantic similarities in effect of sport on body habitus, there are racial and cultural differences when body habitus is operationalised as physical appearance, which need to be "... seen as 'local' responses..." (p.55) to a global view. THEEBOOM, DE KNOP and WYLLEMAN (1995) found when studying the adoption of Asian martial arts in the West, that adaptations have occurred, in which specific spiritual, cultural and artistic characteristics have tended to be disregarded. Such adaptations are explained through "the existence of distinct cultural and situational differences between eastern and western society" (p.65).

Cross-cultural research involving Asian cultures reveals that priority is allocated to academic/intellectual development and not physical achievement. Further, some research reported by CARROLL (1993) revealed that ethnic minority group women in Britain accepted domestic and family duties and responsibilities as part of their lives in ways that males do not. It was found that no female group participated in major team sports and yet in the physical education curriculum in England and Wales, hockey and netball dominate the programme for girls: hockey was disliked for the pain incurred and being played in the mud! Higher participation rates were found amongst Christians and 'Non-believers', lowest rates were amongst Muslims, Sikhs and Hindus. The study concluded that **gender, religion** and **cultural matters** were highly significant determinants. For Muslims in particular, cultural traditions, which relate to privacy of the body, changing facilities, mixed sex sessions and 'Ramadan' are influential factors on participation or rather non-participation. Research findings (CARRINGTON, CHIVERS and WILLIAMS, 1987; CARROLL and HOLLINSHEAD, 1992) suggest

> ... patriarchal relations are culturally reproduced in leisure and equal opportunity policies have little chance of succeeding without taking into consideration cultural and religious traditions and values, and that Asian communities do not value physical education and sport as much as other groups
>
> (CARROLL, 1993, p.61).

Other **societal factors** such as the **socio-economic structure** of the young person's environment and exposure to the **mass media**, especially television may influence an individual's understanding of society. The **physical and social environment** is important because of the range of experience open to young people - hence, a remote rural environment compared with an urban inner city environment exposes individuals to quite different sets of people, institutions and experiences. Off-site visits place young people in different learning environments, which can be both more realistic and appropriate in, and to, the learning process. Youngsters can become part of a sporting environment where there is access to a living and active community, and where they can play an active role throughout their life span. Mass media do bring common experiences perhaps not otherwise observed, and television and commercials in particular can reinforce attitudes and behaviours.

Sporting experiences of young Asian males in Britain are shaped more by **racism** than any other factor (CARRINGTON et al., 1987). For Asians, **class** transcends societies and is a major determinant in sports participation: 75% of the population in India, Pakistan and Bangladesh live on/below the poverty line in rural areas hence, participation in sport is simply not an available option.

Major socialisation occurs as a result of the operation of the **politico-economic system** itself. It is enhanced by the socio-cultural climate, ethos, the ideology and the goals it generates as exemplified in a number of countries. British imperialism socialised whole nations into sport (e.g. cricket). State interventionism in the former GDR, Cuba and the People's Republic of China strictly delimited the nature and scope of participation. Sport commercialism dominating the American market place. Fundamentalism in Muslim States, where it imposes strict constraints on delivery and participation. Australian States and Canadian Provinces, where economic realities have led to rationalisation and determined educational and social priorities to the detriment of physical education programmes.

Factors and Features in Congruence and Diversity: Historical and Contemporary International and Cross-cultural Context

In Britain in the second half of the 19th century, sport came to be regarded as respectable. This respect had its origins in a desire for a healthy and fit nation and in the desire for improved moral education and socialisation. As an area of activity accepted as a 'rational' form of recreation, it was able to provide "... a proper environment for exposure to the superior example, whose values would ultimately be internalised" (BAILEY, 1978, p.41). It was far from coincidental that the new found respectability occurred when moral education came to the fore and physical activity had a significant role to play: playground physical exercises were believed to "extend the moral influence of the teacher" (COMMITTEE OF COUNCIL, 1839-40, p.71). This theme came to be an underlying tenet of 'Muscular Christianity', developed within, and by, English private boarding schools.

Initially, team games provided a means of occupying students in a 'positive' activity, which promoted healthy exercise and was perceived as a healthy antidote to ill discipline associated with the informal pastimes of the early 19th century. From such social control antecedents was derived the belief that competitive sport, especially team games, was thought to have an ethical basis with a transfer of moral behaviour from the playing field to the world beyond. Cricket, for example, was "all part of the business of preparing the young men for the 'great game' to come" (DOBBS, 1973, p.24). 'Official' approval of the values of games was seen in the CLARENDON COMMISSION's (1864) recognition that cricket and football fields are not merely places of exercise and amusement; they help to form some of the most valuable social qualities and manly virtues. The claims here were 19th century forerunners of 20th century developments, in which qualities and virtues to be derived from participation in play, games and sport and which could be transferred into the broader social and institutional world were perpetuated. Physical education and sports-related curricula throughout the world testify to the significance of this legacy. Many of the concepts linking play and sport with transferable positive behavioural outcomes have been shared by the then British Prime Minister, John Major, who was a key figure in the pre-eminent status of Games within the revised (1995) physical education national curriculum in England and Wales. In a prefatory statement to a governmental department policy document on sport, he asserted:

> Competitive sport teaches valuable lessons which last for life ... Sport only thrives if both parties play by the rules and accept the results with good grace. It is one of the best means of learning how to live alongside others and make a contribution as part of a team. It improves health and it opens the door to new friendships. (It) enriches the lives of the thousands of people of all ages ... (and) is a binding force between generations and across borders ... it is ... one of the defining characteristics of nationhood and pride
> (DEPARTMENT OF NATIONAL HERITAGE, 1995, p.2).

The Department of National Heritage policy document endorses the Prime Minister's views by extolling the virtues of school sport, outcomes of which, it claims, are:

- young people's appreciation of the long term benefits of regular exercise and ability to make informed decisions about adopting a healthy and active lifestyle in future years;

- channelling of energies, high spirits, competitiveness and aggression of the young in a socially beneficial way;

- provision of lessons for life which young people are unlikely to learn so well in any other way; team spirit, good sportsmanship, playing within rules, self-discipline and dedication (p.6).

Physical education in England and Wales is identified as having an important role in perpetuating sport to achieve the ascribed outcomes. Competitive sport, especially team games, is given prominence here, because the Government

> ... believes fair play, self-discipline, respect for others, learning to live by laws and understanding one's obligations to others in a team ... can be learnt from team games ...
> (DEPARTMENT OF NATIONAL HERITAGE, 1995, p.7).

Further historical illustration of the relevance of the influence of the cultural climate of the times is embodied in the ideas of Her Majesty's Inspector (HMI) Jolly, articulated in an address to the British (Medical) Association in 1876 in Glasgow. He commented on the deteriorated physique, organic defects, disease, misery and death stemming from ignorance of personal and community hygiene in Britain and contrasted the situation with developments of enlightened physical education programmes for teachers and pupils in every European country except Britain, Spain, Portugal, Turkey and Greece. Britain stood "in this matter in the company of the least enlightened and least advanced European nations!" (JOLLY, 1876, p.16). He pointed to the role of physical education in improving anatomical and physiological functions of the body (physical development), cleanliness (personal hygiene), and social skills (sociability). For JOLLY (1876), 'true physical education' should produce "healthy, shapely, and powerful men" and " healthy, strong, and handsome women" with training administered "equally to both sexes" (p.9). Jolly's ideas stand in contrast to the themes contained within the government's (post-1870 Education Act which heralded a system of state elementary education in England and Wales), instrumental policy permitting 'drill' to be counted as school attendance for grant purposes. This drill (military in form) was the only officially approved form of physical education until 1890. It was introduced to socialise young boys into "habits of sharp obedience, smartness and cleanliness" (COMMITTEE OF COUNCIL, 1870, p.cxxxvi) with the declared aim of inculcating "ideas of order, regularity and discipline without which it was difficult to obtain fully qualified soldiers and sailors" (HANSARD, 1875, col.1203-1204).

In pre-colonial Africa, young people were socialised in informal educational settings, perpetuated by family and tribal elders, into physical and sporting activities as a preparation for surviving the rigours of life and hostilities generated by endemic inter-ethnic group warfare. Missionaries and colonial administrators commenced the process of infusion of European ideals. In British East Africa, a system was imposed in the name of progress towards civilisation and westernisation. It was progression, which included the goals of a healthy sound body (necessary for a responsible and content labour force) and sound character - the ideal colonial citizen. The fact that it lacked any real relevance for the indigenous population was immaterial!

In other countries, physical education has been regarded "as an essential element of education" (K.M.K., 1966) and as "indispensable for the upbringing and education of people" (DEUTSCHER SPORTBUND, 1966). Changes in societal values and a reshaping of education philosophy are cited as the rationale for the German Sports Federation's (DEUTSCHER SPORTBUND) 'Second Action Plan for School Sport', (DEUTSCHER SPORTBUND, 1985). The rationale parallels those expressed for the curriculum changes in the former German Democratic Republic's (G.D.R.) school physical education programme, introduced shortly before (re)-unification. Further parallels are to be seen in physical education curricular aims of the G.D.R. and Länder Guidelines of the Federal Republic: health and physical efficiency; harmonious development; acquisition of sports skills; development of positive attitudes; habituation of pupils to positive behavioural codes and moral concepts such as fair play; and preparation for post-school leisure/life-time engagement etc. In the west, physical education came to have a formative task in the education of 'all-round personality', which embraced the underpinning principles of life enrichment and the sportive active child. Similar principles were to be found in the east, where pupils were to be socialised into "leading a healthy life and to be brought up to regularly and systematically participate in sport during leisure time" (KÖRPERERZIEHUNG, 1987, p.54). The real emphasis, however, was on the cultivation of the 'socialist personality', in which socialist character traits, attitudes and convictions, including socialist patriotism and proletarian nationalism had a part to play. Herein, lies an illustration of the differences influenced by socio-cultural, political and ideological determinants. For the G.D.R. central authorities, the development of the 'socialist personality' encompassed physical, political and moral preparation "for the defence of the socialist fatherland (which was) the patriotic duty and honour of each young person" (MINISTERIUM FÜR VOLKSBILDUNG, 1980, p.7).

To some extent, the former West and East German *differentiations* were mirrored in Hong Kong and the People's Republic of China (PRC). In Hong Kong, physical education was given a role in "building fit individuals" (CURRICULUM DEVELOPMENT INSTITUTE, 1994, p.442). Hence, in the aims of school programmes, physiological and neuro-muscular efficiency and fitness, active life-styles and desirable social attitudes and patterns of behaviour (fair play, sportsmanship, community co-operation and sense of responsibility) feature alongside implicit development of self-esteem through confidence building acquisition of skills. Similar physiological, functional anatomical efficiency and skill development characterise physical education aims in the PRC. However, differentiation in social attitudes is apparent in the promotion of the spirit of unity (of 1.3 billion people), love of the socialist motherland, Chinese people, the Chinese Communist Party, Liberation Army and Chinese leadership as well as the cultivation of communist morality (QU, 1990, pp.62-63). As XIE (1990) so aptly comments, the quality of the labour force depends on the intellectual and physical strength of workers, for which physical training is utilised to achieve: "... it helps the workers master production skills faster and increases attendance and productivity" (p.31).

Nevertheless, and in contrast to the fundamentally influential Mao Gedong's thoughts that moral education and intellectual development are based on physical training, despite their different political economies and ideological persuasion, both Hong Kong and the PRC inherited doctrines embedded in Buddhism, Taoism and Confucianism, common to which are quiet, studious and contemplative life and delicate physique with emphasis on the mind, and antipathy to participation in physical activity. The various incursions of western 'Muscular Christianity' have encountered resistance of the assumed greater importance of intellectual development: "... those who work with their brains rule and those who work with their brawn are ruled" (LI, 1989, p.71); and "those who have brawny extremities are simple minded" (LI, 1994, p.407). Parallels are to be seen here with references in the Anglo-Saxon speaking world to 'Jocks' and 'Muscular Morons'. Under the circumstances of "... All people... being ruled, unless they are scholars" (YE, 1991, p.182), it is hardly surprising that in both cultures, parents stressed academic achievement and that in Hong Kong less than 1% of students elected to take physical education examinations!

In Japan, changes and developments in the Japanese physical education curriculum have been predominantly shaped by political, economic and social demands and are, thus, also representative of the specific culture-bound forces. Prior to 1945, the so-called 'Old Physical Education' was aligned to a national policy to enrich and strengthen Japan and the formation of national morals with an emphasis on loyalty and patriotism.

The post-1945 years of 'New Physical Education' have shown a shift to an over-riding policy of establishing a democratic and peaceful nation and have been marked by three distinct phases. Phase one (1947-1957) was characterised by sound development of the mind and body, and by the moulding of social character. Phase two (1958-1976) emphasised mastery of technical skills and the improvement of strength, the latter representing somewhat of an unpopular return to 'Old Physical Education' days; cultivation of moral (fairness) and social attributes (co-operation, proper behaviour). Phase three (1977-1989) reiterated the development of skills, strength, moral and social qualities, but extended the aims to include preparation for life-long participation in sporting activity. Since 1989, the trend to socialisation for lifetime engagement has accelerated and has been accompanied by promotion of attitudes toward a cheerful, rich and vital life (MAEDA, 1994). Such attitudes along with the cultivation of self-esteem and other attributes to be attained through personal and social development will contribute to the enhancement of the quality of life. Such trends are global, and hence, a degree of congruence is indicated. They are readily discerned in school physical education programmes. Hence, we can read of a central core of curricular aims embracing motivation for active life time participation, healthy well-being, motor competence, development of self-concepts, and social functioning including moral behavioural codes in all continental regions of the world.

Global Crisis in School Physical Education: Congruence?

These developmental trends lead into the third aspect to be addressed and one that is of some concern, a concern that was articulated in the ISCPES Conference Presidential Address in Prague in 1994 (see HARDMAN, 1995b), since when further research has revealed that the situation continues to deteriorate. Physical education practitioners have a vested interest in young people's self-esteem enhancement. Additionally, constructs such as body image and perceived attractiveness, which are related to physical activity, fitness, and health, are emerging as influential determinants of self-esteem from an early age and throughout the life span. The recent trend towards the promotion of life time involvement in sport and exercise as leisure and health-related activity strengthens the case for physical education as a life-span concept for its potential for nurturing a sense of self and related behaviours. Here again, school physical education curricula around the world reveal similarities in aims and purposes in these directions and suggest a degree of congruence. However, it is a congruence, which is paralleled by rapidly increasing threats to the very existence of school physical education in many countries in all continental regions. The Swedish Education Minister's suggestion in 1990 that physical education disappear from the curriculum as a compulsory subject in secondary schools is one illustrative example of the serious nature of this threat. It did not happen, but the mere fact of its consideration in such a country with a distinguished record of school physical education was an alarming development.

There is substantial evidence to suggest that school physical education worldwide is on the decline. Currently, there are numerous examples of the strains and tensions that physical education and physical educators are experiencing. A plethora of commentators (refer, for example, ANDERSEN, 1996; HARDMAN, 1993, 1994a, 1995a, 1995b, 1996; JOHNS, 1995; KAMILOYE, 1993; RILEY and DONALD, 1995; TUOHIMAA, 1993) have argued that physical education has been pushed into a defensive position, that it is suffering from decreasing curriculum time allocation, budgetary controls with inadequate financial, material and personnel resources, erosion of quality standards and pre-dispositions towards alternative physical activity forms, has low subject status and esteem, and is being ever more marginalised and undervalued by authorities. Frequently, physical educators are being called upon to justify the inclusion of physical education within the school curriculum. The strong arguments proffered have met with only limited success. In short, there is a global crisis in physical education.

The tensions are epitomised in CAHPERD President's assertion (1996) that in Canada

> ... physical education is not seen as a priority... in the '90's. It is under severe attack and faces competition for time within the school curriculum. Often physical education is being taught by generalist teachers with little or no preparation in physical education methods. Additionally, budget cutbacks are impacting negatively on the time and resources required to teach a quality physical education programme
> (MACKENDRICK, 1996, p.2).

One not insignificant view of physical education is embraced in a Minister of Education's comment (cited in JANZEN, 1995) that despite the support given to physical education, "the attitudes of society had not been positively affected by their physical education experience within the school system" (p.8). Against such a background, there is little wonder that there has been widespread considerable concern amongst physical educationists. The concern has been manifested, for example, in a conference in Geelong, Australia in 1991, devoted to the theme of Crisis in Physical Education (ALEXANDER & SANDS, 1991), and a special theme within the 1995 winter edition of the BULLETIN of IAPESGW (International Association of Physical Education and Sport for Girls and Women) devoted to the status of physical education and reduction in curriculum time allocation. Clearly a hitherto 'essentially' regarded school curriculum subject is at a crisis point in its history.

If physical education is to sustain its presence both in formal and informal educational settings, then issues have to be confronted, and resistance to change has to be overcome. Application of political skills and argument of the case at local, through national, to international levels will be required. As suggested elsewhere (see HARDMAN, 1995b, 1996), a concerted institutional lobby comprising relevant international, regional and national agencies has an essential and distinctive part to play in persuading those directly involved with decisions. Policy makers, decision takers, committee members, administrators, other subject colleagues and 'clients' need to be lobbied and convinced that physical education is "an authentic educational activity" (KIRK, 1987, p.147). It is widely acknowledged that physical activity can positively influence physical and psycho-social health at **all** stages in the life cycle from infancy to old age. Hence, it seems reasonable to suggest that physical education should have a role to play over the full life span. It is worth remembering that it is not the activity, but the reason for taking part that sustains participation. Research studies around the world indicate changing activity patterns of adolescents with gender distinctions blurring, sport culture and sport settings becoming more differentiated, traditional activities in decline and greater awareness of what is being sought (BRETTSCHNEIDER and BRÄUTIGAM, 1991; KROTEE et al., 1994). Generally, a body concept revolution (including the commercial market) is occurring. The body culture is expanding to incorporate body-building, yoga, tai chi chuan, budo, dance, therapeutic exercises, martial arts, jazz gymnastics etc., health practices, and sports tourism amongst others, and involving a range of social groups and sub-groups (EICHBERG, 1993). Increasing numbers of new groups (women, senior citizens, ethnic minorities, members of different socio-economic strata, people with disabilities etc.) with different abilities and interests have become more physically active in both formal and informal settings. These and other global trends imply convergence, but as others (refer REES and BRANDL-BREDENBECK, 1995) have indicated, at micro levels 'local' cultural responses infer differences and divergence.

For the process of socialisation into life-span physical activity engagement, the school physical education curriculum is in need of re-appraisal both in regard to its fundamental purposes in view of social and peer culture and other projected and hidden changes, and to the pedagogic processes that might best bring about these purposes. There is a need to recognise the importance of contemporary youth culture in structuring a relevant curriculum. Trends in changing activity patterns and body concepts have implications for the future of planned physical education curriculum development. At the very least, any reconstruction of physical education should include strategies to foster **Body/Self-concepts**, promote **Healthy Well-being** and **Moral Education**, which together will contribute to the **Enrichment of Quality of Life**, and stimulate socialisation into habitual regular practice in the pursuit of those values. Any reshaping, however, should recognise local and cultural diversities, traditions as well as different social and economic conditions **and** incorporate a range of aspects related to the all-round and harmonious development of the individual within society.

Any such re-appraisal will inevitably have direct consequences for initial physical education teacher education and training and this important area of potentially positive human influence should also be re-assessed and changes introduced to maximise opportunities for sustained amelioration, a fundamental purpose of comparative study. Central to any developments toward amelioration is the role of research, the fourth issue of concern.

Comparative Physical Education and Sport Research and Methodological Issues

Previously, reference has been made to the neglect of reporting of comparative physical education and sport in academic and research literature (HARDMAN, 1991; 1994b; 1995c). Moreover, numbers of 'comparative' papers presented at major multi-disciplinary international conferences have remained low relative to other areas. This does not signify a dearth of research in the comparative domain. Indeed, the converse is perhaps nearer the truth, for there has been, and is, some excellent cross-cultural research conducted by groups of sports scholars. However, these groups more often than not comprise representatives from disciplines such as history and sociology, and their research is published in the relevant discipline-based journals. Interestingly, at the 1996 pre-Olympic Scientific Congress in Dallas, the International Sport Sociology Association convened a three hour session devoted to the theme *Sport: Cross-cultural, Historical and Global Perspectives* - there were no recognised 'comparativists' amongst the eminent academics on the list of presenters!

Many comparative research studies, albeit excellent in their own right, continue to rely on empirical quantitative approaches. Comparativists should recognise that statistical logic and empirical method are not always the appropriate tools of analysis. Statistical analysis does not explain relationships; it does not reveal causes, nor does it provide evidence about socio-cultural realities, rather it reveals correlations not causes. The qualitative data paradigm aims at understanding and interpretation of processes. Its techniques, in some instances, may be less structured but they are no less systematic than numerical quantitative techniques. There have been significant and welcome methodological developments in recent years, especially in the application of qualitative methods drawn from the social sciences in a comparative context. However, relatively few scholars working in the area of comparative physical education and sport are applying these refined and new methods in cross-cultural research. Sport Sociologists and Sport Historians are taking the 'qualitative' lead in cross-cultural studies.

In order to alleviate some of the concerns about methodological issues, it is suggested here that the emphasis should be on **Research Action** and

Action Research. In the pursuit of pluralism and eclecticism in comparative research, greater attention should be paid to methodologies and methods employed elsewhere within the social sciences. Research methodologies designed by Social and Developmental Psychologists, for example, have particular resonance for cross-cultural research. HASTE's (1987) methodological approach to discourse themes (*scaffolding, negotiation of meaning, and the transfer of cultural representations*) transcends cultural boundaries and has been presented (WEINREICH-HASTE, 1984) as a 'model' of the relationship between three interacting worlds: the **socio-historic** (the domain of cultural mores, culturally defined and historically accumulated), the **interpersonal** (the domain of social interaction, through which cultural norms and social conventions are learned) and **intra-personal** (the domain of assimilation of experiences and construction of understanding). The field of Psychology, specifically KELLY's (1955) personal construct theories and the development of repertory grids, offers further possibilities for cross-cultural research. Being content free and process oriented to facilitate transfer of methodology across cultures, repertory grid techniques have been found (FISHER, 1995) appropriate for cross-cultural investigation. Such models might well serve as methods offering a basis for comparative research studies concerned with the a range of culture-bound issues and help establish a clearer understanding of the shaping forces which produce congruence and diversity.

Concluding Comments

The historically pervasive presence of physical activity as part of the warp and woof of human activity is indicative of congruence over the four points of the compass. The degree of congruence has accelerated under the influence of modern high technology, which has helped to produce the concept of the 'global village'. Nevertheless, the nature, scope and interpretations of that activity reveal overt cultural diversities both between and within geo-political boundaries. Discrete diversities, covered by a superficial veneer of apparently prevailing congruence, are also evident and are demonstrated in deeper meanings, interpretations, attitudes and motivation etc.

The issues and concerns raised and addressed present challenges to all those involved with comparative and cross-cultural studies in physical education and sport. They are challenges, which if accepted, may lead to deeper insights and clearer understanding of physical and sporting activity and its role in various and different cultures throughout the world. They are also challenges which should heed relevant scholarly research and best methodological practice in the social and pedagogical sciences, which, in recent years, have made significant progress in unravelling some of the 'mysteries' of processes in different and various cultural and cross-cultural contexts. Comparativists in physical education and sport have a leading role to play in meeting these challenges to foster the cause of physical education and sport in all cultures.

References

ALEXANDER, K., and SANDS, R.A.: *Report of the recent conference at Deakin University on the crisis in physical education in Australia. Victoria College*, November 1991.

ANDERSEN, D.: Health and physical education in Hungary: a status report. In: *ICHPER•SD Journal*, XXXII (2), Winter, 1996, pp.40-42.

BAILEY, P.A.: *Leisure and class in Victorian England*. London, Routledge and Kegan Paul, 1978.

BRETTSCHNEIDER, W-D., and BRÄUTIGAM, M.: *Sport in der Alltagswelt von Jugendlichen*. Frechen, Rittersbach, 1991.

BULLETIN OF IAPESGW, 5(1), January 1995.

CARRINGTON, B., CHIVERS, T., and WILLIAMS, T.: Gender, leisure and sport: a case study of young people of South African descent. In: *Leisure Studies*, 6(3), 1987, pp.265-279.

CARROLL, R.: Factors influencing ethnic minority groups' participation in sport. In: *Physical Education Review*, 16(1), Spring, 1993, pp.55-66.

CARROLL, R., and HOLLINSHEAD, G.: Equal opportunities: race and gender in physical education. In: EVANS, J., (Ed.), *Equality, education and physical education.* London, Falmer Press, 1992.

CLARENDON COMMISSION: *Report of the Royal Commission on Public Schools.* London, 1864.

COMMITTEE OF COUNCIL: *Minutes,* 1839-40. London, 1840.

COMMITTEE OF COUNCIL: *Minutes,* 1870-71. London, 1870.

CURRICULUM DEVELOPMENT INSTITUTE: *Supporting materials on physical education for secondary schools.* Hong Kong, Education Department, 1994.

DEPARTMENT OF NATIONAL HERITAGE: *Sport raising the game.* London, Department of National Heritage, 1995.

DEUTSCHER SPORTBUND: *Charta des Deutschen Sports.* Frankfurt, D.S.B., 1966.

DEUTSCHER SPORTBUND: *Second action plan for school sport.* Frankfurt, D.S.B., 1985.

DOBBS, B.: *Edwardians at play.* London, Pelham Books, 1973.

EICHBERG, H.: Problems and future research in sports sociology: a revolution of body culture. In: HARDMAN, K., (Ed.), *'Towards a richer and healthier world'. International Sports Science Summit 1991.* Nafferton, U.K., Studies in Education, 1993.

EDITORIAL: Entwürfe der Lehrpläne Sport der Klassen 1 bis 3, 4 bis 6 und 7 bis 10. In: *Körpererziehung,* 37(2/3), 1987, pp.53-120.

FISHER, R.J.: *Physical education in England and Germany: a comparative tale of two schools.* Ph.D. Thesis, University of Surrey, Guildford, 1995.

GAMBETTA, C., and DEPAUW, K.P.: Attitudes toward physical activity among German and United States senior citizens. In: *European Physical Education Review*, 1(2), Autumn, 1995, pp.155-162.

HANSARD: *Parliamentary Debate*. Col. 1203-1204, 1875.

HARDMAN, K.: Students' and teachers' attitudes to interscholastic sports competition - a trans-national comparison. In: FU, F., NG, M.L., and SPEAK, M., (Eds.), *Comparative physical education and sport*, ISCPES, vol.6. Hong Kong, Chinese University of Hong Kong, 1989.

HARDMAN, K.: Physical education within the school curriculum. In: MESTER, J., (Ed.), *'Sport sciences in Europe 1993'- current and future perspectives.* Aachen, Meyer and Meyer Verlag, 1993, pp.544-560.

HARDMAN, K.: Physical education in schools. In: BELL, F.I., & VAN GLYN, G.H., (Eds.), *Access to active living*. Proceedings of the 10th Commonwealth & Scientific Congress. Victoria, Canada, University of Victoria, 1994a, pp.71-76.

HARDMAN, K.: *Comparative physical education and sport: present situation and future direction.* Paper First Asian Conference on Comparative Physical Education and Sport. China Sports Science Society. Shanghai, November, 1994b.

HARDMAN, K.: World crisis in physical education: a bird's eye view in international context. In: VARNES, J.W., GAMBLE, D., & HORODSKI, M.B., (Eds.), *Scientific and pragmatic aspects of ICHPER•SD*, Gainsville, FL, University of Florida, 1995a, pp.79-81.

HARDMAN, K.: Physical Activity for life: North, South, East and West. In: SVOBODA, B., and RICHTECKÝ, A., *Physical activity for life: East and West, South and North*. Proceedings of ISCPES 9th Biennial Conference, Prague, Czech Republic. Aachen, Meyer & Meyer Verlag, 1995b, pp.5-16.

HARDMAN, K.: Comparative physical education and sport: state and status. In: VARNES, J.W., GAMBLE, D., and HORODSKI, M.B., (Eds.), *Scientific and pragmatic aspects of ICHPER•SD*, Gainsville, FL, University of Florida, 1995c, pp.81-82.

HARDMAN, K.: *The fall and rise of school physical education in international context.* Paper presented at the pre-Olympic Scientific Congress, Dallas, Texas, USA, 10-14 July, 1996.

HARDMAN, K., KROTEE, M.L., and CHRISSANTHOPOULOS, A.: A comparative study of inter-school competition in England, Greece and the United States. In: BROOM, E.F., CLUMPNER, R., PENDLETON, B., and POOLEY, C.A., (Eds.), *Comparative physical education and sport.* ISCPES, vol.5. Champaign, IL, Human Kinetics Pub. Inc., 1988, pp.91-102.

HARDMAN, K., and NAUL, R.: Attitudes to interscholastic competition in the Federal Republic of Germany and England: convergence or divergence? In: DUFFY, P., and DUGDALE, L., (Eds.), *Health, physical education and recreation. Moving towards the 21st century.* Champaign, IL, Human Kinetics Pub. Inc., 1994, pp.105-118.

HASTE, H.: Growing into rules. In: BRUNER, J., and HASTE, H., (Eds.). *Making sense.* London, Methuen, 1987.

ICHIMURA, S., and NAUL, R.: Cross-cultural assessments and attributions. In: STANDEVEN, J., HARDMAN, K., and FISHER, D., (Eds.), *Sport for all into the 1990s.* Aachen, Meyer and Meyer Verlag, 1991, pp.204-211.

JANZEN, H.: The status of physical education in Canadian public schools. In: *CAHPERD Journal,* 61(3), Autumn, 1995, pp.5-9.
JOHNS, D.: Moving to the margins: physical education another disposable program? In: *CAHPERD Journal de l'ACSELPD,* Summer, 1995. pp.15-19.

JOLLY, W.: *Physical education and hygiene in schools.* Paper presented at the British Association. Glasgow, September, 1876.

KAMIYOLE, T.O.: Physical educators' albatross in African societies. *International Journal of Physical Education*, XXX (2), 1993, pp.29-31.

KELLY, G.A.: *The psychology of personal constructs*, (volumes 1,2). New York, W.W. Norton, 1955.

KIRK, D.: *The orthodoxy of rational-technocracy and the research practice gap: a critique of an alternative view*. Unpublished Paper, Department of Human Movement Studies, University of Queensland, 1987.

K.M.K.: *Rahmenrichtlinien für die Leibeserziehung an den Schulen der B.R.D.* Bonn, K.M.K, 1966.

KROTEE, M.L., BLAIR, P.F., NAUL, R., NEUHAUS, H-W., HARDMAN, K., KOMUKU, H., MATSUMURA, K., NUMMINEN, P., and JWO, C.: A six-nation study concerning attitudes and participation patterns of youth toward competitive sport. In: WILCOX, R., (Ed.), *Sport in the global village*. Morgantown, WV, Fitness Information Technology Inc., 1994, pp.467-476.

LI, M.: A comparative study of intercollegiate athletics in China and the United States. In: WILCOX, R., (Ed.), *Sport in the global village*. Morgantown, WV, Fitness Information Technology Inc., 1994, pp.403-411.

LI, Z.S.: Controversy of intercollegiate athletics. *Gengshu scientific research of sports and physical education*, 2, 1989, pp.68-71.

MACKENDRICK, M.: Active living + quality daily physical education = the perfect solution. *CAHPERD Journal*, 62(1), 1996, p.2.

MAEDA, M.: *Physical education in elementary, junior high and high schools - their status, aims, and curricula*. Unpublished manuscript. Kochi, 1994.

MINISTERIUM FÜR VOLKSBILDUNG: *Lehrplan Sport: Abiturstufe und Berufsbildung*. Berlin, Volk und Wissen Volkseigener Verlag, 1980.

QU, Z.: Physical education in schools. In: Knuttgen, H.G., Ma, Q., and Wu, Z., (Eds.), *Sport in China*. Champaign IL, Human Kinetics Pub. Inc., 1990, pp.59-74.

REES, C.R. and BRANDL-BREDENBECK, H.P.: Body capital and the importance of sport: a comparison of American and German adolescents. In: *Journal of Comparative Physical Education and Sport*, XVII (2), 1995, pp.50-56.

RILEY, C., and DONALD, M.: Changes in state government policy in Victoria, Australia: its effects on physical education in schools. In: VARNES, J.W., GAMBLE, D., and HORODSKI, M.B., (Eds.), *Scientific and Pragmatic Aspects of ICHPER•SD*. Gainsville, FL, University of Florida, 1995, pp.178-179.

THEEBOOM, M., DE KNOP, P., and WYLLEMAN, P.: Traditional Asian martial arts and the West. In: *Journal of Comparative Physical Education and Sport*, XVII (2), 1995, pp.57-69.

TUOHIMAA, O.: Finnish physical education. At the crossroads? In: *Motion. Sport in Finland*, 2, 1993, pp.40-42.

WEINREICH-HASTE, H.: Morality, social meaning and rhetoric, the social context of moral reasoning. In: KURTINES, W., and GEWIRTZ, J.L., (Eds.), *Morality, moral behaviour and moral development*. New York, Wiley, 1984.

XIE, Q.: Physical culture in the new China. In: KNUTTGEN, H.G., MA, Q., and WU, Z., (Eds.), *Sport in China*. Champaign, IL, Human Kinetics Pub. Inc., 1990, pp. 25-40.

YAN, J.H., and THOMAS, J.R.: Parents' assessment of physical activities in American and Chinese children. In: *Journal of Comparative Physical Education and Sport*, XVII (2), 1995, pp.38-49.

YE, L.: *The general education system in the People's Republic of China*. Unpublished manuscript, East China Normal University, 1991.

PART 1

ISSUES, THEORETICAL AND METHODOLOGICAL CONSIDERATIONS IN COMPARATIVE RESEARCH

Chapter 1

Issues in Comparative Studies in Japan

Hiromitsu Muta

Trends in Comparative Studies: from Introduction to Comparison

Comparative education became popular in Japan after World War II. The Japan Society for Comparative Education was established in 1964. The aftermath of defeat in war and occupation by the American armed forces saw a change in the Japanese education system, which had previously evolved after the Meiji era. When a country has to build a new system, the easiest and the most sensible action is to study systems in other countries. Thus, Japanese scholars studied the education system of the United States (which under occupation had a significant influence on Japan), the United Kingdom, France and the then Soviet Union.

The view that Japan was trailing behind developments in economically advance countries had been prevalent since the Meiji period. Thus, it was not an entirely new phenomenon that arose after World War II. In establishing a modern education system, the Meiji government studied the delivery systems in such countries like the United States, the United Kingdom, Germany and France, and it formed a system suitably modified in accordance with indigenous historical, cultural and climatic features. Scholarly studies of the German system had been undertaken pre-1939 (Germany belonged to the economically developed nations in the Western Hemisphere) and continued after 1945. It was of particular interest to Japanese scholars to observe the changes in the German education system in a post-1945 occupational setting and the respective influences of the four Allied Control Councils.

While the Japanese university system was renewed under American influence after the war, foreign language education reflected the long established practice of European studies. The foreign language programme required university students to study two foreign languages, usually with English as the first foreign language, and German, French or

Russian the second. Normally examinations in two foreign languages were administered as part of graduate school entrance examinations. Studies on education in the United States, the United Kingdom, France Germany and the former Soviet Union formed the core of comparative education studies.

At the time, the *Comparative Education* journal and conference papers focused on educational issues in other advanced countries. Despite the inclusion of the term "comparative", the Japan Society for Comparative Education tended to concentrate on mono-national so-called 'area' studies or educational issues in mono-national settings. Whilst this tendency has since been weakened, it continues to exist to some extent even today. Whereas some critical analysis was undertaken, many studies simply led to the acceptance of foreign practices without question. Implicitly, "comparison" merely related to information gathering on systems and issues. Subject matter of the studies was selected on an 'ad hoc' basis and centred on modern, practical issues such as education policies, administration, management and curriculum with some attention devoted to philosophical, theoretical and historical aspects of education. Additionally, these studies in comparative education focused on educational situations in advanced countries. Thus, although there were scholars, who were specialists on specific countries, very few were making comparisons of Japanese and foreign situations (or of several countries) to discover the important causal factors of differences. Little was also being done to identify problems commonly shared by several countries and to find possible solutions for them. Some Japanese scholars did show interest in developments in Asian countries and particularly in post-1945 changes. However, these represented a small minority and were not especially influential; moreover, their contributions were mainly descriptive reporting of 'area' systems.

The Ministry of Education, Science, Sports and Culture collects information on education in other countries to identify matters, which might effect education policy-making in Japan. As a government ministerial department, it has the ability to obtain current data through diplomatic channels, and hence, is advantaged over research scholars in accessing the latest data. Such ability raises the issue as to whether there is a need for scholars in this field when a ministerial office is already collating the data.

The status of Japan as an increasingly important economic power in the 1960s attracted interest amongst growing numbers of foreign scholars who began to think that the key to Japanese economic success might lie in its education system and research visits ensued. Subsequent dialogue between Japanese and overseas' scholars, however, remained limited in nature and scope: visiting academics were interested in Japanese developments; Japanese academics had inadequate knowledge of the context of issues in Japanese education and with but few exceptions, they had little knowledge and understanding of the historical and cultural settings, from which the foreign visitors came; and there were acute language barriers.

In recent years, the situation has greatly improved and Japanese scholars for a number of reasons are less inhibited in their efforts to engage in 'true' comparative study:

• the advance economic status of a developed country

• decrease in inferiority complex after World War II

• concomitant feature of study out of interest choice and not learning from perceived economically superior other countries syndrome

At the same time as the apparent decline in scholastic achievement and reported high drop-out rates in economically advanced western countries, Japan itself has now come to be recognised as a successful role model, especially in Mathematics and Science, and for its school discipline record.

Since 1992, Japan has been the leading world donor country for the Overseas Development Agency (ODA) and hence, is now one of the major sponsors of educational aid in the world. One outcome is greater Japanese interest in education in developing and neighbouring Asian countries in particular. Comparative research linked to these countries has, therefore, become popular.

Japanese contributions to the ODA distributed not only in Asia but also in Central and South America and Africa have produced an increase in the numbers of scholars and students visiting those areas. Such visits have been accompanied by conference papers on these areas. Studies on western countries are also increasing, a feature which perhaps reflects the increased membership of the Japan Society for Comparative Education. The rate at which the number of studies on Asian countries has increased, however, is by far higher than the rate at which the number of studies on western countries has grown. It might also be added that the economic growth enjoyed by some Asian countries has also drawn the attention of a wider public.

Methodology

Comparative education is interdisciplinary and as such employs a variety of methodologies from the humanities, social and behavioural sciences (ALTBACH, 1991). The methodological approaches include historical, philosophical, sociological, economic, cultural and anthropological orientations. Comparative educationists have actively adapted methodologies developed in other areas of studies to enrich and expand their sphere of interest. The methodologies prevalent in western countries were imported into Japan; however, the emphasis was on adoption and not adaptation to the detriment of production of original studies.

Because of its very nature, comparative education should place emphasis on comparison. By comparing educational situations in two countries, academics should determine where their differences lie, and clarify the historical, cultural and economic background that underpin differences. Additionally, not only is comparison of two countries important but also of several countries. Comparative analysis should attempt to find general principles rather than simply lead to adoption by the 'student' of the 'teacher's' experience. Common issues can be made clear through comparing situations in a number of countries. Hitherto, comparative education has focused on the reasons behind differences. As the world becomes smaller, there are many instances where new problems simultaneously emerge in various regions; now it is necessary to analyse problems and issues that are commonly shared and to learn from each other. For example, the issue of university evaluation has become a major concern not only in western countries but also in Asian countries including Japan.

Some of the characteristics of Japanese education that used to be considered unique to Japan were recognised as such through comparative studies. Such characteristics were often considered "Japanese" simply because they were not shared by western countries. Notably, those characteristics are not necessarily unique to Japan when viewed in the context of countries in East Asia. The message here is that there are many instances where it is more accurate to categorise characteristics as "Asian" or "Confucian" rather than "Japanese". Data collected from a wide range of countries help to avoid errors in interpretative analysis. Nevertheless, it is not an easy task to collate and analyse information from a large number of countries. Moreover, inaccuracies and highly abstract analysis are almost inevitable because of diversity of national education systems, unavailability of official statistics and cultural bias of the researcher (SASAKI, 1994). These problems, however, should not inhibit undertaking such studies for it is important that the differential issues and problems of developing and developed nations be identified as a pre-requisite of mutual concern and understanding.

Comparative study has long been concerned with the determination of similarities and differences through collection and collation of data. Thus, studies employing statistical techniques have become popular. The use of statistical data enables explanation of similarity and disparity in terms of extent to produce more accurate comparison. It is important to emphasise quantitative analysis to maintain the objectivity of the outcome of analysis. Quantitative analyses are particularly suitable for:

a) reporting the present status of school education;
b) monitoring changes in a time series;
c) explaining the causes for conditions or changes;
d) estimating future changes;
e) determining merits and demerits of a system;
f) providing information to decision and policy-makers;
g) defining the concrete objectives of education.

Perspectives to study are just as important as methodology in comparative education studies. Indigenous scholars have advantages of familiarity with delivery, cultural context and language, and knowledge of specific issues. However, 'foreign' researchers can bring a different perspective and interpretation and hence, positively contribute by introducing other dimensions. Often what is behind these perspectives and points of view are studies on educational situations, features or standards in the researchers' own countries.

Many individuals have expressed concern about the fact that comparative education in Japan is centred around studies of foreign countries with a research activity too focused on area studies, utilising imitations of imported foreign methodologies and not comparative analyses (UMAKOSHI, 1992). Whilst mere introduction of facts in foreign countries can be of help to those who know little about them, it is essential to place more emphasis on 'true' comparative analyses and to conduct studies that can stand evaluation not only intra-nationally but also internationally.

Contribution to Society

The purpose of conducting comparative studies should also be addressed. Respect for, or acquisition of knowledge about, foreign countries are sufficient to stimulate motivation for commencing studies in the comparative education domain. Yet such motivation alone will not sustain high quality research. Perspectives for conducting analysis are important in conducting area studies. Among the factors that can lie behind our perspectives is the desire to the resolution of educational problems in Japan and this will lead to comparative analysis. The social value of comparative education lies in the fact that it contributes to the improvement of an education system, and that is one justification for the use of public funds for such studies. Comprehensive explanations for the characteristics and problems of Japanese education and their background are called for not only at home but also internationally. This was the original reason for the existence of comparative education.

What must be done first in striving to improve an education system is to identify problems and causes. Modifications and developments will stem from identification of advantages and disadvantages of the Japanese system. In this process, it is necessary to see if the problems are unique to Japan or if other countries commonly share them. Clarification of the characteristics of the Japanese education system is not only the prerequisite for educational reform in Japan but also helpful information for educational reform elsewhere in the world. The Japanese education system is now attracting the attention of various other countries in the world, and some of them are implementing an adapted Japanese model. Hence, it is necessary to determine the pros and cons of the Japanese education system, its successes and failures, and the reasons for them (ICHIKAWA, 1990). Comparative education should discover facts through the employment of the techniques of the humanities and social sciences, and at the same time it should contribute to society as well as foster theoretical studies.

The _World Conference on Education for All_ sponsored by the World Bank, UNESCO, UNICEF, and UNDP was held in Thailand in 1990. At the end of the conference, the World Declaration on Education for All, aiming to diffuse basic education to all children in the world by the year 2000, was adopted. The development of education, especially basic education, in developing countries is an issue of some urgency, for which international organisations, including international aid agencies in developed countries, should expand their support. The ratio of aid for education in Japan's total bilateral ODA was 6.9% in 1990. This figure was lower than the average (9.8%) of that of the member countries of the OECD. It was proposed that Japan should increase the ratio to 15% by the year 2000 (JICA, 1994). In the fiscal year 1995, it rose to 8.4% and the area of human development, which is centred on education, has become a fast growing area in the ODA activities. The main activities embrace co-operation and extension of aid in the development of school facilities and empowerment of educational administration, development and improvement of the quality of teacher training systems, improvement of their quality, and development of "software" in education such as curricula, textbooks and teaching materials. One of the problems of international development assistance in education is how to find personnel suitable for the tasks. More accurately the leading question is how to develop such personnel because there are hardly any. The fundamental issue is to set curricula for the development of such personnel at university level.

The Japan Society for Comparative Education is an organisation of scholars, which is relatively close to international development assistance in education. Even so its members would not be especially useful in extending co-operation and aid when visiting countries that are the subjects of their studies if they have only studied the educational situations of such countries in isolation. Wide-ranging knowledge and skills in areas such as educational administration, management, and development of teaching materials would be necessary for effectiveness. However, such efficacy could also not be achieved without deep understanding of a country's education system.

The area of educational development is a frontier to be explored by comparative educationists in Japan. The Japan Society should actively pursue investigations in this area as well as the more conventional areas of study. To this end, the number of studies not only in economically advanced countries but also in developing countries should be increased. As the transfer of manufacturing plants overseas and overseas' investments increase, companies are faced with the necessity for educating personnel for "internationalisation" and training of interns from overseas. Thus, there is a growing demand for experts who are conversant with the education issues in foreign countries, and for specialists on teaching methods and curriculum development. There are countries (including the United States) where comparative education is on the wane partly because of decreases in public funding of development assistance. In Japan, however, it is likely that comparative education will grow in popularity.

Studies in educational development are meant to be characterised by action research. It is essential both to clarify the logical characteristics of an educational system and to determine its merits and demerits in the light of the specific political, economic and cultural background. In educational development or assistance and co-operation, it is also necessary to deal with issues by analysing present conditions, identifying problems, formulating policies, evaluating results and analysing the new conditions. This implies that approaches for studies in this area must be changed (USHIOGI, 1995). Comparative studies must embrace diversified approaches and benefit from other areas of study to continue to contribute to the improvement of human development in the world.

References

ALTBACH, P.G: Comparative education research in U.S.A. In: *Comparative Education*, 17, 1991, pp.167-181.

ICHIKAWA, S: A proposal for comparative study concerning Japanese education. In: *Comparative Education*, 16, 1990, pp.5-17.

JICA: *Study on development assistance for development and education.* Tokyo, JICA, 1994.

SASAKI, T: Theories and methodologies in comparative education. In: *Comparative Education*, 20, 1994, pp.7-14.

UMAKOSHI, T: Area studies as the foundation of comparative education. *Bulletin of the School of Education*, Nagoya University, 39(2), 1992, pp.21-30.

USHIOGI, M: Tasks for the research in educational development, co-operation and support. In: *Comparative Education*, 21, 1995, pp.7-14.

Chapter 2

Hermeneutic-oriented Techniques of Data Analysis in Comparative Sport Science Research Methodology

Herbert Haag

Introduction

Research in comparative physical education and sport is relatively complicated because of the variety of socio-cultural factors that have to be taken in to consideration. Furthermore, the situations, to which research is related, are also relatively complex often requiring data coded in words and numbers. Therefore, hermeneutic strategies are central to research methodology for comparative investigation. These strategies are explained in some detail in a four-step approach, in the context of techniques for data analysis, when data are coded in words:

- Techniques of data analysis as part of the *Kiel Model of Research Methodology*

- Hermeneutics as knowledge generating theory

- Function of hermeneutics in the research process

- Theoretical-logical strategies for analysing data coded in words

While statistical strategies to analyse data coded in numbers are widely published, hermeneutics and its strategies are relatively unknown and not systematically well developed as a foundation for techniques of data analysis for verbal coding. Hence, concepts addressed might also contribute to further improve research methodology for sport science in general and for comparative research in sport science in particular.

Techniques of Data Analysis as part of the *Kiel Model of Research Methodology* (KMRM) for Sports Science

In the German Sport Science community, the KMRM is a well-established model for conceptualising research methodology as it relates to sport science (see for example HAAG and PHILIPP, 1996; THOMAS and NELSON, 1996). The model is structured in six steps, which represent a logical procedure for realising research.

Step 1, *Philosophy of Science*, includes theories of knowledge and theories of science. Knowledge generating theories relate for example to hermeneutics, empiricism and phenomenology; theories of science relate for example to subjective idealism, dialectic materialism, critical theory, critical rationalism, logical empiricism, and positivism. Both types of theories provide cues to justify and plan research processes (SEIFERT and RADNITZKY, 1989). Step 2, *Research Methods*, includes basic concepts of methods like description, correlation, experiment and model-method. On a relatively abstract level, the outline procedure for doing research can thus be formulated. Step 3, *Research Design*, relates to the more concrete steps for the research process within a given research method. It is important to plan the steps of the research design in a precise way in order to ensure high quality research. Step 4, *Techniques of Data Collection*, represents an important step in the logical sequence of research in which the specific character of a scientific field plays an important role. These techniques can be with or without apparatus; major forms include questioning, observing and content analysis. Step 5, *Techniques of Data Analysis*, assists in relating data to the stated basic assumptions or hypotheses, and in drawing up the right conclusions. Basically, data can be coded in words and/or numbers. Accordingly two major sets of strategies are available for data analysis:

1. numerical strategies relate to statistical concepts (numbers) from descriptive to inferential forms; these have long been developed and formulated in numerous textbooks (see for example BÖS, 1987; MOREHOUSE and STULL 1975; STEMMLER, 1980);

2. non-numerical strategies relate to so called hermeneutic strategies, which have still to be specifically introduced to sport science (BAUERSFELD, 1987; ZIMMER and KLIMPEL, 1987).

Step 6, *Science Transfer*, means the ways of application of research results to reality. This last step is frequently neglected but is necessary if science is to meet its obligations.

The KMRM represents a logically sequenced model, which covers all important aspects of research.

Hermeneutics as Knowledge Generating-Theory

Hermeneutics can only be fully understood if a theoretical framework is developed, which consists of aspects of meta-theory of science such as scientific theories and knowledge generating theories. Within this framework, hermeneutics can then be explained as a specific way to generate scientific knowledge (GELDSETZER, 1989; HAAG, 1994b). *Theories of Science* are related to four main issues or questions:

- the function of science (teleology)

- the body of knowledge of science (subject-matter)

- generation of scientific knowledge (research methodology)

- the application of research results (science transfer)

The following six positions are examples for theories of science as they relate to research in sport science. They are named in a logical order from idealistic to positivistic positions that can be seen as endpoints of a continuum.

a) Subjective idealism is a position, which is strongly individually oriented, where science is mainly undertaken for science sake. The discovery as well as the application of context is considered. The methodological approach is predominantly hermeneutic.

b) Dialectic materialism is a position where science is serving the 'Diamat' in order to prove the superiority of this scientific position and the respective political system. The theory is society oriented, embraces the discovery and application context, and uses a wide range of research methodologies from hermeneutic to empirical approaches.

c) Critical theory is position bound to social necessities. It recognises the discovery and application context. In the main, it applies the hermeneutic approach, but also acknowledges empirical oriented methodologies.

d) Critical rationalism, as a position, accepts knowledge as true as long as it is not proven wrong or falsified. The discovery context is acknowledged; the application context, however, is neglected. In regard to research methodology, there is a preference for the empirical approach.

e) Logical empiricism is characterised by connecting theoretical and empirical dimensions in scientific work. The discovery and application context is considered to some extent. It is based on pluralism in research methodology with a predominance of the empirical research approach.

f) Positivism is, as a position, strictly based on the empirical research approach. Aspects relating to the before or after the research process are of no interest at all.

These six positions are just examples for scientific theories. It is not necessary to subscribe to these elaborated positions. What is, however, necessary in a research process is that every researcher spells out his/her scientific position because this has consequences for the type of research process to be realised.

Within these theories of science, the theories of generating scientific knowledge also play an important part, by indicating how certain theories of science value certain ways of generating scientific knowledge. It is an important task for sport science to deal with these issues (see GRUPE, 1986; HEINEMANN, 1985; KUNATH, 1988; WILLIMCZIK, 1992).

Knowledge-Generating Theories are of importance in understanding the research process in general and the techniques of data analysis in particular. These knowledge-generating theories have been described by HAAG (1994a,) as follows:

> ... In regard to epistemology, i.e., the issues of ultimate interest and importance, namely how knowledge can be gained scientifically, three positions can be distinguished on a continuum: hermeneutics is the one pole, empiricism the other pole, and phenomenology is in the middle of this continuum. A short explanation of the three positions is given in the following:
>
> Hermeneutic means that one can gain knowledge on the basis of understanding and interpreting available material, mostly texts and documents (example: UNESCO International Charter for Physical Education and Sport. This is done either informally or by following formal procedures such as content analysis.
>
> Empirical means that on the basis of the sensory ability of seeing (partly also hearing) a clear observation can be made; these observations are exact and can be tested in their perception by other individuals (degree of inter-subjective examination) (example: measuring a long jump or stopping a time).
>
> Phenomenological means that one is perceiving something empirically and at the same time one attempts to understand and interpret it hermeneutically (example: perceiving a movement and interpreting it as a coach does when giving corrections or as movement in pantomime).
>
> Phenomenological on the continuum of hermeneutical and empirical is somewhat in the middle; it is a reconciliation of seeing and understanding, since both aspects play a role in phenomenology. The phenomenological approach is used quite often in daily life. It is, however, also one unique approach to gaining scientific knowledge, besides hermeneutic and empirical as two separate approaches. It is becoming clear that there is not a better or worse, a more valuable or not so valuable way to gain knowledge. A plurality in scientific approaches is necessary; the issue to be investigated decides on how knowledge in regard to these issues is gained scientifically.

(pp.99-100).

The following figure indicates how these tracks of epistemology are related to basic contents of sport science expressed in the seven-theory-field model.

Figure 1.
Relation between theory of sport science and epistemological positions

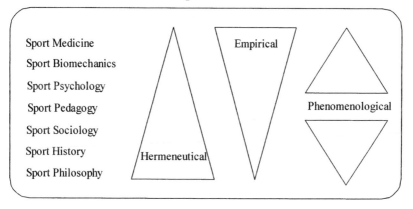

(HAAG, 1991, p.295)

The Function of Hermeneutics in the Research Process

This position is explained in figure 2, which indicates *the Research Sequence* (LRS) in a detailed way. This explanation of the research process in four major parts (introductory steps, theoretical planning, practical work, analysis and presentation) facilitates the location of rule function I of hermeneutics, the special function of hermeneutics and the rule function II of hermeneutics.

Figure 2.
Logical research sequence

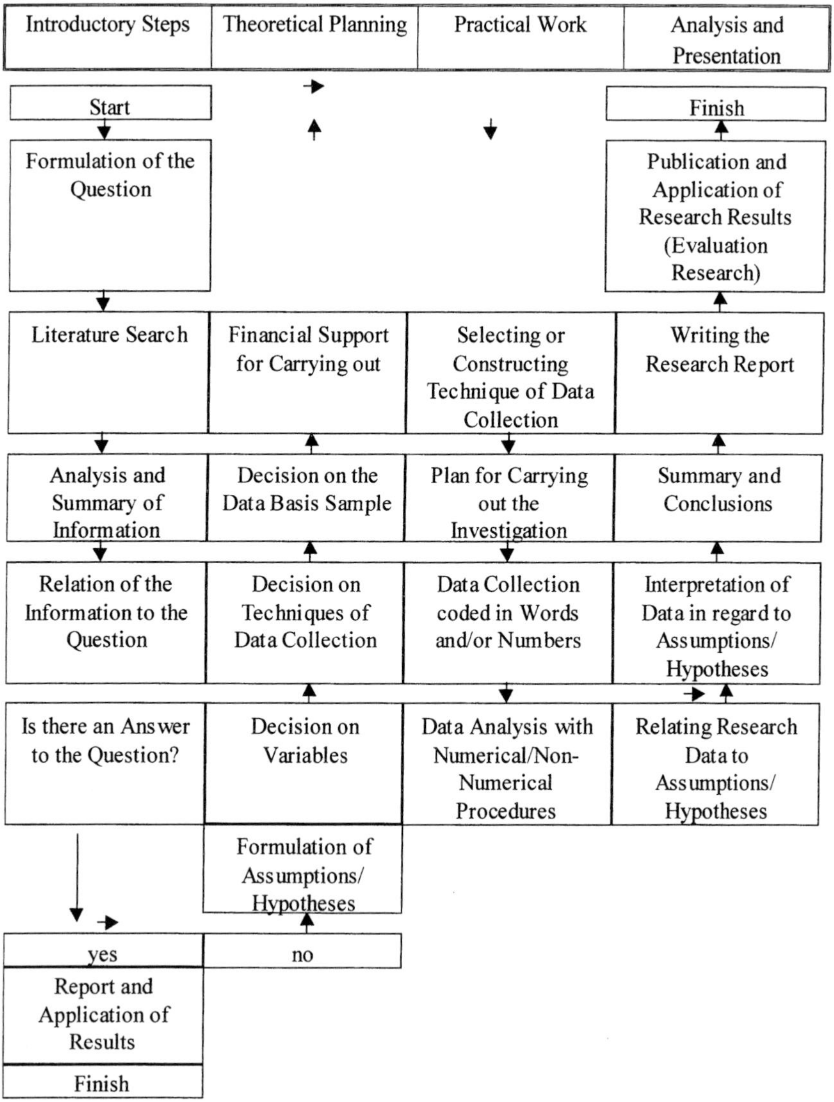

Introductory Steps	Theoretical Planning	Practical Work	Analysis and Presentation
Start			Finish
Formulation of the Question			Publication and Application of Research Results (Evaluation Research)
Literature Search	Financial Support for Carrying out	Selecting or Constructing Technique of Data Collection	Writing the Research Report
Analysis and Summary of Information	Decision on the Data Basis Sample	Plan for Carrying out the Investigation	Summary and Conclusions
Relation of the Information to the Question	Decision on Techniques of Data Collection	Data Collection coded in Words and/or Numbers	Interpretation of Data in regard to Assumptions/Hypotheses
Is there an Answer to the Question?	Decision on Variables	Data Analysis with Numerical/Non-Numerical Procedures	Relating Research Data to Assumptions/Hypotheses
	Formulation of Assumptions/Hypotheses		
yes	no		
Report and Application of Results			
Finish			

Rule Function 1 of Hermeneutics

The acquired scientific knowledge is available in different types of writings, respectively documents. Whoever is undertaking research (no matter if it is hermeneutic-theoretical or empirical-analytical) has to be informed about the knowledge already available in regard to the issue of the planned research. This so-called 'review of literature' is important, because from this the theoretical framework for research is established and the necessary derivation of basic assumptions (data coded in words) or hypotheses (data coded in numbers) is undertaken. Therefore, everyone engaging in a research process to gain scientific knowledge has to understand hermeneutic analyses (see also rule function II).

Special Function of Hermeneutics

This special function consists of document content analysis (MAYRING, 1985). Content analysis of texts can be undertaken with use of numbers (quantitative content analysis, e.g. how often certain terms are used in a text). However, the hermeneutic technique of collecting data coded in words is still used. For complex questions, triangulation is often used. This process usually involves data collected from a range of sources, which can provide a data based comprising words and numbers.

Rule Function II of Hermeneutics

This function relates to the interpretation of research results, a procedure that is necessary in any type of research: hermeneutic-theoretical or empirical-analytical. Rule function II means explanatory analysis of the results of the scientific research. It is carried out objectively, so that a high degree of inter-subjective objectivity is obtained.

Rule function II is related to the theoretical-logical strategies described in the next section of this analysis. For this rule function, it is important that the stated basic assumptions and/or hypotheses are used in order to interpret their respective acceptance or rejection. In this context, it is important that the narrow paradigm of causal-effect analysis be enlarged so as to arrive at explanations (based on an experimental design), since explanation is the result of research of a hermeneutic-theoretical nature. Here, explanation is based on the paradigm of plausibility. In summary, rule function II applies to any type of research thus, hermeneutics again, as in rule function I, are applied in general research.

Theoretical-Logical Strategies for Analysing Data Coded in Words

These strategies are linked to verbal expressions, to texts, to words as one form of coding data (ANSHEL, 1991; BEYER, 1987; HAAG, 1987; EBERSPÄCHER, 1997, RÖTHIG, 1992). These words are central to the hermeneutic-theoretical approach to research. However, words also play a role in the empirical-analytical research approach, in conducting the review of literature, formulating hypotheses, and interpreting the data in light of the stated hypotheses. Dealing with language, either in daily use or in regard to scientific work (daily language - scientific language) entails dealing with language in the form of letters, words, sentences or texts. This can be done by using theoretical-logical strategies as explained in the following eight examples (ZIMMER and KLIMPEL, 1987).

1. Basically there are three ways for acquiring information or informing oneself: reference publications (e.g. dictionaries), literature (derived from literature data banks) and organisations. Informing is a basic cognitive procedure to acquire knowledge.

2. Systematising has three terms, which clarify this cognitive procedure: system, systematics and order. Systematising means reducing, ordering and structuring of verbal information to facilitate systematic analysis.

3. In summarising, the following requirements have to be met: congruence of single aspects with the whole, clear writing, referring to the stated objective and indicating steps that have to be taken; formal summaries are supposed to include aim(s), database, research methods, results, discussion of results and evaluation.

4. Comparison is a very basic procedure within the research process and can be seen in three ways: (i) comparison of available scientific

literature with the stated research question - review of literature; (ii) comparison of results with the stated assumptions/hypotheses; (iii) comparison of results to prepare a final statement. Comparison can result in difference, equivalence or similarity. It is applied as a cognitive procedure in descriptive, correlational and experimental research. Comparison is close to evaluation as a highly important cognitive action.

5. Interpretation is applied in relation to objects of nature, actions, maxims, and texts. The following elements are related to interpretation: observation and analysis of the object; knowledge of the interpreter; pre-understanding in relation to the topic; examination of this pre-understanding. It is possible to distinguish six kinds of interpretation:

• causal interpretation (e.g. outcome of training methods)

• functional interpretation (e.g. importance of co-ordination for playing basketball)

• structural interpretation (e.g. structure of training processes)

• genetic interpretation (e.g. detecting the development of motor performance)

• modelling interpretation (e.g. model for analysing teaching-learning processes in sport

• relating interpretation (e.g. anticipation as part of co-ordination)

Thus, the theoretical-logical strategy of interpretation is very close to explanation.

6. Explanation in a scientific sense means the relating of subject matter to nomologic expressions. Hitherto, explanation has largely been reserved for experimental method. However, to explain something is always the main purpose of research. The difference between explanation as a result of an experimental, and descriptive study only, is a different degree in the possibility of inter-subjective validation of

the result. Besides this broad understanding of explanation, the nomologic-deductive and the statistical-inductive explanation provide a more narrow understanding. This narrow understanding is related to the results of research, where data are coded in numbers. For the analysis of data coded in words, however, comparable procedures should be applied to arrive at research results, which have a high level of validity.

7. Justification is a theoretical-logical strategy in which the argument is rational, with the aim of obtaining agreement related to the validity of the arguments. Two forms of justification can be distinguished:

a) mathematical-oriented logical reasoning for research with data coded in numbers (compare positivism);

b) normative justification on the basis of understanding within hermeneutic-theoretical research based on data coded in words (compare constructivism). Four aspects of this process of justification can be identified:

(i)   reason or generally accepted principles (proven by science);
(ii)   concrete situation which is described by data;
(iii)   rules to construct the connection of (i) and (ii);
(iv)   conclusion containing the statement for or against which one is arguing.

Thus, justification is a cognitive operation using language; it is essential to the analysis of data coded in words.

8. Proof is applied in daily life situations and in law. In science, proof embraces a sophisticated process to prove a statement (basic assumption/hypotheses) against possible contradictions. It is used in all different types of sciences (from natural to cultural sciences). The following criteria are important for proof as a theoretical-logical strategy:

• completeness of deductive proof

• a single step not further divisible

- explicit naming of the assumptions

- using only proven statements and axioms

- completeness of proof

- obtaining assured results

- finality of the proof

In proving, deductive proof is also distinguished from the so-called inductive proof. Complete induction is characteristic of mathematics. Incomplete induction is characteristic within many sciences and cannot prove things forever, since changeable experience is linked to incomplete induction.

These eight examples for theoretical-logical strategies represent avenues for analysing data coded in words. These strategies can be compared with statistical concepts, which are used when data are coded in numbers. It is relatively difficult to describe these theoretical-logical strategies in an operational way. However, application of the KMRM may help to upgrade hermeneutic- theoretical research by introducing clear action steps in the logical sequence of research.

Concluding Comments

Data analysis is the fifth step in the Kiel Model of Research Methodology (KMRM) for sport science in general and in comparative research in particular. This chapter reports on recent research findings related to the conceptualisation of techniques of data analysis, if data are coded in words. The intention is to secure equal recognition of hermeneutic-theoretical and empirical-analytical research, since the quantitative versus qualitative paradigm is a misleading one (LAMNEK, 1988, 1989; OLAFSON, 1991). As comparative and cross-cultural data are quite often coded in words, hermeneutic-oriented techniques of data analysis are an important addition to improving comparative research in the form of cross-cultural studies related to movement, play, and sport.

References

ANSHEL, M.H., (Ed.): *Dictionary of sport and exercise sciences.* Champaign, IL, Human Kinetics Pub. Inc., 1991.

BAUERSFELD, K-H.: Forschungsmethoden in den sportmethodischen Wissenschaftsdiszipline. In: *Wissenschaftliche Zeitschrift der Deutschen Hochschule für Körperkultur*, 28(3), 1987.

BEYER, E., (Ed.): *Dictionary of sport science.* Schorndorf, Hofmann, 1992.

BÖS, K.: *Handbuch sportmotorischer Tests.* Göttingen, Hogrefe, 1987.

EBERSPÄCHER, H.: *Handlexikon Sportwissenschaft.* Reinbek, Rohwohlt, 1987.

GELDSETZER, L.: Hermeneutik. In: SEIFFERT, H., and RADNITZKY, G., *Handlexikon zur Wissenschaftstheorie*, München, Ehrenwirt, 1989, pp.127-139.

GRUPE, O.: Künftige Aufgaben und Probleme der Sportwissenschaft. In: HEINEMANN, K., and BECKER, H., (Eds.), *Die Zukunft des Sports. Materialien zum Kongress 'Menschen im Sport 2000'.* Schorndorf, Hofmann, 1986, pp.262-268.

HAAG, H.: Development and structure of a theoretical framework for sport science ('Sportwissenschaft'). In: *Quest*, 31, 1979, pp.25-35.

HAAG, H.: *Schülerduden der Sport.* Mannheim, Duden-Verlag, 1987.

HAAG, H.: Qualitativ und quantitativ - Ein falscher Gegensatz in der forschungsmethodologischen Diskussion der Sportwissenschaft. In: SINGER, R. (Ed.), *Sportpsychologische Forschungsmethoden. Grundlagen, Probleme, Ansätze*, Köln, bps, 1991, pp.69-76.

HAAG, H.: *Theoretical foundation of sport science as a scientific discipline. Contribution to a philosophy (meta-theory) of sport science.* Schorndorf, Hofmann, 1994a.

HAAG, H.: Der hermeneutische Zweig. In: STRAUSS, B., and HAAG, H., (Eds.). *Forschungsmethoden - Untersuchungspläne - Techniken der Datenerhebung in der Sportwissenschaft.* Schorndorf, Hofmann, 1994b, pp.39-47.

HAAG, H. and PHILIPP, T.: The naturalistic and rationalistic research paradigm. A possible theoretical framework for scientific methods in cross-cultural comparative sport science research. In: SVOBODA, B., and RYCHTECKY, A., (Eds.), *Physical activity for life: East and West, South and North*, Aachen, Meyer and Meyer Verlag, 1996, pp.99-103.

HEINEMANN, K.: Entwicklungsbedingungen der Sportwissenschaft. In: *Sportwissenschaft*, 1(3), 1985, pp.33-45.

KUNATH, H.: Differenzierung und Integration in der Sportwissenschaft. In: *Theorie und Praxis der Körperkultur*, 6, 1988, pp.366-373.

LAMNEK, S.: Qualitative Sozialforschung. Band 1, *Methodologie.* München, Psychologie Verlags Union, 1988.

LAMNEK, S.: Qualitative Sozialforschung. Band 11, *Methoden und Techniken.* München, Psychologie Verlags Union, 1989.

MAYRING, P.: *Qualitative Inhaltsanalyse.* Weinheim, Beltz, 1985.

MOREHOUSE, C.A., and STULL, A.: *Statistical principles and procedures with application for physical education.* Philadelphia, Lea and Febiger, 1975.

OLAFSON, G.: Triangulation in comparative research: mixing qualitative and quantitative methods. In: STANDEVEN, J., HARDMAN, K., and FISHER, R., (Eds.), *Sport for all into the 90's.* Aachen, Meyer and Meyer Verlag, 1991, pp.39-44.

RÖTHIG, P. (Ed.): *Sportwissenschaftliches Lexikon*. (6. Auflage), Schorndorf, Hofmann, 1992.

SEIFFERT, H. and RADNITZKY, G. (Eds.): *Handlexikon der Wissenschaftstheorie*. München, Ehrenwirt, 1989.

STEMMLER, R.: *Statistische Methoden im Sport*. Berlin, Sportverlag, 1980.

THOMAS, J.R., and NELSON, J.K.: *Research methods in physical activity*. Champaign, IL, Human Kinetics Pub. Inc., 1996.

WILLIMCZIK, K.: Interdisciplinary sport science - a science in search of its identity. In: HAAG, H., GRUPE, O., and KIRSCH, A., (Eds.), *Sport science in Germany. An interdisciplinary anthology*. Berlin, Springer, 1992, pp.7-36.

ZIMMER, H. and KLIMPEL, P.: Theoretisch-logische Methoden. In: *Wissenschaftliche Zeitschrift der DHFK*, 28(3), pp.49-62.

Chapter 3

Methodology in Comparative Physical Education and Sport: Keeping up with the Field

Richard J. Fisher

Introduction

Arguably, research in the domain of Comparative Physical Education and Sport suffers from insufficient credibility in relation to other fields to the extent that it might be seen to be inferior. Indeed, in some fields, e.g. Development Psychology, some excellent comparative research employing sophisticated approaches and methods well advanced from those utilised in comparative physical education and sport is being carried out. In such a context, comparativists in physical education and sport have to consider the concept of 'field' beyond that of the so-called parent area, comparative education and with a greater level of sophistication if they aspire to the 'real action'. This contribution looks at some key issues in comparative methodology in relation to a piece of research which attempted to come to terms with what was happening in other fields. It is offered as one way of attempting to locate research in physical education (PE) and sport within recent trends elsewhere.

Methodological issues

Methodology is defined as a "body of methods used in a particular branch of activity", whilst a method is viewed as a "special form of procedure" (OXFORD CONCISE DICTIONARY, 1991). Methodology, then is an overarching conception of how to address a problem, in this case how pupils and teachers in two different cultures, England and Germany (the former German Democratic Republic - GDR), were interpreting PE in the face of new curricula promulgated by fundamental social change. More importantly perhaps, it is located within the general developments in comparative and international research outlined by CROSSLEY and BROADFOOT (1992), who proposed a broader relationship between the hitherto fairly discrete world of comparative education and social science in general. In doing so, they underlined the increasing mutual interdependence of nations and the value of comparative study, but pointed to the marginal nature of many courses and much of the research. Furthermore, they claimed broad support for the development of better, more systematic frameworks and techniques for cross-cultural research, especially the use of research styles which combine appropriate paradigms, and which focus on cross-cultural studies that are sensitive to more subtle elements within the phenomenon under investigation. This allows also for a greater diversity of approaches, which ALTBACH and KELLY (1986) regard as important, since it allows the application of more qualitative approaches, phenomenological perspectives in particular, within an international framework. This move to a greater level of integration with broader social science perspectives provided a sound basis for the research presented here. It also sits well with a growing trend in research to focus on the importance of acknowledging the wider social pressures impinging upon PE (see KIRK and TINNING, 1990, p.2, for example), as well as the meanings that PE holds for those who are a part of it - pupils and teachers.

The approach to research in the comparative field presented here is one way of responding to these developments and conducting more qualitative, interpretative investigations in a cross-cultural context and is intended as a contribution to the integration of existing comparative theories into larger social science perspectives. In an operational sense, the task was to assemble relevant contextual information, which would inform the central focus of the research, detailed analysis of teachers' and pupils' interpretations of PE. Consequently an adaptation of the approaches taken by BROADFOOT (1990) and MENLO and POPPLETON (1990), which are methodologically compatible with the position advanced by HOLMES (1991), appeared to be both fruitful and in line with the intentions outlined above. To this end, a framework was devised around HOLMES' (1965; 1981; 1991) approach to comparative research, since it recognises the importance of relationships between different aspects of a social system, utilises suitable categories of data within a proposed taxonomy, and facilitates the portrayal of internal and external aspects of a school. It is a dynamic model, which emphasises the significance of social change in creating problems; a synchronous response to such change in different parts of the social system being the seats of tension. In this sense, it was particularly relevant to the schools investigated, since both were experiencing significant change of one type or another: one from the unification of Germany; and other from the implementation of a new national curriculum. The schools were selected on the basis of commonly used criteria such as public/private, rural/suburban etc. It was not intended that the schools should represent each nation or cultural system, but more that they should portray a good example of PE within their respective systems, and upon which reasonable assumptions could be made. Indeed, it is one of the major claims for case studies that to understand one circumstance well is to be able to abstract to broader circumstances

Within HOLMES' (1991) model, four major patterns are identified and the relationships within and between these patterns, particularly the existence of tension, are important features to investigate, although the focus of any study determines which patterns are used and how. One of these patterns, the environment, was not particularly germane to this study, the others being normative, institutional and mental states. The normative pattern includes general notions about the type of person valued by a society, the political ideology promoted and legislative requirements for various aspects of that society, including education. In short, it represents "what ought to be the case" (HOLMES, 1991, p.22). The institutional pattern represents the way these essential beliefs or aims are operationalised. Economic, political, educational and religious institutions are all important, and at a lower level there will be specific institutions, actual schools for example, which function within this general pattern. HOLMES' (1991) final pattern, a critical one for the research, was based on his conviction that:

> ... the deeply held beliefs or mental states of individuals influenced the successful implementation of policy ... My view is that they cannot be derived from attitude tests which reveal normative beliefs ... Mental states, however, motivate behaviour and must therefore be known if new aims are to be achieved

> (p.2).

The final model adopted for the comparative analysis then, was one where interpretations of the participants, a critical element in the mental states pattern, were overlaid with normative and institutional patterns which were used, therefore, to contextualise the reality of life in schools.

Of central importance, of course, are issues of validity and these occur at several interrelated levels. It should be said, however, that research in PE has probably entertained rather restricted notions of validity. SPARKES (1992) captured the key issues apposite to this investigation with his view that validity should be seen as different sets of meanings, which vary with research based on different conceptual frameworks. He suggested that the way in which researchers perceive the phenomenon under investigation guides the mode and style of the enquiry and the way in which validity is conceived. Furthermore, he emphasised KUHN's (1970) position that each paradigm embodies its own 'disciplinary matrix' encompassing beliefs, assumptions and methodologies. In line with these views, MAXWELL (1992) cites BRINBERG and MCGRATH (1985) in claiming a consensus on determining validity in such contexts: "... Validity is not a commodity that can be purchased with techniques... Rather, validity is like integrity, character, and quality, to be assessed relative to purpose and circumstances" (pp.280-281).

Entering the Pupil's World - Personal Meanings of PE

The core issues were related to exploring pupils' interpretations of PE and are located within POPE and DENICOLO's (1986) view of individuals as active exploring entities; the "person as scientist" (p.164). The decision to pursue a more qualitative line was based on the nature of the research and the most appropriate data to be collected. The value of qualitative research in PE and associated issues has been well argued elsewhere (see EVANS and PENNEY, 1992, for example) and cannot be dealt with here. Pupils' interpretations were educed in part from a 'Like/Dislike' exercise, participant observation and informal conversations, but extensive experience over a number of years of trying to find the best way to enter the private worlds of pupils had confirmed that an approach rooted in personal construct psychology and based on repertory grid techniques should be the core method, since such techniques are:

(i)   suitable for cross-cultural comparison since a method is transferred across cultures rather than content, so the point of comparison is differential responses to the application of a common method;

(ii)   sensitive to a range of possible differences in individual and group interpretations of the subject;

(iii)   particularly suitable for uncovering the personal meaning that the subject has for pupils;

(iv)   appropriate for use with adolescents of mixed abilities.

In view of all the issues associated with these techniques and the general thrust of the methodology, it was sensible to focus specifically on one class in each school. It is clear from existing research that middle adolescence is a critical period for pupils' interpretations of PE (see FOX, 1994) and this guided the decision to select the particular class in question. Moreover, notwithstanding the important methodological issues involved, it was also clear that access to the German school would not be easy. Hence, it was better to contain the investigation within the confines of one group and to use the main advantage of case study, namely, to understand a particular circumstance very well.

The actual method of uncovering and representing these interpretations in PE is rooted in personal construct psychology, based on the seminal work of KELLY (1955). There has been a growing interest in the last decade in the applicability of KELLY's work to educational research in general, although very little use appears to have been made of this approach in PE and sport. Studies such as FEIXAS, JAUME and VILLEGAS (1989) and BALSDON and CLIFT (1992) are among the few pieces of research to adopt this approach in PE and sport. In the cross-cultural study of PE and sport this would appear to be virgin territory. KELLY (1955) maintains that people evolve their own sense of reality through sets of constructions of the world which are retained or discarded as they allow them to anticipate events successfully or otherwise. Without ignoring the relevance of early experiences or environmental influences, KELLY emphasises this constantly evolving representational map of the world which people create, and which guides their behaviour as they anticipate events and the likely consequences of their actions. As BANNISTER and FRANSELLA (1980) pointed out: "... we cannot apprehend reality directly. We can only construe and interpret it, usefully or uselessly, inventively or routinely, humorously or soberly" (p.43).

Essentially, it promotes the notion of individuals as scientists, seeking to observe, interpret, predict and control behaviour in the face of a nexus of social and environmental contexts. The theory itself is explicated in a fundamental postulate and 11 corollaries. The fundamental postulate states that a person's processes are psychologically channelled by the ways in which events are anticipated. Three of these corollaries are particularly significant here (using KELLY's, 1955, original numbering):

1. "Construction Corollary: A person anticipates events by construing their replications" (p.50). Construing involves an interpretation of features from a series of elements in terms of similarity and contrast. Constructs are thus erected as bi-polar in nature thereby allowing a logical system of differentiation. Once we recognise recurrent themes it is possible to predict them in terms of their "replicative aspects" and so to anticipate events.

10. "Commonality Corollary: To the extent that one person employs a construction system which is similar to that employed by another, his psychological processes are similar to those of the other person" (p.90). This is an implicit ramification of the fundamental postulate and allows for the fact that two or more people can construe events in a similar fashion. Clearly this was important to the present study since a class spends a good deal of time together and one may assume the possibility of some commonality, as researchers such as SALMON and CLAIRE (1984) and BURKE, NOLLER and CAIRD (1992) have done.

11. "Sociality Corollary": To the extent that one person construes the construction processes of another, he may play a role in a social process involving the other person" (p.95). Common or similar cultural backgrounds may give rise to similar behaviour patterns, but in order for meaningful social interaction there must be some mutual acceptance of the other's outlook. The emphasis here is on interpersonal understanding and in the present research context this

supports the existence of group or class interpretations, particularly where there is extensive and continuous interaction on a daily basis.

Essentially in this study, the concern was to uncover the constructs relevant to a particular set of elements, which in this case were PE and subjects in the curriculum. In its simplest sense, a construct is bi-polar in nature and is a way in which two elements are similar and contrast with a third. In this way, the approach complemented the overall thrust of the research, which is comparative and, therefore, a process of comparison and contrast. To operationalise this process the Role Construct Repertory Test was used. It has no pure form, being rather a flexible method of, as POPE and KEEN (1981) put it "... entering the phenomenological world of an individual by exploring the nature and inter-relationships between various elements and constructs elicited by the method" (p.31).

Many forms of grid have developed over the years and a full analysis of the principles is contained in POPE and KEEN (1981), including such things as the purpose of the grid, choice of elements and constructs, scaling, method of elicitation and methods of analysis. In short, the traditional 'triadic' method was adopted to elicit a series of grids, which were merged into a consensus grid with the approval and co-operation of the class. Cards were presented to pupils three at a time and they were asked to consider ways in which two might be similar or different from the third, leading to a bi-polar construct. Since the main focus of attention was PE, this card was included in every triad with the other two cards changing each time. Pupils were offered the chance to select their own pairs of cards to go with PE, but were quite happy addressing those that came up naturally. Pupils worked alone or in a group of no more than three, identifying and discussing each pole as it arose and resolving their thoughts with prompting from the researcher, either directly or through 'laddering'. Once the emergent and contrasting pole had been uncovered, 'boring... fun' for example, this was recorded on the grid sheet, which had been designed with large number indicators of 1 and 5 on each side to help pupils focus on an appropriate point of the rating scale when this part of the process arrived. After two or three constructs had been identified, they were 'laddered' before moving on. The process continued until the pupils kept repeating themselves or became fed up, or both, although most managed an hour and appeared to enjoy doing it. Such grid conversations allow a good exploration of pupils' construct systems through uncovering the poles of each construct, and then being able to discuss whether they are what the individual intended and if they reflected accurately the original meaning ascribed to them. Working with a class to develop a consensus grid meant that additional care had to be taken to ensure that the final grid was meaningful to all members. Once a consensus grid had been agreed it was offered to all the class for completion - rating each element (subject) on each construct, on a scale of 1-5 (more towards one pole or another). At the same time, pupils were asked to rank what they considered to be the six most important constructs, which would give an extra dimension to the analysis. A similar process was followed in both schools, except that, pupils in the German school mainly preferred to come in twos and threes for the initial conversations.

Three main steps were involved in the analysis of grids: stages two and three using a computer package - Rep.Grid 2 (SHAW, 1989):

a) initial scrutiny of the grids was undertaken to see which constructs were ranked highest on average, and what the mean class rating was on each of the constructs; these average figures were viewed as descriptive statistics only and simply used to help identify likely patterns within the class and to get a feel for the data;

b) all the grids were focused using Rep.Grid 2; focusing is based upon an analysis of similarities between elements and between constructs in a grid, in order to reorganise the display to highlight particular patterns which may be contained within an individual's responses (refer THOMAS and HARRI-AUGSTEIN, 1985, for a full explanation of the nature of the process);

c) the 'Socio' option in Rep.Grid 2 compares grids having elements, constructs, or both in common and, like a socio-net, shows up which pupils' grids link up in terms of construct ratings.

Some Important Results

Some of the more important outcomes of the research process serve to demonstrate the value of the approach adopted.

(i) For the English pupils most important constructs included:

Exciting .... Boring (Ranked 1)

Very Serious .... Can have fun (Ranked 2)

Can take part in lessons .... Mostly writing and slow
                                                                           things (Ranked 4)

The girls actually ranked 4 as slightly more important than 1, not so the boys.

For the German pupils, most important constructs included:

Mentally Exhausting .... Fun (Ranked 1)

Can make a personal contribution .... Topics are fixed
                                                                            (Ranked 2)

Can let yourself go .... Being Necessary
                                                                            (Ranked 3)

The girls were much more definite about the importance of number 2.

(ii)   The focused grids gave a good insight into pupils' interpretations
         of PE within the curriculum. Those who liked it placed it alongside
         such subjects as drama, where you learned about yourself. Those
         who disliked PE often placed it alongside the sorry tale that became
         history or often in Germany with the 'dry' scientific subjects.

(iii)   The focused grids showed a greater consensus of construing PE
         among the German pupils than the English. In the 'Socio' analysis
         of relationships between grids, the German pupils checked in
         quicker and in greater numbers than their English counterparts who
         demonstrated a broader range of interpretations. It seemed
         reasonable to explain this by way of the nature of the educational
         diet that had been fed to the two sets of pupils, the one rigid and
         definite, the other more exploratory and pupil centred.

(iv)   The most marked result was that each class threw up two sub-
          sets of girls, one that liked being active, especially in a modern
          context such as dance, and one that really disliked practical work
          completely, or at least in this context. There were similarities of
          construal between both groups, whilst the bulk of the boys in both
          schools viewed the subject in a positive and constructive light - do
          we have a common adolescent interpretation of PE in Europe
          subdivided into three major social groupings?

This is only a selection of all the findings and discussion points available,
but it highlights the value of utilising a different sort of research
paradigm from the social sciences to those which have been employed in
comparative work in the main until now. The aim was to use comparative
study to look at the nature of PE in two different contexts of changing
socio-political circumstances, with particular regard to the interpretations
of the participants, and with a view to making recommendations for
practice. The methodology was in line with developments in the main
field of comparative and international studies, and the methods of
investigation were well suited to the declared purpose and applied within
the precepts of accepted practice in the respective fields.

Closing the Circle

LYONS (1992) recognition of an evolutionary process that starts with
what is effectively intrusion, but develops into co-operation and then
intervention with an inevitable progression from research on teaching to
research with teachers was evident in this investigation. Feedback on
what PE meant for their pupils was given to teachers in the form of a
written summary of essential information as an aid to programme review.
Fundamentally, it allowed completion of the circle of investigation by
informing teachers of the implications of their teaching, and offered the
possibility of fuelling a process of development and professional learning
in both schools. This is in keeping with the philosophy underpinning
HOLMES' (1965) approach to comparative education and, indeed, with
the ethos of personal construct psychology. In examining and analysing
education, there are no end points only positions in a process.

References

ALTBACH, P.G., and KELLY, G.P.: *New approaches to comparative education*. Chicago, University of Chicago Press, 1986.

BALSDON, A.J., and CLIFT, S.M.: Assessing pupils' games performance in the secondary school: an exploration using repertory grid technique. In: WILLIAMS, T., ALMOND, L., and SPARKES, A., *Sport and physical activity: moving towards excellence*. London, E & FN Spon, 1992, pp.145-157.

BANNISTER, D., and FRANSELLA, F.: *Inquiring man: the psychology of personal constructs*. Harmondsworth, Penguin, 1980.

BROADFOOT, P.: Research on teachers: towards a comparative methodology. In: *Comparative Education*, 26(2/3), 1990, pp.165-169.

BURKE, M., NOLLER, P., and CAIRD, D.: Transition from practitioner to educator, a RepGrid analysis. In: *International Journal of Personal Construct Psychology*, 5(2), 1992, pp.159-182.

CROSSLEY, M., and BROADFOOT, P.: Comparative and international research in education: scope, problems and potential. In: *British Education Research Journal*, 18(2), 1992, pp.99-112.

EVANS, J., and PENNEY, D., with BRYANT, A.: Physical education after ERA? In: *British Journal of Physical Education, Research Supplement*, 13, Autumn, 1993, pp.2-5.

FEIXAS, G., JAUME, M., and VILLEGAS, M.: Personal construct assessment of sport teams. In: *International Journal of Personal Construct Psychology*, 2, 1989, pp.49-54.

FOX, K.: Understanding young people and their decisions about physical activity. In: *British Journal of Physical Education*, 25(1), Spring, 1994, pp.15-19.

HOLMES, B.: *Problems in education*. London, Routledge and Kegan Paul, 1965.

HOLMES, B.: *Comparative education: some considerations of method.* London, George Allen and Unwin, 1981.

HOLMES, B.: Comparative education methodology and physical education. In: STANDEVEN, J., HARDMAN, K., and FISHER, R., (Eds.): *Sport for all. Into the 90s.* Aachen, Meyer and Meyer Verlag, 1991, pp.19-32.

KELLY, G.A.: *The psychology of personal constructs*, vols.1 and 2. New York, W.W. Norton and Co. Inc., 1955.

KIRK, D., and TINNING, R., (Eds.): *Physical education, curriculum and culture: critical issues in the contemporary crisis.* London, The Falmer Press, 1990.

KUHN, T.: *The structure of scientific revolutions.* Chicago, University of Chicago Press, 1970.

LYONS, K.: Telling stories from the field. In: SPARKES, A., (Ed.), *Research in physical education and sport: exploring alternative visions.* London, Falmer Press, 1992, pp.248-270.

MAXWELL, J.A.: Understanding and validity in qualitative research. In: *Harvard Education Review*, 62(3), Fall, 1992, pp.279-300.

MENLO, A., and POPPLETON, P.: A five-country study of secondary school teachers in England, the United States, Japan, Singapore and West Germany (1986-1988). In: *Comparative Education*, 26(2/3), 1990, pp.173-182.

OXFORD CONCISE DICTIONARY, Oxford, Clarendon Press, 1991 (3rd edition).

POPE, M.L., and KEEN, T.R.: *Personal construct psychology and education.* London, Academic Press, 1981.

POPE, M., and DENICOLO, P.: Intuitive theories - a researcher's dilemma: some practical methodological implications. In: *British Educational Research Journal*, 12(2), 1986, pp.153-166.

SALMON, P., and CLAIRE, H.: *Classroom collaboration.* London, Routledge and Kegan Paul, 1984.

SHAW M.L.G.: Interactive elicitation and exchange of knowledge. In: *International Journal of Personal Construct Psychology*, 2, 1989, pp.215-238.

SPARKES, A.: Validity and the research process: an exploration of meanings. In: *Physical Education Review*, 15(1), 1992, pp.29-45.

THOMAS, L.F., and HARRI-AUGSTEIN, E.S.: *Self-organised learning: foundations of a conversational science for psychology.* London, Routledge and Kegan Paul, 1985.

PART 2

CROSS-CULTURAL STUDIES IN SPORT

Chapter 4

Reconstructing Femininity and Masculinity in Sport - Women and Football in Germany and France during the Inter-war Years

Gertrud Pfister

Introduction

Body and movement may be grounded in biology, but body techniques and body ideals as well as forms and traditions of movement are predominantly shaped by culture. This means that, on the one hand, the gender order leaves its special imprint on the bodies of men and women and that, on the other, body culture contributes towards maintaining the sexual hierarchy. Since both body culture and movement culture are "engendered", certain forms of movement are given a masculine connotation while others are given a feminine connotation. As a result, types of sport develop either a masculine or feminine image and thus have a different appeal for the members of the two sexes. In the history of European physical culture, the participation of men and women in certain types of exercise and sport was, from the very beginning, tied to a great number of rules and norms. It was women especially who were excluded from sporting activities, the reasons given being the prevailing roles of the genders and the myths surrounding them.

One type of sport, which is still regarded today in many countries as "typically male", is the game of football. In addressing the development of the game in France and Germany, this contribution focuses on women's participation in the "unfeminine" regarded sport, football, in the two countries and particularly on social and gender orders.

The Development of Football

The rise of modern sport was connected with the processes of social and economic change, which took place in England at the end of the 18th and the beginning of the 19th centuries. In the wake of modernisation processes affecting all fields of society, the old games resembling football (played in many places on public holidays without any strict rules and often with large numbers of people taking part) lost their appeal. The idea of the game of football was taken up by the public schools in the middle of the 19th century. It was here that this national game was codified, ritualised and regulated for use as a means of disciplining schoolboys. The year 1863 saw the founding of the Football Association, which established standardised rules, thus making a clear distinction once and for all between soccer and rugby. Initially, football was the preserve of the upper echelons of society. However, the increasing popularity of the game and the enthusiasm shown by large sections of the population soon led to a striving towards professionalisation, which, especially after the introduction of a system of leagues in 1888, produced a democratisation of the game and a wider distribution of the social background of the players. By the end of the 19th century, thousands of football clubs had been formed engaging workers in a healthy and sensible form of recreation. Football subsequently became a working man's game and it was the workers who "made the game an integral part not only of the national culture but also of class culture" (EISENBERG, 1994, p.181).

Moreover, football became a significant factor in a boy's education towards manhood and the appropriation of masculinity:

> Boys learnt how to drink and tell jokes as well as the language of physical aggression ... Football clubs were only a part of the wider process of male socialisation which took place in the workplace, the pub and the world of hobbies
> (WILLIAMS and WOODHOUSE, 1981, p.89).

In England, rugby, too, offered young men the opportunity, in addition to football, to build up and participate in a sub-culture of mythical demonstrated masculinity and male identity (DUNNING, 1986).

What was to become the 'world game', spread rapidly throughout the 'empires' of the 19th century (see GUTTMANN, 1994). It was Englishmen who, as businessmen, students or tourists, introduced the game of football into Germany in the 1880s and, at first, both soccer and rugby were played, i.e. football played with and without picking up the ball. One of the first football centres in Germany was the capital, Berlin, where young men were already playing the game in the 1880s on Tempelhof Field, an area in the south of the city otherwise used for military exercises. Soon the first clubs were founded and in a relatively short time these began to concentrate on Association Football. After much argument, the German Football Federation was established in 1900. The game soon became increasingly popular with both players and spectators and was established as Germany's national game (PFISTER, 1987) with between 800,000 and 900,000 football players, (the majority of them belonging to the middle classes), members of the German Football Federation in the 1920s (NERZ, 1927).

In its rapid diffusion throughout the world, football reached France in the 1870s. "Ce sont les agents de l'expansion économique britannique dans le monde qui assurent la diffusion du football", so noted WAHL (1990, p.30) in his brief history of football. In France, too, by the start of the First World War, the classical form of football without picking up the ball was predominant. Football players were organised at first in various associations, among others, from 1894 onwards, in the Union des Sociétés Françaises Sportives et Athlétiques, founded in 1889. It was not until 1919 that the founding of the French Football Association brought them independence and unity. In 1922, the Association had a membership of 30,000.

The Beginnings of Women's Sport in Germany and France

In the 19th century, women were in many respects the "weaker sex" both in Germany and in France. In the world of politics, just as in the family, they were deprived of equal rights. The myth of female weakness and the conditions of women's lives had many effects, including the effect on women's opportunities for practising sport.

1. Germany

In Germany, the first concepts of systematic physical education date back to the late 18th and early 19th centuries. Girls and women, however, were excluded not only from the gymnastic activities of the Philanthropists but also the German 'Turnen' (Gymnastics). The latter was generally held to be a man's affair, not least since, besides its emphasis on masculinity and producing able-bodied men capable of defending their country, it also pursued political objectives.

In its early years, the 'Turnen' movement exhibited many features of a "male alliance". Nevertheless, even although at the end of the century male 'Turner' were still adamantly pursuing the cause of education towards and demonstration of masculinity, the number of female 'Turner' began to rise steadily from the 1880s onwards. Gradually, women 'Turner' began to alter the image of the 'Turnen' movement and the way it saw itself. Now it was the new types of sport from England, which were labelled "unfeminine", especially the ones (with the exceptions of the upper class sports of golf, hockey and tennis) related to performance and competition. The first sporting contests with women competitors, therefore, (for example the "Ladies' Sports Festival" organised by the Berlin club SC Komet in 1904) met with great opposition (DER LEICHTATHLET, 1926). The women's 400m. event held during the festival even prompted the German Athletics Authority, in its newsletter Sport im Wort, to formulate its basic rejection of all foot races for women, calling them an "aberration of emancipation wrongly understood" (BERNETT, 1987, p.202). In most other sports, women were also confronted with problems and obstacles specific to the sport they wished to practise. In swimming it was people's concern about decorum and morals that made the participation of women at swimming competitions appear problematic among other things because of the bathing costumes they wore. Nevertheless, women were allowed to compete in public for best times and first place in the swimming contests of the 1912 Olympic Games. Rowing, on the other hand, was considered too strenuous for the "weaker sex" and women rowers were, therefore, restricted to competitions in which precision of movement rather than speed counted. Cycling events for women, quite popular in the 1890s, were discontinued after the turn of the century in spite of protests from women cyclists (PFISTER and LANGENFELD, 1980).

Despite the opposition, girls and women became increasingly interested in sport, including the so-called traditional activities involving running, throwing and jumping. In 1913, these were then incorporated in the first guidelines to be drawn up for girls' physical education. In the wake of the processes of modernisation, which followed the First World War, great changes took place both in the situation of women and in the situation of women's sport. In 1919, for example, the German Athletic Authority urged all athletic clubs to set up women's sections (BERNETT, 1987). In 1920 the first women's athletic championships were held in Dresden, albeit in only three disciplines (DER LEICHTATHLET, 1928). The 1920s saw the founding of not only a great number of women's sections affiliated to men's sports clubs but also independent women's sports clubs such as, for example, the German Ladies' and the German Women's Sports Club in Berlin, both of which could boast of first class athletes as members (NEITZKE, 1984). The women's sections and the independent women's clubs (with the exception of rowing clubs) were members of the sports associations of the male athletes.

In the 1920s, too, there was general consensus among not only sports officials, doctors, sports journalists and the general public but also many women gymnastics coaches and women athletes that the femininity of girls and women should on no account suffer from exaggerated sporting activities. Numerous precautionary measures were introduced in order to prevent an imagined masculinisation of women athletes. It was the renowned athlete and later functionary Karl Ritter von Halt who, in the 1920s, observed that "men were born to compete; competition is alien to a woman's nature" (PFISTER, 1993). According to the general consensus, women should be excluded not only from all contests but also from those types of sport "not suited to women's natures, which have an alienating and distorting effect and therefore should be better left to the male sex" (SPORT UND GESUNDHEIT, 1932, p.16).

2. France

Since its beginnings in the early 19th century, the French gymnastic movement was closely connected with military fitness. One of the first and most important propagators and teachers of gymnastics was Francisco Amoros, whose work focused on the physical preparation of soldiers. In the 19th century, physical activities played a marginal role only in the lives of women and girls. Some authors, like Clias, Laisné, Paz and Docx, recommended gymnastique douce, i.e. exercises, which did not endanger health, grace and beauty of the female participants. Books like Calisthénie (CLIAS, 1828) or Gymnastique des jeunes filles et des Demoiselles (DOCX, 1873) aimed at the education of strong mothers. Physical education should have been integrated in girls' schools from 1882, but it is not clear to what extent this law was realised (LUZ, 1989). Whereas at the end of the 19th century different types of female gymnastics were promoted, modern competitive sport was a male preserve. This is reflected in the fact that Baron Pierre de Coubertin, the most famous French sports official, fundamentally rejected any participation of women in the Olympic Games. His criticism was addressed above all to athletic contests, which he described as an "unworthy spectacle" (COUBERTIN, 1912).

Although Coubertin's views were endorsed by many people (see L' EDUCATION PHYSIQUE ET SPORTIVE FÉMININE, 1921), in France, too, a wide variety of different gymnastics and sports activities for girls and women began to develop even before the First World War. In France, in contrast to Germany, independent women's sports associations were founded which competed with each other with regard to both their objectives and their programmes. The *Union Française des Sociétés de Gymnastique Féminine* was established in 1912, which amalgamated with the *Fédération Féminine Française des Sports Athlétiques* in 1921 to become the *Fédération Féminine Française de Gymnastique et d' Education Physique*. This association promoted gymnastics and "pratiques sportives modérées, éducatives" and completely rejected both exaggerated competitiveness in sport as well as "masculine" sports: "... Elle estime tout à fait inutile, et même nuisible, d'exalter les prouesses individuelles" (L'EDUCATION PHYSIQUE ET SPORTIVE FÉMININE, 1923, p.1). In spite of this hostile attitude towards sport, there were some areas in which gymnastics and women's sport did find common ground. The gymnastics club *En Avant*, for example, founded a branch, which offered its members athletics among its various activities. *Fémina Sport*, one of the biggest and most successful sports clubs for women (in 1928, it had 5,000 members), also had its origins in *En Avant*, breaking away in 1912 (see DURRY, 1992).

The members of *Fémina Sport* received coaching in a variety of gymnastics systems and were also given the opportunity of practising numerous "masculine" sports ranging from a game similar to rugby called *barette* to cross-country running and ice hockey. In 1915, a further independent sports club for women was founded (on the initiative of a journalist) with the neo-Hellenistic name of *Académia* (LEIGH and BONIN, 1977, HOLT, 1991; DURRY, 1992). Women's sport in France experienced a first blossoming during the First World War, when competitions were held in *barette* and various track and field events. "Those were heroic times, when women ran the 1,500m, the 400m and the 300m, when the same athlete thought nothing of taking on six or seven different competitors on the same day" (MILLIAT, 1928). The founders of the women's sports clubs - five men, all of them well-known promoters or officials of French sport - subsequently founded, in 1917, an association of women's sports (*the Fédération des sociétés françaises des sports féminins - FSFSF*). The Association held championships in disciplines, which included cross-country running and, a year later, athletics. Alice Milliat, a rower from the Fémina sports club, was appointed treasurer of this new association and at the first members' assembly in 1921, she was unanimously elected its President. In the years that followed, she was to play a major role in not only French but also international women's sports as president of the Fédération Sportive Féminine Internationale.

Women and Football - The Early Years

1. Germany

The German games movement, which from the beginning of the 1880s had promoted physical exercise, especially with games derived from 'Turnen', also sought to attract girls and women because of the belief that strong off-springs can only be born of strong mothers. Among the activities that were recommended for girls were ball games in which the ball was only allowed to be moved by kicking it with the feet, for example football. Like all 'Turnen' games, this type of football game completely lacked both a competitive impulse and any orientation towards performance.

The women playing soccer at the end of the 19th century in England were criticised and ridiculed in German journals. *SPORT IM BILD* (1895), for example, recommended strongly that ladies "should leave the game of soccer to the male sex and to be satisfied with appropriate and feminine games" (p.334).

While proponents of sports as well as of the games movement wished to restrict 'proper' football to boys and men, there were also advocates of women's football to be found among the first women doctors who were in favour of physical fitness for women. These included FISCHER-DÜCKELMAN (1905) and ADAMS-LEHMANN (undated), both of whom encouraged the women readers of their popular guidebooks to practise sports as they pleased, and keep active, building up strength and stamina through exercise. FISCHER-DÜCKELMANN (1905) even went as far as recommending football for woman, provided that they wore the right clothing. Evidence that this unconventional proposal was ever put into practice has not been found; throughout the 1920s there was absolutely no question about the fact that the football field was no place for women.

"All types of sport which exceed women's natural strength, such as wrestling, boxing and football, are unsuitable sports for women and are, moreover, unaesthetical and unnatural in appearance", is Vierath's (1930, p.61) lapidary comment in his book, *Moderner Sport*. Reasons why women should be prohibited from playing football were seldom given. In 1927 an article appeared in *Sport und Sonne* (1927) under the heading "Should the female sex play football?" The rhetorical question had been prompted because of the "great women's football associations which exist" in England. According to the article, German women disapprove of football, firstly, because the "rough way" in which the game is played is contrary to women's sensibilities and, secondly, because the game is not suited to the "build of the female body" (p.24).

A rare reference to women football players - and one, moreover, which did not contain a fundamental rejection of the game played by women - is to be found in a 1930 issue of the journal *LEIBESÜBUNGEN*. A report on the founding of a women's football club in Frankfurt included the following comment: "... The lady footballers... intend to play a cheerful, combative kind of football. Whether it will be worse than hockey, we will have to wait and see... It will be interesting to see what will come of this venture" (p.108).

Today we know that nothing came of this venture. Thirty-five young women from Frankfurt between the ages of 18 and 20 founded a women's football club in 1930. The club members trained regularly on Sundays on a field called Seehofwiese in a Sachsenhausen district of Frankfurt. Reports of this "scandal" in the press led to a "storm of indignation", and many of the players yielded to pressure from both their families and the general public and left the club, which was subsequently dissolved in 1931 (SCHREIBER-RIETAG, 1993). Thus, generally, there were only very sporadic initiatives to establish women's football in Germany.

2. France

In spite of such eminent opponents as Baron Pierre de Coubertin, a women's football movement was established in France during the First World War. Numerous women's teams were founded, not only those belonging to the renowned Paris women's sports club Fémina but also in other clubs such as Académia, En Avant, Fauvettes, etc. - and not only in Paris but in the provinces as well, for example in Reims, Marseille and Toulouse. Many of the early women footballers also practised other sports: Delapierre, for instance, one of the best known and finest track and field athletes, was a member of the team which played against Dick Kerr's Ladies in 1930. She later became secretary-general of the FSFI.

After the first football matches had taken place in 1917/18 *en privé*, the first women's match (between two teams belonging to the Fémina sports club) (FÉMINA SPORT, 1926) was held in public on 28 April 1918 before the start of the men's international between France and Belgium. The French women's sports association FSFSF, founded in 1917 (which in 1922 became the FFSF), introduced the first official football championships in 1918 (LA FEMME SPORTIVE, 1921). In 1922, two association cup matches were added to the list of championships, the cups bearing the names "La Francaise" and "L'Encouragement".

In its numerous reports, Sportives (renamed *Fémina Sport* and later *L'Education Sportive Féminine*), the official journal of the French women's sports association, presents a dynamic picture of women's football in France. There is, for example, a report of a great sports festival organised by the Fémina sports club in 1922 in which, besides hockey, basketball and 'barette', a football match was played. In the same year, it also published a report on the "match interrégional: Reims - Navarre". Furthermore, there are regular lists of football results as well as the results of the French championships. These championship matches, which from 1926 to 1929 were won by Fémina Sport, were attended by roughly 10,000 spectators (see FÉMINA SPORT, 1926). In 1930, there was a comment in L'EDUCATION SPORTIVE FÉMININE:

> ... En football, comme dans les autres sports, les Championnats se poursuivent avec acharnement. Paris, qui a cette année reçu l'engagement de onze équipes, fait, chaque dimanche, poursuivre le cours de son important Championnat dont le leader Fémina Sport tient la tête
>
> (p.1).

That women's football had become an acknowledged sport can be seen in a review summarising developments in the sport during the year 1929. Here, it is reported that a great number of women players had acquired "dans la pratique de ce sport, une assurance d'ellesmêmes et une force physique incomparable" (L'EDUCATION SPORTIVE FÉMININE, 1930, p.3). It might be claimed by opponents of women's football, the review continued, that the game had a detrimental effect on motherhood, but there were enough examples to show that both training and the matches themselves did not cause any harm even to the most eager players. Nevertheless, only women in good health should play football. For this reason the French women's sports association only issued a player's licence after a medical examination (L'EDUCATION SPORTIVE FÉMININE, 1930).

Besides playing local, regional and national games, women's football teams also took part in numerous international events. In 1920, for instance, a French team led by Alice Milliat, who was later to become president of the international women's sports association, travelled to Preston in England to play against the famous Dick Kerr's Ladies, the team members of which all worked for Dick Kerr's munitions factory (Williamson, 1991). Like all women's football matches in England, the matches between Dick Kerr's Ladies and their French guests were charity performances. On their arrival in Preston, the French women were greeted with enthusiasm. In one week they played four matches in four English towns in front of a total of 61,000 spectators. In October of the same year, the players from Preston travelled to France on an exchange visit, which also turned out to be a great success for women's football (WILLIAMSON, 1991). In the following year, matches were played between a French team and the Plymouth Ladies. Other popular opponents were Belgian women's teams. In 1929, for example, the Atalante de Bruxelles team, winners of the Belgian championships in 1927 and 1928, came to Paris to play against Fémina, the French women's champions.

In addition to these games, 'selection' matches were also played in the 1920s "pour former l'équipe de France" (LES SPORTIVES, undated). In 1931, the French team played and won 4:0 against Belgium (LE MIROIR DES SPORTS, 1931).

Prior to the formation of a Women's Football Association, the organisation of women's football in France was supervised by the women's sports association, an application to join the French Football Association having been turned down. In the 1920s, conflicts arose between the different women's sports organisations. Unfortunately, the history of French women's sport has not yet been written and, therefore, little is known about the causes and the background of these conflicts.

In spite of the close relations existing between the French women's sports association and its international counterpart, the FSFI, football was not added to the list of the sports supervised by the international organisation. In 1932, England had submitted a proposal to the FSFI recommending the inclusion of football in the Women's World Games.[1] At the FSFI Congress in 1932, however, the delegates were in favour of postponing the decision on women's football until a survey had been conducted on attitudes towards women's football in member countries. Nothing is known, unfortunately, about the results of this survey.

In the early 1930s, opposition to women playing football in France seems to have increased. In 1932, only eight teams are believed to have taken part in the French women's championships. The objections raised appear to have centred on the clothing and on the "street urchin-like" carriage and gait of the young women (SPORT UND GESUNDHEIT, 1932, p.16). In an interview given in 1934, Alice Milliat, President of the FSFI, named a further reason for the disappearance of women's football:

> ... I have given up football now...but not because I have been won over by the critics. I still think that football is a perfectly safe game for women: The reason that football is abandoned in France is that we have no fields
>
> (INDEPENDENT WOMAN, 1934).

In France, too, the question of whether women ought (or should even be allowed) to play football caused heated debates, which have briefly been mentioned earlier. Here, too, there was a widespread conviction that "la femme n'est point construite pour lutter mais pour procréer" (PRUDHOMME, 1996, p.113). It was feared that women football players might forfeit grace, charm and elegance - in short, their feminine image. Just as elsewhere, the women were prepared to defend themselves; in their view, football was a healthy and rewarding game. In spite of the opposition, and in contrast to what happened in Germany, French women succeeded in keeping women's football alive all through the 1920s.

Nevertheless, in the 1930s, reports and news about women's football began to dry up. Whether women continued to play football, unnoticed and unmentioned, is hitherto unknown. Further factors which may have contributed towards the withdrawal of women from what had traditionally been defined as a man's sport were the effects of the Great Depression and the rise in unemployment as well as a reappearance of conservative attitudes which drove women back to their customary roles.

In other European countries, too, women tried to have a share in the game of football in the 1920s. During the First World War, English women were successful in establishing their football matches as charity events. In the 1920s, however, not least on account of the opposition of the English Football Association, women's football suffered a serious decline and right up to the 1970s, English women football players were doomed to a life in the shadows (see WILLIAMSON, 1991; WILLIAMS and WOODHOUSE, 1991).

Women's Football - Similarities and Differences between France and Germany

Opposition to women's football was closely connected to the characterisation of the game as an aggressive and combative sport. In contrast to the games of the 'Turner', which were played all over Germany, football was considered to be combative, strenuous, aggressive and potentially dangerous. On these grounds, football suffered from disapproval in Germany by 'Turner' and 'Turnen' coaches, even for boys. Neither in Germany nor in France did football, based as it was on performance and competition, appear to be reconcilable with the prevailing ideals of femininity. In 1928, for example, FISCHER attested to the "markedly combative character" of football (p.73). He advised women to play handball, an "altogether more subdued and civil game" FISCHER, 1928, p. 78). It did not matter, of course, for such images to be effective, whether the qualities attributed to the different games were based on imagination and association, and did not necessarily have much to do with the reality of the games.

Today football still connotes roughness and aggression and this is a reason for judging women's football sceptically or even rejecting it. Even today, women, who do not shun physical confrontation, reserve the right for themselves to be robust and tenacious, and have nothing against the display of sweat and exhaustion in public, do not correspond to the dominant ideals of beauty and femininity.

The body, physical activity and forms of presenting oneself - and thus sport, too - play a major role in the re-production of the gender order, which, in both France and Germany, is based upon the division of work and tasks in the family. Ideologies and myths concerning the body and limits of physical achievement with regard to both sexes are key factors in shoring up patriarchal structures. From the very beginning, people were afraid that women's sport would have adverse and undesirable effects on both gender identity and the sexual hierarchy. Sport (or certain sports at least), has continuously provided a means, right up to the present day, of constructing and demonstrating masculinity. As Dunning (1986) was able to reveal using the example of rugby, sport is especially vital as a resource in shaping male identity in times in which the balance of power between the sexes is undergoing change. Football teams (and this can be seen in the rituals that they enact) may be regarded as male preserves and male allegiances. Male allegiances are formed precisely through the exclusion of women and the rejection of femininity and all the qualities attached to it such as softness and tenderness. Efforts to keep women away from football fields can, therefore, be interpreted as attempts to preserve and protect the domains and the privileges, which men have secured for themselves.

Further, it must be taken into consideration that in both countries football is a national sport - the sport with which the (male) population identifies. National sport and myths of masculinity are intricately interwoven:

> ... Each country's national sport contributes towards producing and securing the male identity specific to that particular country. This explains not only why in all societies the national sport is a male preserve ... but also why it is linked to sexual demands, needs and anxieties
>
> (KLEIN, 1983, p.18).

On the whole, the aim seemed to preserve the gender order both inside and outside sport. That the differences between the sexes should disappear, that women should become more masculine, that "certain limits" should be exceeded, was more or less strictly rejected (FISCHER, 1928).

In many respects, the general view of football as a male combative sport and attitudes toward women football players were quite similar in both countries. Why, then, was women's football tolerated in France but spurned in Germany? Were French women more "emancipated" than their German contemporaries?

In a study of family structures and family life in Germany and France, KAELBLE (1991) came to the conclusion that French women played a more modern role than German women: "... French married women seemed not only to be tied up more intensively in their jobs but also to take a more active part in social and public life" (52). Among the evidence for his view, are the percentages of women who went out to work: in 1907, 45% of all employable women and 26% of all married women in Germany were employed outside the home. By contrast, in

France the percentage of employable women who went out to work was 56%, while the percentage of married women who were employed was 50% (figures for 1906). In France, a far greater number of women worked as entrepreneurs than in Germany. Furthermore, at the turn of the century, university studies for young women had become relatively widespread - 5% of all students were female at a time when in Germany the doors of universities were completely closed to women.

However, in the 1920s processes of modernisation began to be felt in Germany, which also had an effect on the situation of women. For example, women won the right to vote in 1919, whereas French women had to wait until 1944 before they could vote (SINEAU, 1995). The great changes that took place in women's roles in Germany also led to a relatively liberal attitude towards women's sport, which is to be seen, for example, in the promotion of women's athletics. It is probable, however, that the development of independent women's sports associations and the key positions held by women in French women's sport are to be seen in connection with the different feminine ideals and women's roles in both countries.

It is also probable that the short success of women's football in France was made possible by the particular historical constellations and specific contexts. Here, the First World War undoubtedly played a considerable role: if women had to take the places of men in numerous fields of life, then why not in sport, too? In France, women began to play football; in Germany after the war, athletics were recommended for women. That it did not occur to German women to play football may have been connected with the widespread misgivings which people had about this combative game. Even men's football was not accepted by everyone in Germany at that time. Moreover, German women were provided with a real alternative to sport, which emphasised performance and competition in the form of 'Turnen'.

The constellations prevailing in French sports politics no doubt furthered the development of women's football. First, the independent women's sports organisations, some of them founded and sponsored by men, had succeeded in becoming firmly established. In Germany, there was no women's sports association that could have organised and supervised women's football. Secondly, a women's sport culture had developed in

France, which showed no great fear of sports with a masculine connotation. Characteristic of Fémina Sport or the FSFSF was the fact that both "feminine" and "masculine" physical activities were practised side by side. At the "Fête du Printemps", for example, held by the FSFSF in the Pershing Stadium in Paris, the activities included not only athletic contests and basketball matches but also group gymnastics and ballet performances. It was perhaps this mixture of activities, combined with the moderate goals of the FSFSF and the FSFI, which took the wind out of their opponents' sails. Another puzzle in the picture of women's sport in France is the social exclusiveness of some types of sports. As DELAPLACE (1996) emphasises

> ... le développement des pratiques sportives féminines entre les deux-guerres s'intègre totalement dans le mouvement d'emancipation civique et social qui s'illustre aussi bien dans la mode vestimentaire que dans la littérature, dans l'éducation comme dans le syndicalisme. Encore convient-il de rappeler que c'est le fait de quelques progressistes, intellectuelles, grandes burgeoises ou femmes de gauche.

To participate in an "unfeminine" sport would be a challenge for some extravagant ladies. In Germany, female athletes seem to come rather from middle or lower middle classes, and sport stars did not reach the social prestige and the glamour of a Suzan Lenglen. Finally, it can also be assumed that the competition between the various women's sports organisations and thus, too, between different definitions of femininity and movement cultures, encouraged attempts by some women to mark themselves off from others by, for example, taking up the game of football. It must also be borne in mind that in France football was by no means followed with the same enormous nation-wide enthusiasm as in Germany. France's national sport par excellence was cycling, and the nation's heroes were not football players but cyclists. This meant, of course, that the intrusion of women on the football field did not pose the same fundamental threat to the gender order as it did in Germany.

In the early 1930s, because of factors, which included economic difficulties, social upheaval and political developments, traditional ideals of womanhood and the family greatly increased in significance in both

France and Germany. In a period in which criticism of emancipation and civilisation was rife, there was no room for women's football. Only many years after the Second World War did a revival of women's football take place. In the 1970s, a new movement developed which was not restricted to France and Germany but embraced the whole world - and which in the meantime has even succeeded in having women's football accepted as an Olympic discipline.

Note

1. The FSFI had organised its own World Games for women (in Paris in 1922, Gothenburg in 1926, Prague in 1930 and London in 1934) since the IOC and the IAAF refused to include athletics, or at least certain track-and-field disciplines, in the women's Olympic programme; refer PFISTER, 1996.

References

ADAMS-LEHMANN, H.B.: *Das Frauenbuch.* Stuttgart, Pfautsch (undated).

BERNETT, H.: *Leichtathletik im geschichtlichen Wandel.* Schorndorf, Hofmann, 1987.

CLIAS, P.: *Calisthénie.* Paris, Audot, 1828.

DE COUBERTIN, P.: Les femmes aux Jeux Olympique. In: *Revue Olympique,* Juli, 1912, pp.109-110.

DELAPLACE, J. M.: Les acteurs du développement du sport entre les deux-guerres en France (1919-1940): défenseurs et adversaires. In: KRÜGER, A., and TEJA, A., (Eds.), *La Commune Eredità dello Sport in Europa.* Rome, CONI, 1997, pp.351-359.

DER LEICHTATHLET, 39(3), 1926.

DER LEICHTATHLET, 43(5), 1928, pp.19-20.

DIE LEIBESÜBUNGEN, 1930, 108.

DOCX: *Guide pour l'enseignement de la gymnastique des filles.* 4th ed. Namur, Classique et Scientifique de A.D., 1882.

DUNNING, E.: Sport as a male preserve: notes on the social sources of masculine identity and its transformations. In: ELIAS, N., and DUNNING, E., *Quest for excitement.* Oxford, Basil Blackwell, 1986, pp.267-307.

DURRY, J.: Le combat des femmes et l'évolution des struktures. In: HUBSCHER, R., (Ed.), *L'histoire en mouvements.* Paris, Armand Colin, 1992, pp.287-313.

EISENBERG, C.: *Fussball in Deutschland* 1890-1914. In: Geschichte und Gesellschaft, 20, 1994, pp.181-210.

FÉMINA SPORT: 3, 1926.

FISCHER, H.W.: *Körperschönheit und Körperkultur.* Berlin, Deutsche Buch-Gemeinschaft, 1928.

FISCHER-DÜCKELMANN, A.: *Die Frau als Hausärztin.* Dresden/Stuttgart, Süddeutsches Verlags-Institut, 2nd edition, 1905.

GUTTMANN, A.: *Games and Empires.* New York, Columbia University Press, 1994.

HOLT, R.: Women, men and sport in France, c. 1870 - 1914: introductory survey. In: *Journal of Sport History,* 17, 1991, pp.121-134.

INDEPENDENT WOMAN, October, 1934.

KAELBLE, H.: *Nachbarn am Rhein. Entfremdung und Annaherung der französischen und deutschen Gesellschaft seit 1880.* München, Beck, 1991.

KLEIN, M. (Ed.): *Sport und Geschlecht.* Reinbek, Rowohlt,1983.

LA FEMME SPORTIVE, 1, 1921, p.2.

LAISNÉ, N.: *Gymnastique des Demoiselles*. Paris, Le Lièvre, 1854.

L'EDUCATION PHYSIQUE ET SPORTIVE FÉMININE, 21, 1921, p.2.

L'EDUCATION PHYSIQUE ET SPORTIVE FÉMININE, 23, 1923, p.1.

L'EDUCATION SPORTIVE FÉMININE, 1930, pp.1-3.

LEIGH, M. and BONIN, T.: The pioneering role of Madame Allice Milliat and the FSFI in establishing international track and field competition for women. In: *Journal of Sport History*, 4, 1977, pp.72-83.

LE MIROIR DES SPORTS, 587, 1931, p.190.

LES SPORTIVES (no publication date given).

LUZ, K.: *Turnen und Sport in Frankreich von 1800 bis zum Ende der dritten Republik unter besonderer Berücksichtigung von Mädchen und Frauen*. Staatsexamensarbeit, Berlin, 1989.

MILLIAT, A.: In *DER LEICHTATHLET*, 39(5), 1928, p.19.

NEITZKE, C.: *Berliner Frauensportvereine in Vergangenheit und Gegenwart*. Examensarbeit, Berlin, 1984.

NERZ, 0.: Fussball. In: NEUENDORF, E. (Ed.), *Die deutschen Leibesübungen*. Berlin/Leipzig, Wihelm Andermann, 1927, pp.338-356.

PFISTER, G.: Sport auf dem grünen Rasen. Fussball und Leichtathletik. In: PFISTER, G., and STEINS, G., (Eds.), *Vom Ritterturnier zum Stadtmarathon. Sport in Berlin*. Berlin, Forum für Sportgeschichte, 1987, pp.68-96.

PFISTER, G.: Der Kampf gebührt dem Mann... Argumente und Gegenargumente im Diskurs über den Frauensport. In: RENSON, R., (Ed.), *Sport and Contest*. Madrid, INEF, 1993, pp.349-365.

PFISTER, G.: Physical activity in the name of the fatherland: Turnen and the national movement (1810-1820). In: *Sporting Heritage*, 1, 1996, pp.14-36.

PFISTER, G., and LANGENFELD, H.: Die Leibesübungen für das weibliche Geschlecht - ein Mittel zur Emanzipation der Frau? In: UEBERHORST, H., (Ed.), *Geschichte der Leibesübungen*, 3(i). Berlin/München/Frankfurt, Bartels and Wernitz, 1980, pp.485-521.

PRUDHOMME, L.: Sexe faible et ballon rond. Esquisse d'une histoire du football féminine. In: ARNAUD, P. and.TERRET, T., (Eds.), *Histoire du Sport Féminin*. Vol.1. Paris, L'Harmattan, 1996, pp.111-126.

SCHREIBER-RIETIG, B.: Die Suffragetten spielten Fussball. In: *Olympisches Feuer*, 2, 1993, pp.36-41.

SINEAU, M.: Recht und Demokratie. In: DUBY, G., and PERROT, M., (Eds.), *Geschichte der Frauen*. Vol.5. Frankfurt, Campus, 1995, pp.529-559.

SPORT IM BILD: 22.11.1895, p.334.

SPORT UND GESUNDHEIT, 1, 1932, p.16.

SPORT UND SONNE, 3, 1927, p.24.

VIERATH, W.: *Moderner Sport*. Berlin, Oestergaard, 1930.

WAHL, A.: La balle au pied. Histoire du football. Gallimard, 1990.

WILLIAMS, J., and WOODHOUSE, J.: Can play, will play? Women and football in Britain. In: WILLIAMS, J., and WAGG, S., (Eds.), *British football and social change*. Leicester, Leicester University Press, 1991, pp.85-111.

WILLIAMSON, D.J.: *Belles of the ball*. Devon, R & D Associates, 1991.

Chapter 5

Physical Fitness of Asian Youth and their Attitude toward Sport

*Yoshiro Hatano, Zou Da Hua, Lu Da Jiang, Frank Fu,
Chen Ji Zhi and Shi De Wei*

Introduction

The Asian Health-Related Youth Fitness Test was first proposed by the Asia Regional Board of the International Council for Health, Physical Education and Recreation (ICHPER) in 1989. The primary purpose of developing such a test was not to compare or encourage competition among the subjects of various nations (regional groups), but rather to encourage respective school children to become more health and fitness conscious.

The test battery was formulated to comprise: an endurance run (800m. for children aged 10-11, 1,000m. for girls aged 12-17 years, and 1,500m. for boys, aged 12-17); number of sit-ups in 60 seconds, pull-ups (modified pull-ups for girls of all ages and boys, aged 10-11 years); sit-and-reach test of flexibility in a sitting position; and skin-fold measurements (sum of triceps and calf). Together with the fitness test, a questionnaire survey on the cultural background (inclusive of attitudes to, and behaviour in, sport and physical activity, with a focus on efficacy for health, relaxation, strength development, socialisation and any negative perceptions of outcomes such as harmful effects and tedium) to youth fitness, was administered to the sample group.

In 1991, the Japanese survey was conducted as an official project under the name of "Asia Youth Fitness Japan", within the Test and Measurement Research Division of the Japanese Society of Physical Education. Testing involved 2,149 boys and girls, attending elementary, junior high and senior high schools in urban areas. In 1992, Zou Da Hua of the Shanghai Research Institute of Sports Sciences directed the Chinese part of the survey with 3,168 Chinese students attending public schools in the Shanghai area. Lu Da Jiang, a graduate student in physical education, then at the Tokyo Gakugei University Computer Center, undertook the data analysis. The findings of the Japanese and Chinese studies were included in a report published by the Test and Measurement Research Division of the Japanese Society of Physical Education in 1993 (HATANO). Summary reports (HATANO, 1994; ZOU, 1994) were also published in the ICHPER•SD (ICHPER changed its name to embrace Sport and Dance in 1993) Journal.

The Hong Kong group study took place in 1990-91 under the direction of Dr. Frank Fu of Hong Kong Baptist College, with the assistance of the Hong Kong Education Department and the co-operation of school principals and teachers; the Hong Kong sample comprised 20,304 school children. A summary report (FU, 1994) was also included in the ICHPER•SD Journal; the full report was published by the Department of Physical Education, Hong Kong Baptist College (FU, 1994).

The Macao group study was undertaken under the supervision of Dr. Chen Ji Zhi of the Shanghai Institute of Physical Education in 1994-95, with a sample of 1,547 boy and girl subjects of the same age levels as the other studies. The testing took place in autumn 1994 and the findings were included in a report (SHI, 1995) published by the Macau Polytechnic Institute.

The current comparison has omitted the Hong Kong group sports culture study, because the detailed report of this section was unavailable at the time of data analysis. Otherwise, the data of each national group sample, as they appeared in each published report, were used for comparative procedural purposes.

Results

For each female and male sample group, mean and standard deviation and results of all the test and measurement parameters for each age level of the four different regional subject groups, together with t-test results for difference between means, were calculated and subjected to analysis (females) and (males). In the endurance run test for girls, a discrepancy arose in the running distance among the regional groups, therefore, t-test for difference between means was omitted. In certain other cases, the number of subjects for a particular test item for respective age/sex group was not large enough for statistical treatment.

The inter-regional group comparison of test results on the age groups continuum and by activity are shown in figures 1-10. The results of inter-regional comparison (the Hong Kong group excepted) of cultural aspects of physical education/sports participation feature in figures 11-16 for selected age groups. In figures 11-16, the rating scale 1 represents "strongly disagree", and rating scale 5 represents "strongly agree".

Discussion

In general, the Chinese group exceeded the other three groups and the Macao group underscored all groups in almost all the fitness parameters. These findings were suggestive of some significant tendencies in this aspect. In terms of the Japan-Hong Kong comparison, the Japanese group appears to score more highly in endurance run and sit-and-reach tests than the Hong Kong group. However, the Hong Kong group outscored Japan (and China, for some age levels) in the pull-up test. In the skin-fold thickness measurement, Japanese and Chinese groups have similar scores and recorded a larger amount than the other two national group samples; in the Macao group, all age levels recorded the thinnest measurements.

It is difficult to draw any definitive conclusion about the cultural differences that may influence the health-related fitness results of the young people comprising the total sample. However, one speculative supposition may be made that the Chinese group is strongly "physical" conscious, at least relative to the interregional groups, which are the subject of the study. The Macao group seemed to lag behind other groups; perhaps this stems from less emphasis in health and fitness consciousness in school education and education of youth in society in general.

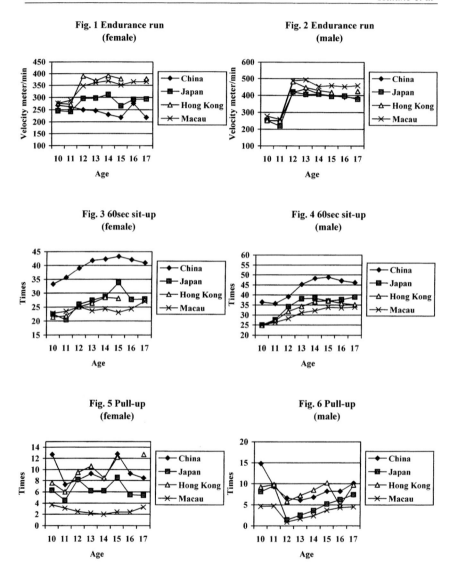

Fig. 1 Endurance run (female)

Fig. 2 Endurance run (male)

Fig. 3 60sec sit-up (female)

Fig. 4 60sec sit-up (male)

Fig. 5 Pull-up (female)

Fig. 6 Pull-up (male)

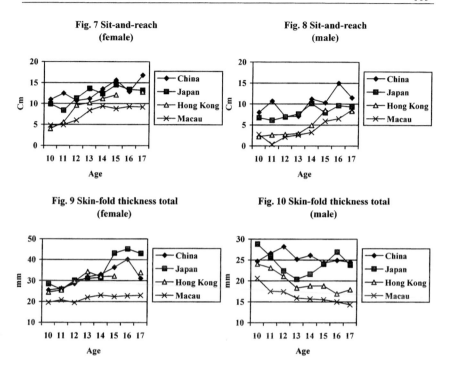

Fig. 7 Sit-and-reach (female)

Fig. 8 Sit-and-reach (male)

Fig. 9 Skin-fold thickness total (female)

Fig. 10 Skin-fold thickness total (male)

With regard to the significance of exercise and sport, the Chinese group indicated a rather negative view; the responses tended to suggest such physical activities are discomforting, too difficult and tedious. TheJapanese group regards physical activities as a natural part of training. The Macao group indicated that physical activities are conducive to relaxation. In other words, in China exercise and sports are regarded as a necessary hardship (while the fitness level is seen to be the highest of all the groups). In Japan, they are considered to be a part of training and in Macao, they are associated more with relaxation activities (while the fitness level is less favourable than in the other groups). Nevertheless, despite such differences, physical activities are deemed by all the sample groups to be enjoyable and useful for promotion of relaxation, health and fitness.

Fig. 11
11-Year old girls

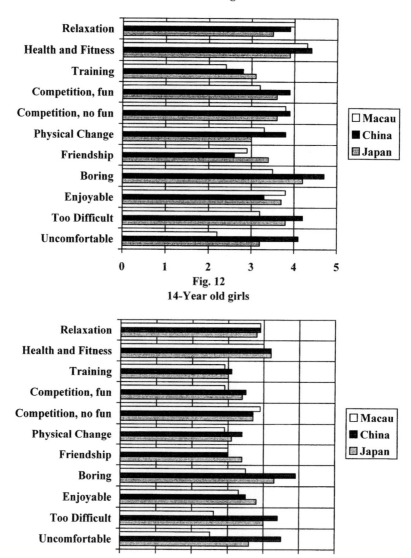

Fig. 12
14-Year old girls

Fig. 13
17-Year old girls

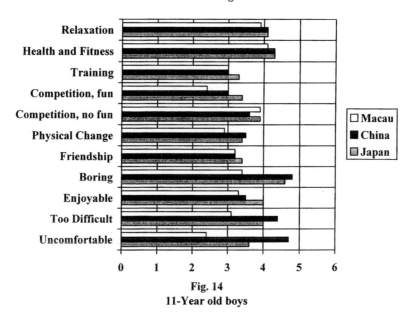

Fig. 14
11-Year old boys

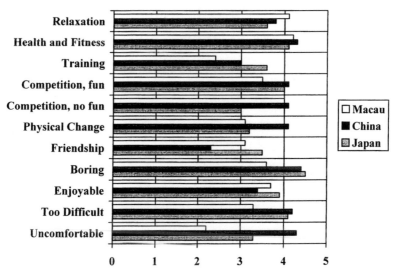

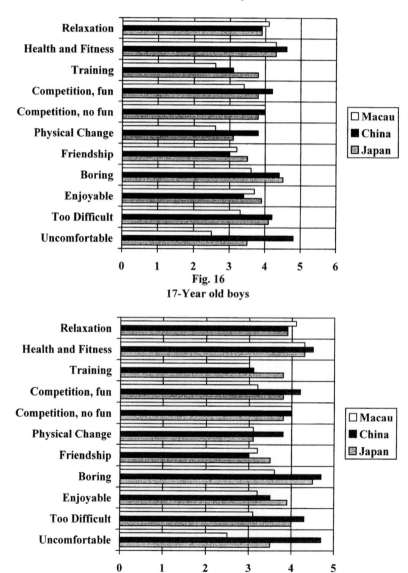

Fig. 15
14-Year old boys

Fig. 16
17-Year old boys

For the time length of time (hours per week) spent on sports activities, the Japanese group recorded the longest, followed by the Chinese and then Macao. In the case of Japan, there was a broad range of engagement: there were both longest (13+ hours per week) and rather short (2-4 hours per week) time groups. The Chinese group was concentrated in the 2-4 and 5-8 hours per week ranges and Macao in the 0-2 and 2-4 hours per week ranges. All three groups indicated that schools provide the greatest proportion (80-90%) of sports facilities in their respective societies.

The Chinese male group indicated their frequent participation in soccer, track and field athletics and basketball, and the female group, in track and field, gymnastics and basketball in rank order. The Japanese male group ranked baseball, soccer and tennis, and the female group, tennis, basketball and volleyball. The Macao male group listed basketball, soccer and track and field athletics, and the female group, track and field athletics, badminton and basketball.

Concluding Comments

A total of 27,168 school children, aged 10-17 in four different nations/regions in eastern Asia were subjected to the ICHPER·SD Health-related Fitness Test and respective cultural backgrounds were surveyed by the use of a 20-item questionnaire. The results can be summarised as follows:

1. The Chinese group generally recorded the highest fitness levels of the four regional groups and Macao the lowest. Japanese and Hong Kong groups were similarly ranked, though Hong Kong young people performed rather well in the pull-up test and the Japanese in the endurance run. In terms of skin-fold thickness, Japanese and Chinese groups recorded the highest (thickest) values.

2. As for the significance of physical activities, all groups consistently felt that such activities are enjoyable, useful for health and fitness promotion and relaxing. The Chinese group, however, indicated that such activities are administered compulsorily and are tedious. The Japanese group regarded the activities as part and parcel of training and the Macao group as relaxation.

3. In terms of the weekly duration of time spent on physical activity, the Japanese group showed a diverse tendency patter with the longest mean value, followed by China and then Macao with the least amount.

4. For sports activities in general, in all three regions the most frequently used facility is exclusively provided in schools, suggesting other facilities are yet to be developed.

5. The sports activities with most frequent participation were as follows: a) Chinese group - soccer, track and field athletics and basketball for boys, and track and field, gymnastics and basketball for girls; b) for the Japanese group - baseball, soccer and tennis for boys, and tennis, track and field athletics and volleyball for girls; c) for the Macao group - basketball, soccer and track and field athletics for boys, and track and field athletics, badminton and basketball for girls.

References

FU, F.: ICHPER•SD Asia youth health-related fitness test: implementation in Hong Kong. In: *ICHPER•SD Journal*, 30(3), 1994, pp.22-27.

HATANO, Y.: *Asia youth health-related fitness test study project report.* Asia Youth Fitness Japan, Test and Measurement Research Division, Japanese Society of Physical Education, 1993.

HATANO, Y.: ICHPER•SD Asia youth health-related fitness test: construction of norms for Japanese students. In: *ICHPER•SD Journal*, 30(3), 1994, pp.8-15.

SHI, D. W.: *General report of Macao youth fitness test.* Macao College of Physical Education Youth Fitness Testing Team, 1995.

ZOU, D. H.: ICHPER•SD Asia youth health-related fitness test: test results of Chinese students. In: *ICHPER•SD Journal*, 30(3), 1994, pp.16-21.

Chapter 6

Leisure Constraint Factors on the Sporting Activity of English and Iranian Students

Mohammed Ehsani, Ken Hardman and Bob Carroll

Introduction

In recent years, the themes of leisure constraints and the extent of participation in leisure activities have been of growing interest to researchers, with the consequence that there has been a concomitant increase in related literature (JACKSON 1988, 1991, 1993; GOODALE & WITT, 1989; WADE, 1985; HENDERSON, STALNAKER and TAYLOR, 1988). This literature has indicated that any factor, which inhibits a person's ability to participate in leisure activities, can be defined as a constraint. The term "constraints" is recognised (CRAWFORD and GODBEY, 1987) as more inclusive than "barriers" and is now preferred. The concept of constrained leisure has emerged with a research emphasis on the types of leisure constraints and the extent to which they act as barriers to participation in recreation activities. Many researchers have noted that constraints can be reduced by the action of leisure providers thus, leading to developed participation levels in leisure activities (e.g. MCGUIRE and O'LEARY, 1990). The concept of constraints also comprises such phenomena as constraints to leisure satisfaction and enjoyment of current activities (FRANCKEN and VAN RAIIJ, 1981; WITT and GOODALE, 1981).

Leisure constraints surveys have been carried out mostly in the United States and Canada, and to a lesser extent in England and The Netherlands at national, regional, and local levels. There has also been an attempt to develop sophisticated methodological, theoretical, and conceptual models of leisure constraints over the past decade (e.g. CRAWFORD, JACKSON and GODBEY, 1991). Studies have been developed and conducted within different conceptual models of leisure constraints. Some authors have acknowledged a need to examine the operation of, and relationship among, forms of constraints (see for example,

CRAWFORD and GODBEY, 1987; HENDERSON, STALNAKER and TAYLOR, 1988; JACKSON, 1990).

FRANCKEN and VAN RAIIJ (1981) have divided constraints into "internal" and "external". "Internal" constraints include personal capacities, abilities and knowledge; "external" constraints include such items as lack of funds and time, lack of facilities and geographical distance. CRAWFORD and GODBEY (1987) have suggested that constraints can be understood within the broad context of a leisure preference participation relationship. Theirs was the first systematic attempt to classify leisure constraints into three categories, according to the way they affect preference and participation.

a) **Intra-personal constraints** "... involve individual psychological states and attributes which interact with leisure preferences rather than intervening between preferences and participation" (p.122).

CRAWFORD et al., (1991) have added the notion of 'psychological orientations' to intra-personal barriers thus, broadening the earlier definition. The psychological orientation comprised at least three subjective evaluations: i) the beliefs a person has about what he or she and others ought to do; ii) what the individual likes or wants to do; and iii the extent to which the person has the competence, or the ability, to perform a particular behaviour (p.314). Examples of intra-personal constraints are stress, anxiety, depression, religiosity, perceived self-skill and subjective evaluations of the appropriateness of various leisure activities.

b) **Interpersonal constraints** "... are the result of interpersonal interaction or the relationship between individuals' characteristics... Barriers of this sort may interact with both preference for, and subsequent participation in, companionate leisure activities... and the concept of interpersonal barriers is applicable to interpersonal relations in general" (p.123). The term is applied to individual barriers such as lack of partner and peer group. This is when a person is unable to find a partner to engage in specific activity, possibly due to dissimilarity of preferences, different time-table and skill levels, and so on.

c) **Structural constraints** "... represent constraints as they are commonly conceptualised, as intervening factors between leisure preference and participation" (p.124). Structural constraints include environment, financial resources, of opportunities, work timetable and reference group attitudes concerning the appropriateness of certain activities.

CRAWFORD and GODBEY (1991) have developed these three discrete dimensions into a single model of constraints interacting within a sequential hierarchy from preferences to participation. Their proposed model is based on a hierarchical decision-making process and a hierarchy of experienced constraints. It moves from proximal constraints, which affect preferences, to distal constraints, which affect participation. Each level of constraint must be overcome in order for an individual to face the subsequent level of constraints. CRAWFORD et al., (1991) have addressed the hierarchy of importance within the model. **For intra-personal** constraints "... leisure preferences are formed... when interpersonal constraints... are absent or their effects have been confronted through some combination of privilege and exercise of the human will" (p.313). For **interpersonal constraints** "... the individual may encounter constraints at the interpersonal level... it is only when this type of constraint has been overcome (if appropriate to the activity) that structural constraints begin to be encountered" (p.313). For **structural constraints** "... participation will result in the absence of, or negotiation through, structural constraints" (p.313). They proposed that the levels of constraints are managed from most proximal (intra-personal) to most distal (structural), and intra-personal constraints on leisure participation as the most proximal are the most powerful of the three, and structural constraints as the most distal are the least powerful. Despite this claimed hierarchy of importance of leisure constraints, a number of other studies has shown that "structural constraints" such as lack of time, lack of money, lack of facilities, limited access to transportation and so on, were consistently the more important "reasons" given for inhibited leisure participation (BUCHANAN and ALLEN, 1985; MCGUIRE, 1984; MANNELL and ZUZANEK, 1991). Whatever, the process model itself, the concepts of intra-personal, interpersonal and structural constraints might provide leisure researchers with a new foundation on which to base research investigating the nature of constraints on leisure (RAYMORE et al., 1993). As a result, people would not reach the stage of encountering higher order constraints, which might (or might not, depending on the nature and strength of these constraints), prevent them from doing what they would like in the way of leisure. However, because empirical support for both of these versions of the model is inadequate, the model is potentially open to modification.

A few investigations show how leisure involvement might be analysed in intra-personal, interpersonal, and structural constraints terms. The investigation by JACKSON, CRAWFORD and GODBEY (1993) provided empirical support for the model. The investigators tried to develop the three discrete categories (intra-personal, interpersonal, and structural constraints) into a single model of constraints interacting within a sequential hierarchy. They refuted the idea of constraints as insurmountable barriers to leisure. Constraints were conceived of as phenomena that are more likely to result in modified participation than non-participation. Hence, leisure constraints are best conceived as those intra-personal, interpersonal and structural constraints that people recognise as potentially limiting their behaviour.

Relationship between Constraints and Participation

Although the relationship between constraints and participation is emphasised in the literature, few empirical studies have been conducted in the area. BOOTHBY, TUNGATT and TOWNSEND (1981), GODBEY (1985), and MCGUIRE (1984) have suggested that a significant practical contribution could be made by an empirical study of leisure constraints. A few attempts have been made to identify the link between perceived barriers and participation. These studies challenged the assumption that constraints always prevent participation and provided evidence that the assumption of a link between perceived constraints and participation may be problematic. There has been some focus on the nature of leisure constraints. JACKSON et al., (1993), for example identified lack of money, lack of facilities, lack of time and a transportation problem, as structural constraints, which were found to be most important constraints. The absence of constraints was seen to imply higher levels of participation. Nonetheless, other types of constraints (intra-personal and interpersonal) may be related to participation. Participation in actual recreation activity might well be related to the absolute importance of specific constraints' variables. Social theory and sociological studies have noted that social structures such as gender, age, lifestyle, occupational status, income and education affect people's decision-making and options in their life.

There is some evidence to show that there is a direct and negative link between the level of participation in leisure activities and the reporting of constraints in the literature (SHAW, BONEN and MCCABE, 1991). However, KAY and JACKSON (1991) have suggested that reported constraints are likely to come not only from non-participants but also from participants. Moreover, the authors expected that high levels of constraints were related to frequent participants, because participation exposes individuals to constraints. For instance "lack of facilities" as a constraint may affect individuals, either by reduction or non-participation in a specific activity, which may lead to an increase in participation in another one. JACKSON et al. (1993) attempted to identify in detail the leisure decision-making process. The main suggestion was that negotiation of leisure constraints took place. Often the literature has emphasised the conception of constraints as insurmountable barriers to leisure participation, but Jackson et al. (1993) suggested that negotiation resulted very often in modified participation rather than non-participation. They also suggested that motivation is one of the most important factors in the decision-making process, and the outcome of the negotiation process is dependent on the interaction and relationship between the strength of motivation and constraints' participation.

A Comparative Study between English and Iranian Students

As indicated earlier, the majority of published studies have been conducted in North America and to a more limited extent in England. No studies have been reported in Iran. The model has been developed in North America and has not been empirically tested in different countries or different cultures. England and Iran are two countries with different economic, religious and socio-cultural cultural settings. It was, therefore, decided to conduct a comparative investigation of leisure constraints on sport participation in these two countries to see whether the theoretical models could be supported there. Sport participation was selected to narrow leisure behaviour to activities available in both countries.

Four main research questions were investigated:

- Which constraints are experienced by English and Iranian participants in relation to recreational sporting activities?

- How do the participant and non-participant samples in England and Iran perceive constraint factors in terms of their importance?

- How do the English and Iranian samples compare on constraints to participation in recreational sporting activities in terms of three categories: intra-personal, interpersonal and structural constraints?

- How do the participants and non-participants in recreational sporting activities compare in terms of their constraint factors?

The aim of the study was to develop a cross-national empirical study in constraints' factors in recreational sporting activities. More specifically, it tested the new model of constraints (intra-personal, interpersonal, and structural) and their relationship with actual participation levels in specific recreational sport activities in the two countries.

Two samples of data were collected. Sample ES (English Students) and IS (Iranian Students) consisted of random samples at Manchester (England) and Esfahan (Iran) Universities, both of which are among the largest universities (approximately 15,000 undergraduate students) in their respective countries. The students were undergraduates and ranged in age from 18 to 24. A self-administered questionnaire was used to collect data from the subjects in the two universities. A total of 180 questionnaires (90 each for male and female students) were distributed in each university. There was an approximate 90% response rate from ES (n=161) and a 91% response rate from IS (n=164) samples. Incomplete collected questionnaires (4 ES and 13 IS) were not subjected to analysis. Thus, the analysed samples consisted of 157 (ES) and 151 (IS) individuals.

The "constraints on participation in sporting activities" (CPSA) questionnaire was designed to collect information related previously published research. The instrument included a list of thirty-eight (38) constraints recognised both in the literature (WITT and GOODALE,

1981; MCGUIRE, 1984; HENDERSON et al., 1988; RAYMORE et al., 1993; JACKSON and RUCKS, 1993) and through interviews conducted prior to the study. For linguistic purposes, the instrument was checked through the back-translation procedure. Scoring of the constraints scale was on a 4-point Likert type scale, ranging from 4 (most important) to 1 (least important). Respondents were asked to indicate whether each constraint was "A = Very Important = 4 ", "B = Quite Important = 3", "C = Somewhat Important = 2", "D = Not Important = 1".

Participation in sporting activities was addressed with regard to desire to participate in sporting activities, and related to actual participation in sporting activities during the previous year (i.e. a yes or no response). The respondents were classified into two groups: first (non-participation); second (participation).

Whereas in general, facilities, facilities use costs, and distance between accommodation and facilities for sporting activities are more or less similar in the Manchester and Esfahan Universities, there are two important differences. First, in Esfahan University, the facilities are used by students free of charge for four credit hours compulsory sport, a pre-requisite for graduation in all four-year university courses in Iran, during the academic year. Secondly, Iran is a Muslim country and all sports activities involving males and females are separated.

Results

Data for constraint factors were subject to varimax rotated factor analysis (SPSS, version 6.0 for Windows). The study utilised empirical methods of classification because they are deemed to be more reliable than single items (JACKSON, 1993). All factor analysis coefficients and loading matrix are shown in table 1 (for ES) and table 2 (for IS) samples.

When the thirty-eight items concerning constraints were factor analysed, nine factors were isolated: " time" (5 related items); "interest" 4 related items); "money" 4 related items); "transportation" (3 related items); "facilities" (3 related items); "social (lack of partner) (3 related items)"; "awareness" (5 related items); "skill/abilities" (5 related items); and "health/fitness" (6 related items). All factors were similar to the factors of leisure constraint, which have been most commonly identified in previous studies. All factors in both ES and IS samples had eigenvalue greater than 1.0, and nine factors accounted for (ES) 65%, and for (IS) 63.4% of the variance (see tables 1 and 2).

Table 1.

Factor analysis of constraints on participation in sporting activities (English students)

	Time	Interest	Finance	Transport	Facility	Social	Aware	Skills/ Abilities	Health/ Fitness
Time: work/studies	.64								
Time: family commitments	.59								
Time: domestic commitments	.65								
Time: social commitments	.49								
Time: because of time table	.65								
Not interested		.80							
Not enjoyed in the past		.75							
Not interrupt routine		.66							
Not interest available activity		.66							
Cannot afford			.80						
Cost of transportation			.79						
Cost of equipment			.81						
Admission fee			.78						
No opportunity near my home				.72					
No car				.83					
Transportation takes much time				.82					
Facilities inadequate					.83				
Facilities crowded					.79				
Facilities poorly kept					.78				
Nobody to participate with						.80			
Friends do not have time						.78			
Friends do not like participating						.85			
Social unease						.68			
Social situation (opportunity) limit						.52			

	Time	Interest	Finance	Transport	Facility	Social	Aware	Skills/ Abilities	Health/ Fitness
Not known where to participate							.87		
Not known what is available							.91		
Not known where I can learn it							.88		
Not skilled enough								.86	
No one to teach me								.69	
Do not feel confident								.86	
Generally poor ability								.82	
Shy because of lack of ability								.86	
Not fit									.72
Health problems									.64
It makes me feel tired									.77
Too tired for recreation									.66
Afraid of getting hurt									.46
Not concerned about health									.44
Eigenvalue	9.21	4.30	2.38	1.77	1.64	1.54	1.33	1.30	1.17
% of Variance explained	24.2	11.3	6.3	4.7	4.3	4.1	3.5	3.4	3.1
Cumulative % of Variance explained	24.2	35.6	41.9	46.5	50.8	54.9	58.4	61.9	65

Table 2.
Factor analysis of constraints on participation in sporting activities (Iranian students)

	Time	Interest	Finance	Transport	Facility	Social	Aware	Skills/ Abilities	Health/ Fitness
Time: work/studies	.50								
Time: family commitments	.53								
Time: domestic commitments	.55								
Time: social commitments	.58								
Time: because of time table	.48								
Not interested		.59							
Not enjoyed in the past		.73							

	Time	Interest	Finance	Transport	Facility	Social	Aware	Skills/ Abilities	Health/ Fitness
Not interrupt routine		.64							
Not interest available activity		.68							
Cannot afford			.87						
Cost of transportation			.82						
Cost of equipment			.83						
Admission fee			.82						
No opportunity near my home				.76					
No car				.85					
Transportation takes much time				.81					
Facilities inadequate					.77				
Facilities crowded					.79				
Facilities poorly kept					.70				
Nobody to participate with						.77			
Friends do not have time						.72			
Friends do not like participating						.68			
Social unease						.51			
Social situation (opportunity) limit						.53			
Not known where to participate							.80		
Not known what is available							.79		
Not known where I can learn it							.84		
Not skilled enough								.80	
No one to teach me								.71	
Do not feel confident								.74	
Generally poor ability								.77	
Shy because of lack of ability								.74	
Not fit									.63
Health problems									.64
It makes me feel tired									.75
Too tired for recreation									.72
Afraid of getting hurt									.64
Not concerned about health									.43
Eigenvalue	8.28	2.97	2.66	2.13	1.90	1.77	1.64	1.49	1.21
% of Variance explained	21.8	7.8	7.0	5.6	5.0	4.7	4.3	3.9	3.2
Cumulative % of Variance explained	21.8	29.6	36.7	42.3	47.3	51.9	56.3	60.2	63.4

Conceptual Framework

These factors have been classified as intra-personal, interpersonal, and structural constraints simultaneously (see table 3). Factors 2, 8, and 9 (lack of interest, lack of skill/abilities and health/fitness problems) corresponded with "intra-personal" constraints. Factors 1, 3, 4, and 5 (lack of time, lack of money, geographical distance, lack of facilities) were conceptualised as "structural" constraints, whereas factor 6, "social" (lack of partner), interacts between preferences and participation and is "interpersonal". Factor 7, "awareness " (lack of information) as opposed to the objective absence of recreation activities opportunity, can be recognised as either environmental or individual. CRAWFORD and GODBEY (1987) have argued that some of these constraints (e.g. availability, appropriateness) can be considered both as intra-personal and structural constraints. In the present study, items of the "awareness" cluster were considered and all of items related to perceived lack of knowledge and subsequently unawareness were classified as "intra-personal" constraints.

Table 3.

Conceptual framework

Intrapersonal Constraints	Interpersonal Constraints	Structural Constraints
Factor 2: Lack of Interest	Factor 6: Social (lack of partner)	Factor 1: Lack of Time
Factor 7: Unawareness		Factor 3: Lack of Money
Factor 8: Skill/Abilities		Factor 4:Transportation
Factor 9: Health/Fitness		Factor 5: Facilities

The factor analysis results were produced for the whole scale and each sub-scale, and also the internal reliability of each scale evaluated. As can be seen in table 4, there were satisfactory levels of the Cronbach's alpha coefficients: the ES sample ranged from .58 to .88 and the internal solidity reliability of the whole scale was .91; the IS sample ranged from .45 to .87 and the internal solidity reliability of the whole scale was .89.

Table 4.

Reliability analysis (English students)

SUB-SCALES	Cronbach's alpha (ES)	(IS)	Number of Items
Lack of Time	0.58	0.45	Five
Lack of Interest	0.69	0.61	Four
Lack of Money	0.81	0.87	Four
Transportation	0.72	0.75	Three
Lack of Facilities	0.73	0.65	Three
Social (lack of partner)	0.78	0.65	Five
Unawareness	0.87	0.75	Three
Lack of Skill/Ability	0.88	0.82	Five
Health/Fitness	0.69	0.72	Six
Whole Scale	0.91	0.89	Thirty Eight

In the ES sample, 73.5% (n=111) were designated "participants and 26.5% (n=40) as "non-participants". For the IS sample, figures were 36.1% (n=53) participants and 63.9% (n=94) non-participants. Further analysis (chi square) of the data indicated there was a significant relationship ($p<.001$) between participants and non-participants and the country.

Perception of Constraint Factors, Total ES and IS Samples

Table 5, in terms of mean scores in the ES, reveals that the factor of "lack of money" was the strongest constraint to participation in sporting activities (mean = 2.16) and "lack of facilities"-related problems were perceived as the second important constraint to participation in sporting activities (mean = 1.93). This was followed by "lack of time" (mean = 1.89), "skill/abilities" (mean = 1.79), "social" - lack of partner - (mean = 1.76), "transportation" (mean = 1.71), "lack of interest" (mean = 1.69), "health/fitness (mean = 1.61) and "unawareness" loaded as the lowest (mean = 1.55). All the factors were perceived as placing constraints on participation in sporting activities.

Table 5.
The perception of constraint factors (total samples of English and Iranian students).

Mean Scores (ES)	Rank	Constraint Factors	Mean Scores (IS)	Rank
2.16	1	**Lack of Money**	2.52	3
1.93	2	**Lack of Facilities**	2.74	1
1.89	3	**Lack of Time**	1.90	7
1.79	4	**Skill/Abilties**	2.14	5
1.76	5	**Social (lack of partner)**	2.16	4
1.71	6	**Transportation**	2.62	2
1.69	7	**Lack of Interest**	1.73	9
1.61	8	**Health/Fitness**	1.79	8
1.55	9	**Unawareness**	1.98	6

In the IS samples, the factor of "lack of facilities" was the most important constraint to participation in sporting activities in terms of mean scores (mean = 2.74). This supports previous studies. The second strongest constraint was perceived as "transportation-related problems" (mean = 2.62), followed by "lack of money" (mean = 2.52), "social" (lack of partner) (mean = 2.16), "skill/abilities" (mean = 2.14), "unawareness" (mean = 1.98), "lack of time" (mean = 1.90), "health/fitness" (mean = 1.79); the "lack of interest" (mean = 1.73) was perceived as the lowest of factor constraints to participation in sporting activities. Iranian scores were higher in each factor.

The mean scores of the two ES sample groups (participants and non-participants) in the constraint factors were calculated and the significance of the differences found evaluated, using an independent sample t-test (SPSSx). The mean scores and the standard deviation of the two groups in each of the constraint factors, the t values for the t-tests and the significance level are indicated in table 6.

Table 6.
T-test of constraint factors (mean scores): English students' samples

Factors	Participants n=111		Non-Participants n=40		t.	p.
	Mean	S.D.	Mean	S.D.		
Lack of Time	1.84	0.46	1.99	0.55	-1.63	n.s.
Lack of Interset	1.75	0.71	1.53	0.57	1.75	n.s.
Lack of Money	2.06	0.79	2.41	0.73	-2.44	0.016
Transportation	1.62	0.68	1.90	0.83	-2.05	0.042
Lack of Facilities	1.88	0.71	2.07	0.79	-1.42	n.s.
Social (lack of partner)	1.72	0.65	1.87	0.78	-1.15	n.s.
Unawareness	1.51	0.74	1.60	0.72	-0.72	n.s.
Lack of Skill/Ability	1.85	0.85	1.62	0.66	1.55	n.s.
Health/Fitness	1.63	0.55	1.53	0.50	0.93	n.s.
Total Constraints Scale	1.77	0.44	1.82	0.41	-0.65	n.s.

Table 7 indicates the mean scores and the standard deviation of the two IS groups (participants and non-participants) in each of constraint factors, together with the t values for the t-tests, and the significance level. The mean scores of two groups were calculated, and the significance of the differences found was evaluated using an independent sample t-test (SPSSx). In terms of whole scale, the results indicated that there were no significant differences between the participants (mean = 2.08) and the non-participants (mean = 2.12). In terms of the sub-scales, statistically again there were no significant differences found between participants and non-participants groups.

Table 7.

T-test of constraint factors (mean scores): Iranian students' samples

Factors	Participants n=53		Non-Participants n=94		t.	p.
	Mean	S.D.	Mean	S.D.		
Lack of Time	1.79	0.57	1.94	0.41	-1.70	n.s.
Lack of Interset	1.78	0.67	1.67	0.69	0.94	n.s.
Lack of Money	2.38	1.05	2.53	0.96	-0.88	n.s.
Transportation	2.55	1.00	2.64	0.95	-0.53	n.s.
Lack of Facilities	2.69	0.81	2.72	0.87	-0.24	n.s.
Social (lack of partner)	2.11	0.79	2.19	0.71	-0.60	n.s.
Unawareness	2.06	1.02	1.92	0.81	0.90	n.s.
Lack of Skill/Ability	1.99	0.88	2.17	0.83	-1.25	n.s.
Health/Fitness	1.80	0.64	1.74	0.64	0.61	n.s.
Total Constraints Scale	2.08	0.51	2.12	0.41	-0.60	n.s.

For the whole scale, the results showed that there was no significant difference in the scores of the participants (mean = 1.77) and the non-participants (mean = 1.82). In terms of sub-scales, statistically significant differences were found in two factors namely, "lack of money" (t = -2.44, p<. 05), "transportation" (t = -2.05, p<. 05), with non-participants scoring higher in both dimensions.

The mean scores of the two IS and ES sample groups (participants and non-participants), in the nine constraint factors were calculated, and the significance of the differences found were evaluated using a two-way ANOVA test (SPSSx). In sub-scales, the results, shown in table 8, indicated that constraints between participants and non- participants were found to be significant in "lack of time" (p<. 05), and "lack of money" (p<. 05). In terms of the sub-scales statistically significant differences between IS and ES samples were found in "lack of money" (p<. 05), "transportation" (p<. 01), "lack of facilities" (p<. 01), "social (lack of partner)" (p<. 01), "unawareness" (p<. 01), "lack of skill/ability" (p<. 01), and "health/fitness" (p<. 05).

Table 8.
2-Way ANOVA of constraint factors (mean scores) participants and non-participants: Iranian and English samples

Factors	IRAN		ENGLAND		Main Effectes Significance	
	P N=53 Mean	NP N=94 Mean	P N=111 Mean	NP N=40 Mean	IS & ES	P & NP
Lack of Time	1.79	1.94	1.85	2.00	n.s.	0.014
Lack of Interest	1.78	1.67	1.76	1.54	n.s.	n.s.
Lack of Money	2.39	2.54	2.07	2.42	0.039	0.031
Transportation	2.55	2.64	1.62	1.90	0.000	n.s.
Lack of Facilities	2.69	2.73	1.88	2.08	0.000	n.s.
Social (lack of partner)	2.11	2.19	1.72	1.87	0.000	n.s.
Unawareness	2.06	1.93	1.51	1.61	0.000	n.s.
Lack of Skill/Ability	2.00	2.18	1.86	1.63	0.002	n.s.
Health/fitness	1.81	1.74	1.63	1.54	0.011	n.s.

Discussion

This comparative investigation into leisure constraints with respect to a model identifying intra-personal, interpersonal, and structural constraints in England and Iran revealed a number of similarities and differences. The most fundamental similarity was in the factor structure of the constraints scale, where the factor structure is identical with similar individual item loadings on each factor and the same order of importance in relation to the percentage of variance (see tables 1 and 2). This is particularly interesting in view of the respective cultural settings, but it may relate to the fact that both samples were composed of university students, who may be regarded as being in a special situation. Therefore, it is not known whether this factor structure would apply to the general population in both countries. Although it is difficult to compare directly results from one study to another because of differences in methodology, the factors classified here have been found in other studies in North America, for example, JACKSON (1993) and by ALEXANDRIS and CARROLL (1997) in a study in Greece. This would suggest that there is a possibility of a universal applicability and crossing of cultural divisions.

As noted in the literature review, the factors have been categorised further into intra-personal, interpersonal and structural. This categorisation was also found to be appropriate in this study. In terms of the relative importance of constraints, there is again some similarity in relation to the three broad categories, as "structural" was the most important, with "interpersonal" and "intra-personal" being less so in each sample. For ES samples, the factors of "Money", "Facilities", and "Time" as structural were found to be the most important constraints to recreational sport participation. "Social" (lack of partner) as interpersonal was a less important constraint, and "Interest", "Health/Fitness", and "Awareness" as intra-personal were reported as the weakest constraints to recreational sport participation.

IS samples identified the factors of "Facilities", "Transportation", and "Money" as the most important constraints to recreational sport participation. "Social" (lack of partner) as interpersonal was a less important constraint, and "Awareness", "Health/Fitness", and "Interest" as intra-personal were found as the weakest constraints to recreational sport participation. This analysis clearly showed similar constraints amongst both ES and IS samples with respect to the three categories (structural, interpersonal, and intra-personal constraints), as reasons for ceasing participation and as barriers to participation in sporting activities, although individual factors were in a slightly different order. However, it should be noted that the Iranian students scored consistently higher in all factors except "Time" and "Lack of Interest" (see table 5), which implies they were considerably more constrained in all the remaining factors.

In a majority of previous studies, structural constraints such as, "Money", "Facilities", "Time" and "Transportation", have been found to be the most

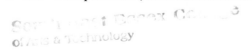

important constraints to participation in recreational sporting activities. NEWBY and LILLEY (1980) (lack of time and money), HULTSMAN, (1992) and JACKSON and RUCKS (1993) (lack of money and transportation), SCHREYER (1986) and JACKSON, (1993) (lack of time, money, and facilities) supported this investigation in this way.

Interpersonal constraints such as, "Social isolation" (related to "lack of partner") have been found by several researchers (e.g. JACKSON, 1993). Intra-personal constraints such as, "Skill/Abilities", "Unawareness", "Health/Fitness", and "Lack of interest", were experienced in the current investigation. "Lack of interest" which had been excluded in many previous studies (RAYMORE et al., 1993), was found to be of minor importance as a leisure constraint factor for both IS and ES samples. Both participants and non-participants in the two samples reported the full range of constraints. In the Iranian students' sample, there were no significant statistical differences between participants and non-participants in any of the factors, whilst in the English students' sample, the only significant statistical difference between these two groups was in the money and transport factors using independent t-tests (see tables 6 and 7). For the English non-participants, "money" and "transport" were more of a constraining factor than for the participants. Overall, and certainly in relation to the Iranian sample and all but two of the factors in the English sample, there is little difference in the perceived constraints between participants and non-participants. As already indicated, few studies have related the constraints directly to sport participation. However, the present results are in contrast to ALEXANDRIS and CARROLL (1997) and tend to support SHAW et al., (1991) and KAY and JACKSON (1991) in their proposition that participation exposes individuals to constraints and that these constraints are overcome through negotiation.

The hierarchical model of constraints proposed by CRAWFORD et al. (1991) cannot be supported by this study. They suggested that the intra-personal constraints would be the most powerful and proximal and would intervene with preferences. In this case non-participants should report statistically significant higher levels of intra-personal constraints than participants should. However, in the present investigation, this was not the case. In fact, higher levels (though not statistically significant) were shown by the participants in the Iranian sample in terms of "lack of interest", "unawareness" and "health/fitness", and by the participants in the English sample in "lack of interest", "lack of skill" and "health/fitness". It would appear that participation exposes individuals to these intra-personal factors just as readily as non-participants do. This may mean that constraints are inter-related (SCOTT, 1991) or met in combination. Whether there are any differences in gender has not been addressed in this investigation. This could have accounted for some of the differences between Iranian and English results, particularly in view of the different values attached to religion in the two countries.

Conclusions and Suggestions for Future Research

This comparative investigation has confirmed a model of constraints consisting of three general categories - intra-personal, interpersonal and structural constraints simultaneously - and a number of constraint factors, which were perceived by participants and non-participants. Non-participants were found to be more influenced by structural constraints. However, the investigation did not support a hierarchical model of leisure constraints.

Support is given to structural constraints as the most powerful perceived constraints, which are more likely to affect leisure participation. Intra-personal and interpersonal constraints are seen to be less important. Despite the two countries' different socio-cultural, religious, language, economic, ideological and political etc. contexts, structural, interpersonal, and intra-personal constraints have appeared in the same hierarchy of importance. According to JACKSON (1988), these findings can help the management of recreation sporting activity services when constraints related to participation are understood. The university authorities in both Esfahan and Manchester could examine these constraints and attempt to help the students overcome them if they wish to increase their participation. Attention may well focus on structural constraints: e.g., increase facilities, increase accessibility, and decrease costs.

Similar issues exist in this study when compared with the results of findings of previous studies. Further research with qualitative methodologies could offer possibilities for clarification and refinement of such findings. The knowledge gained from the current investigation provides an initial insight that could give rise to measures, which could increase leisure participation, from which society as a whole could benefit. However, there were limitations to this study in respect of the measurement of participation. Participation during the last previous year was used as the index of participation and non-participation. Further refinement of this measure to include frequency of participation would be useful.

For future studies, it will be necessary to investigate multiple factors such as these types of constraints (intra-personal, interpersonal and structural) simultaneously, in the hierarchical model proposed by CRAWFORD et al. 1991. These types of constraints become more or less important depending on the precise stage of the leisure decision-making process at which they are experienced (JACKSON and RUCKS, 1993).

There are undoubtedly other items of factor constraints, which were not included in this study. There is potential, therefore, for modification of the model. Although in this investigation structural constraints were consistently the highest recorded constraints and supported some previous studies (RAYMORE et al., 1993), other aspects of constraints (intra-personal and interpersonal) should be noted. Samples in the current study were limited to a student population, age group 18-24, i.e. educated young people. Further empirical study is required in both comparative and simultaneous investigation of all three constraints types (intra-personal, interpersonal, and structural), and to expand this analysis to include a full range of groups in terms of gender, age, education level, single, married, with/without children and so on. This study suggests that the model can cross "the Atlantic divide" (BECKERS, 1995) but further cross-cultural studies are required to confirm this.

References

ALEXANDRIS, K., and CARROLL, R.: An analysis of leisure constraints based on different recreational sport participation levels: results from study in Greece. In: *Leisure Sciences*, 19(1), 1997, pp.1-16.

BECKERS, D.: Back to basics: international communication in leisure research. In: *Leisure Sciences*, 17, 1995, pp.327-336.

BOOTHBY J., TUNGATT, F.M., and TOWNSEND, R.A.: Ceasing Participation in Sports Activity: Reported Reasons and their Implications. In: *Journal of Leisure Research*, 13, 1981, pp.1-14.

BUCHANAN, T., and ALLEN, L.R.: Barriers to recreation participation in later life cycle stages. In: *Therapeutic Recreation Journal*, 19, 1985, pp.39-50.

CRAWFORD, W.D., and GODBEY, G.: Reconceptualizing barriers to family leisure. In: *Leisure Sciences*, 9(2), 1987, pp.119-127.

CRAWFORD, W.D., JACKSON, L.E., and GODBEY, G.: A hierarchical model of leisure constraints. In: *Leisure Sciences*, 13(4), 1991, pp.309-320.

FRANKEN, A.D., and VAN RAIJJ, F.M.: Satisfaction with leisure time activities. In: *Journal of Leisure Research*, 13(4), 1981, pp.337-352.

GODBEY, G.: Non-use of public leisure services: a model. In: *Journal of Park and Recreation Administration*, 3(2), 1985, pp.1-12.

GOODALE, L.T., and WITT, A.P.: Recreation non-participation and barriers to leisure. In: Jackson L.E, and Burton L.T., (Eds.). *Understanding leisure and recreation: mapping the past, charting the future*. State College, PA, Venture Publishing Inc., 1989.

HENDERSON, A.K., STALNAKER, D., and TAYLOR, G.: The relationship between barriers to recreation and gender-role personality traits for women. In: *Journal of Leisure Research*, 20(1), 1988, pp.69-80.

HULTSMAN, W.Z.: Constraints to activity participation in early adolescence. In: *Journal of Early Adolescence*, 12(3), 1992, pp.280-299.

JACKSON, L.E.: Leisure constraints: a survey of past research. *Leisure Sciences*, 10(3), 1988, pp.203-215.

JACKSON, L.E.: Variations in the desire to begin a leisure activity: evidence of antecedent constraints. In: *Journal of Leisure Research*, 22(1), 1990, pp.55-70.

JACKSON, L.E.: Leisure constraints/constrained leisure. In: *Leisure Sciences*, 13(4), 1991, pp.273-278.

JACKSON, L.E.: Recognizing patterns of leisure constraints: results from alternative analyses. In: *Journal of Leisure Research*, 25(2), 1993, pp.129-149.

JACKSON, L.E., CRAWFORD, W.D., and GODBEY, G.: Negotiation of leisure constraints. In: *Leisure Sciences*, 15, 1993, pp.1-11.

JACKSON, L.E, and HENDERSON, A.K.: Gender-based analysis of leisure constraints. In: *Leisure Sciences*, 17, 1995, pp.31-51.

JACKSON, L.E., and RUCKS, C.V.: Reasons for ceasing participation and barriers to participation: further examination of constrained leisure as an internally homogeneous concept. In: *Leisure Sciences*, 15, 1993, pp.217-230.

KAY, T., and JACKSON, G.: Leisure despite constraint: the impact of leisure constraints on leisure participation. In: *Journal of Leisure Research*, 23(4), 1991, pp.301-313.

MANNELL, C.R., and ZUZANEK, J.: The nature and variability of leisure constraints in daily life: the case of the physically active leisure of older adults. In: *Leisure Sciences*, 13(4), 1991, pp.337-351.

MCGUIRE, A.F.: A factor analytical study of leisure constraints in advanced adulthood. In: *Leisure Sciences*, 6(3), 1984, pp.313-325.

MCGUIRE, A.F., and O'LEARY, T.J.: What the constraints literature says to the leisure service provider. In: *Leisure Challenges: bringing people, resources, and policy into play*. Proceedings, Sixth Canadian Congress on Leisure Research, Ontario Research Council On Leisure, 1990, pp.374-376.

NEWBY, F.L., and LILLEY, W.D.: *Cross-country skiing trend data: planning for participant needs*. Proceedings of 1980 National Outdoor Recreation Trends Symposium 2, 1980, pp.125-133.

RAYMORE, L., GODBEY, G., CRAWFORD, D., and VON EYE, A.: Nature and process of leisure constraints: an empirical test. In: *Leisure Sciences*, 15, 1993, pp.99-113.

SCHREYER, R.: *Motivations for participation in outdoor recreation and barriers to that participation - a comment on salient issues.* President's Commission on Americans Outdoors: A Leisure Review, 1986.

SCOTT, D.: The problematic nature of participation in contract bridge: a qualitative study of group-related constraints. In: *Leisure Sciences*, 13(4), 1986, pp.321-336.

SHAW, M.S.C., BONE, A., and MCCABE, F.J.: Do more constraints mean less leisure? Examining the relationship between constraints and participation. In: *Journal of Leisure Research*, (4), 1991, pp.286-300.

WADE, M.G.: *Constraints on leisure.* Springfield, IL, Charles C. Thomas, 1985.

WITT, A.P., and GOODALE, L.T.: The relationships between barriers to leisure enjoyment and family stages. In: *Leisure Sciences*, 4(1), 1981, pp.29-50.

Chapter 7

A Cross-cultural Study of the Socialisation Process of Female Tennis Players

Nicole M. LaVoi, March L. Krotee, Adel Elnashar and Keith Gilbert

Introduction

A number of studies have been undertaken delving into myriad of aspects of sport involvement, its antecedents and consequences, participation patterning, and the sociological and psychological variables related to the athlete's role in a specific sport, society and/or culture. However, very little research has broadened the scope to include trans-national data, especially in regard to the socialisation processes of female athletes. Cross-cultural comparative research increases perspectives concerning the sporting experience and provides a richer field of exploration (BENNETT, HOWELL and SIMRI, 1983; HAAG, 1994; KROTEE and BART, 1979; LUESCHEN, 1980; POOLEY, 1987).

As technological advances in communication and travel help to bring people of diverse nations together, it is inevitable that cross-cultural studies will take on more importance and significance. As diverse people search to find commonalties, communicate and share information, cross-cultural research can begin to facilitate and provide a foundation on which to further understand one another. Since sport is a fundamental activity and has been noted in nearly every society (BENNETT et al., 1983), sport provides the perfect context in which to reveal trends from nation to nation on a wide range of values, issues, attitudes and beliefs.

In addition to the cross-cultural value of sport studies, further insight may be gained by studying the female athlete. The rapid expansion of girls' and women's sports, higher participation rates, increased number of sport programmes available to females, changing roles of the female in society, and the increase in positive female role models provide a rich field for cross-cultural sport investigation. However, with the current general state of socialisation research in mind, "... it is not surprising to find that we are only now beginning to unravel the processes by which individuals become active participants in sport" LEWKO and GREENDORFER (1986, p.288).

Historically, early sport studies were designed primarily using male samples and findings were then generalised onto female populations. The early findings that did incorporate females into population samples, treated the female results as "atypical" and too difficult to fit in the traditionally male sport framework (GREENDORFER, 1987). Until the last decade, researchers mistakenly assumed that female sport experiences and reasons for involvement were the same as their male counterparts. Currently the view concerning the variance of sport experience of male and females is receiving some deserved attention. BROWN (1982) implies that vital information is missing on how women perceive, engage in and move through sport processes and involvement. Few cross-cultural studies concerning the female athlete have been undertaken and the exploratory study reported here is an attempt to fill this void and add significantly to the literature.

Purpose

The purpose of the study was to examine the socialisation processes, psycho-social attributes and sport involvement backgrounds of female tennis players to determine if significant similarities and differences existed across nations. Data were collected from volunteer tennis players (n=198), ages 14-18, from Australia, Egypt and the United States.

Procedures

The instrument employed in the study was the K-N-L Sociological Tennis Questionnaire (K-N-L STQ). This instrument was modified to accommodate the sport of tennis from the original K-N Questionnaire developed by Krotee and Naul in 1991 to explore various aspects of the socialisation processes of the female athlete as well as their participation patterning and attitudes. The K-N STQ was used because of its previous success in collecting a wide range of information concerning the socialisation process and attitudes of female soccer players (KROTEE, HUANG and NAUL, 1992).

The K-N-L STQ consisted of 34 open-ended and fixed alternative questions. The K-N-L STQ was translated and back translated in Arabic for the Egyptian sample to ensure accurate meaning was garnered and reliability maintained for use cross-culturally. Data were treated using descriptive statistics and where applicable Chi-square analysis was employed with categorical data items. Results were reported for both the entire sample as well as for each individual country.

The questionnaire was administered to volunteer female tennis players ages 14-18 from a variety of high school, club and tournament sport specific situations. The areas selected for the study were the metropolitan areas of Minneapolis, Minnesota for the United States sample, Cairo, Egypt and Brisbane, Australia for the other respective samples. A total of 198 respondents were included in the data pool.

Table 1.

Sample sizes

Country	U.S.A.	Egypt	Australia	Total
Sample Size	100	82	16	198

Results

1. Personal and Family Background

Age, weight and height of respondents were similar across country. The means were as follows: age (15.72 years), height (165cm) and weight (56kg). Across country, 52% of respondents lived in a highly populated (200,000 people or greater) areas. Ninety-nine percent of Egyptian tennis players lived in highly populated areas, vastly different from Australian (31%) and US (17%).

Parents of the female tennis players across country were found to be highly educated. Of all respondents' parents, only 2% did not possess a degree of any type and 73% of mothers and 85% of fathers held

University degrees (B.A., B.Sc., M.A., Ph.D.). Of significance, 100% of Egyptian mothers and fathers held University degrees. Occupations of mothers and fathers were similar across country. The most common categories of occupation for mothers across all countries were teacher (33%), homemaker (23%) and professional (16%). The most common categories of occupation for fathers were professional (49%), self-employed/other (22%) and teacher (12%).

2. Playing Experience

Across country a large percentage (52%) of respondents initially began playing tennis through private lessons. However, in the United States, 49% of the respondents began tennis in a community-based programme. This was clearly not the pattern in Egypt (1%) or Australia (6%). The respondents also indicated being actively involved in other competitive sports as well as tennis. Overall 53% reported participation in another sport. Australia reported the highest rate of dual-sport competition (75%), followed by the United States (63%) and Egypt (37%). The most popular sports indicated across country are shown in table 2.

Table 2.

Participation in other competitive sports

Sport	Sample		USA		EGY		AUS	
	N	%	N	%	N	%	N	%
Track	70	35	19	19	16	20	0	0
Basketball	41	21	29	29	11	13	1	6
Volleyball	19	10	7	7	7	9	5	31
Softball	20	10	16	16	0	0	4	25
Soccer	13	7	10	10	1	1	2	13
Swimming	8	4	5	5	0	0	3	19
Netball	6	3	0	0	0	0	6	38
Athletics	5	3	0	0	0	0	5	31
Golf	6	3	6	6	0	0	0	0

Some 90% of the subject's coaches across country were male. Respondents in the United States indicated 19% female coaches whereas

Australia (6%) and Egypt (0%) reported significantly less opportunity for same gender coaching.

Incidence of prejudice, barriers and obstacles encountered by players across country varied. Australian (31%) and US (24%) players reported the highest incidence, whereas the Egyptian (0%) players reported no incidence. The most common prejudice cited was "boys are better than girls". Elitism, lack of money, and social class were also frequently cited prejudices. Injuries, poor coaching, poor sportsmanship and favouritism were the most commonly perceived barriers and obstacles.

3. Psycho-social Influences

Data concerning the psycho-social attributes often associated with female tennis players indicate both similarities and differences across country. Overall, 76% of the respondents indicated that "athletic" was the most prominent psycho-social attribute describing female tennis players. The breakdown by country for the "athletic" response was United States (77%), Egypt (73%) and Australia (86%). Subsequent attributions concerning female tennis players across country appear to be dissimilar and are shown in table 3.

In the United States, ensuing high-ranking attributes most often noted were "intelligent" (61%), "aggressive" (61%), "strategic" (57%), and "smart" (57%). With the Egyptian sample, only "confident" (10%), and "intelligent" (4%) elicited any responses. The Australian data yielded "strong" (56%) and "quick" (50%) as popular attributes.

Lowest ranking attributes seemed consistent across country and included "graceful" (10%), "feminine" (10%), "impulsive" (8%), "tentative" (6%), and "elegant" (3%). These findings were consistent with the KROTEE et al., (1992) study of female soccer players, which found elegance, grace and fairness to be ranked at the bottom of attributes associated with female soccer players.

Table 3.
The psychosocial attributes associated with female tennis players

	Sample		USA		EGY		AUS	
	n	%	n	%	n	%	n	%
Athletic	151	76	77	77	60	73	14	86
Confident	71	36	56	56	8	10	7	44
Strong	67	34	53	53	5	6	9	56
Intelligent	68	34	61	61	3	4	4	25
Aggressive	66	33	61	61	0	0	5	31
Strategic	65	32	57	57	1	1	7	44
Smart	64	32	57	57	0	0	7	44
Quick	61	30	53	53	0	0	8	50
Powerful	61	30	44	44	0	0	7	44
Controlled	60	30	55	55	0	0	5	31
Decisive	42	21	37	37	0	0	6	38
Fair	41	21	35	35	0	0	6	38
Clever	36	18	34	34	0	0	2	13
Graceful	20	10	18	18	0	0	2	13
Feminine	20	10	17	17	0	0	3	19
Ingenuous	18	9	18	18	0	0	0	0
Rough	16	8	16	16	0	0	0	0
Impulsive	15	8	15	15	0	0	0	0
Tentative	12	6	12	12	0	0	0	0
Elegant	5	3	4	4	0	0	1	6

* Egyptian respondents chose only one attribute, whereas US and Australian respondents chose as many as they deemed applicable.

Significant differences of family involvement in tennis were apparent across country. The involvement of the female members of the family across country appeared to be most different. Not one Egyptian mother (0%) was indicated as an "active" tennis player, compared with mothers in Australia (27%) and the United States (24%). In addition, Egyptian sisters (11%) were significantly less involved as "active" players than their American counterpart sisters (47%) and Australia (40%). Male family members were more involved as "active" tennis players than female family members in Egypt and Australia. Active participation between gender appears to be most similar in the United States.

Table 4.

Family members as active tennis players

	USA	Egypt	Australia
Mother	24%	0%	27%
Sister	47%	11%	40%
Father	25%	27%	38%
Brother	43%	33%	55%

Conclusions and Discussion

The results of the study concerning personal and family background
suggested that families of female tennis players tend to be similar in
socio-economic and educational background. The data appear to imply
that tennis is typically an upper-class endeavour. This finding is
consistent with sport research which suggests that sport participation is
often a reflection of education, occupation and social class status
(HASBROOK, 1987; MCPHERSON, CURTIS and LOY, 1989).
Findings in this study across country indicated a high level of education
both for player and parent as well as a high level of occupational
achievement for parents.

The tennis respondents indicated injury as an obstacle to sport
participation. This finding was consistent with results from KROTEE et
al. (1992), who studied female soccer players. In the soccer study, injury
was among the top two obstacles reported across American, Chinese and
German female athletes. It may be possible that coaches are placing their
athletes at risk from injury because of a lack of knowledge concerning
sport science and training principles. Furthermore, it may be of interest to
study whether female athletes receive the same level of quality coaching,
teaching, attention, and access to qualified coaches and athletic medical
personnel to help prevent and treat injuries obtained during practice or
competitions.

The results also indicated the apparent acceptance of the female tennis
player in the sporting process across country. However, programmes for
youth within large urban areas were found lacking and are still requisite

for advancement of the game as well as equal access and opportunity for all diverse populations. In this regard, tennis In the United States appeared to be more effectively organised and more widely available to people in metropolitan, rural and urban areas than in Australia or Egypt. This might imply that access to tennis, or sport for that matter, may be a function of organisation and management of the delivery systems within each nation's sport infrastructure.

The findings further indicated that parents and family are significant socialising agents in the lives of female tennis players. This notion supports existing research that parents are the most significant socialising agents for girls (LEWKO and GREENDORFER, 1988). The data revealed that female family members in the United States were just as likely to be involved as active tennis participants as were males. However, female family members in Egypt and Australia were less involved as active tennis participants than male family members. This was most apparent in the Egyptian sample, and may be indicative of societal beliefs concerning females in sport and the roles of females in society. Additionally, it might indicate that sport participation is more encouraged and deemed appropriate by society for boys and men, than for girls and women (ELNASHAR, KROTEE and SHAHIZAH, 1996).

Tennis is a unique sport because of its international and professional status for women. Much can be learned about the female tennis participant across many nations where cultural variables may be very different. By comparing the similarities and differences concerning the female athlete, information can be derived about how the female athlete enters into, and moves through, the sport participation process, the development and maintenance of her attitudes and perceptions regarding her sport experiences, as well as learning about the nuances of the role of sport in society. The assumption that sport impacts all women in the same way (LOHN, 1995) should not be made. It is crucial professionals learn more about the dynamic of the growing female sport potential within the global village so that all involved in the sporting process can develop to their fullest potential.

References

BENNETT, B.L., HOWELL, M.L., and SIMRI, U.: *Comparative physical education and sport* (2nd ed.). Philadelphia: Lea & Febiger, 1983.

BROWN, B.K.: Female sport involvement: A preliminary conceptualization. In: DUNLEAVY, A.O., MIRACLE, A.W., and REES, C.R., (Eds.), *Studies in the sociology of sport*. Fort Worth, TX, Texas Christian University Press, 1982, pp.121-138.

ELNASHAR, A.N., KROTEE, M.L., and SHAHIZAH, D.: Keeping in stride with the Olympic games: An Islamic impression. In: *ICHPER Journal*, 4, 1996, pp.17-19.

GREENDORFER, S.L.: The case of female socialization into sport. In: *Psychology of Women Quarterly*, II, 1987, pp.327-340.

HAAG, H.: Triangulation: a strategy for upgrading comparative research methodology in sport science. In: WILCOX, R., (Ed.), *Sport in the Global Village*. Morgantown, WV, Fitness Information Technology, 1994, pp.501-507.

HASBROOK, C.: The sport participation-social class relationship among a selected sample of female adolescents. In: *Sociology of Sport Journal*, 4, 1987, pp.37-47.

KROTEE, M.L., and BART, W.M.: (1979). Some contributions of ethnology. In: KROTEE, M.L., (Ed.), *The dimensions of sport sociology*. West Point, NY, Leisure Press, 1979.

KROTEE, M.L., HUANG, C., and NAUL, R.: A cross-cultural study of the socialisation process of female soccer athletes. In: STANDEVEN, J., HARDMAN, K., and FISHER, R., (Eds.), *Sport for All. Into the 90s*. Aachen, Meyer und Meyer, Verlag, 1992, pp.243-248.

LEUSCHEN, G.: The system of sport. In: LEUSCHEN, G., and SAGE, G.H., (Eds.), *Handbook of the Social Science of Sport*. Champaign, IL, Stipes Publishing Company, 1980, pp.204-266.

LEWKO, J.H., and GREENDORFER, S.L.: Family influences in sport socialization of children and adolescents. In: SMOLL, F.L., MAGILL, R.A., and ASH, M.J., (Eds.), *Children in Sport.* Champaign, IL, Human Kinetics Books, 1988, pp.287-300.

LOHN, M.: *Women's research center is up and running.* Minnesota, Minnesota Women's Press, 1995.

MCPHERSON, B., CURTIS, J.E., and LOY, J.W.: *The social significance of sport.* Champaign, IL, Human Kinetics Books, 1989.

POOLEY, J.C.: The use and abuse of comparative physical education and sport. In: *Journal of Comparative Physical Education and Sport,* 9(1), 1987, pp.5-24.

Chapter 8

Participant Motivation in High School Interscholastic Sport in the U.S.A. and the U.K.

Paul A. Potrac and Robyn L. Jones

Introduction

From its largely English origins, organised competitive interscholastic sport has come to have broad international significance. However, physical educators have recently expressed concern about the ethos of competition within and between schools, and about the internal and external pressures to which this ethos is subjected (HARDMAN and NAUL, 1992). Consequently, the area of inter-school competition has become a focal point for research, with many studies investigating both teachers' and students' attitudes towards the subject (HARDMAN, KROTEE and CHRISSANTHOPOULOS, 1988; HARDMAN and NAUL, 1992). This research has generally focused on the perceived purposes of such sporting activity, the potential for enhancement of status and contact as a consequence of involvement, the propensity for identity with school values and the extent of commitment to competition. The perceived benefits of interscholastic sports participation have also been an area of contention. Generally, however, recent research has tended to conclude that high school sports do not do much to build character in adolescents, in either pro- or anti-social ways (COAKLEY, 1993; EITZEN and SAGE, 1994; FREY and EITZEN, 1991).

Despite such scholarly interest in school-based competitive sport, relatively little investigative research has been carried out in the principal component motivations for the involvement of athletes in interscholastic sport, particularly from a comparative viewpoint, though studies by HARDMAN et al., (1988), HARDMAN and NAUL (1992), and BLAIR et al., (1992) deserve mention. The dearth of comparative research in this area of participation motivation prompted the study reported here. The study aimed to provide updated information concerning the principal components motivations of participants in interscholastic sport in the United States (U.S.) and the United Kingdom (U.K.), thus, providing greater insight and understanding of involvement, and how the related casual attitudes may be subject to social construction. Furthermore, accepting the influence of culture upon respective social actions and perceptions, it was hypothesised that, reflecting wider social tenets, American athletes would place greater emphasis on the competitive nature of interscholastic sport, while their counterparts in the U.K. would attach a greater importance to the recreative nature of school sport.

The historical link between school and sport in both the U.S. and the U.K. has been well researched (GLAMSER, 1986; FREY and MASSENGALE, 1988; FIGLER and WHITAKER, 1991). Other significant areas of enquiry have centred on the values attached to interscholastic sport in the respective countries (GLAMSER, 1986; FIGLER and WHITAKER, 1991; COAKLEY, 1994; EITZEN and SAGE, 1994). These enquiries have generally concluded that a competitive emphasis is evident in the U.S. (FIGLER and WHITAKER, 1991), while in the U.K., the accent is on the process rather than the result (JONES, 1984; HARDMAN and NAUL, 1992).

Methodology

The subjects for the study comprised 120 high school athletes (n=60 from the U.S, n=60 from the U.K.) from the Washington D.C. and London suburban areas respectively. The athletes ranged from 15-18 years of age, had represented their respective schools in sporting competition, and were divided equally between the genders. Additionally, the proportion of subjects in each country was similarly divided between the sports of soccer, basketball, track and field, field hockey and tennis.

The instrument employed in the study was an adaptation of the questionnaire model designed by KENYON (1968) for measuring the relative importance of the component motivations for participation in physical activity. This model breaks down the concept of physical activity (sport) into several categories (i.e., as a social experience, for health and fitness, as an ascetic experience, as an aesthetic experience, as catharsis, and as the pursuit of vertigo), to which were added competitive and recreative classifications. The catharsis category was excluded. This was done to better measure the attitudes of athletes regarding their participatory motivations in keeping with the hypothesis stated earlier. Additionally, KENYON's (1968) encompassing term 'physical activity' was replaced by that of 'sport', the specific area with which the study was concerned. Just as the decision to select Kenyon's now superseded model as the main instrument of research, the terminological modification was introduced to meet with the specific purposes of the study.

Regarding the administered procedure, athletes from both countries were requested to complete the questionnaire by ranking the several component factors based on Kenyon's (1968) model in order of importance as to the purpose of their involvement in interscholastic sport. The most important factor was rated as seven; the least important ranked as one. The final ranking for each component was calculated by totalling the ranking accorded to each component. The subjects in both countries were given identical instructions as to how to complete the questionnaire, and were requested to do so individually. Hence, it was attempted to keep contact with the respondents in both countries minimal and standardised in order to maintain methodological uniformity.

Results

Table 1.
The principal component motivation for involvement in interscholastic sport of male and female athletes in the U.K.

Component	Male (n=30) (Ranking)	Female (n=30) (Ranking)
Health and fitness	1	1
Competitive experience	2	2
Recreative experience	5	3
Social experience	4	4
Aesthetic experience	7	7
Ascetic experience	3	6
Pursuit of vertigo	6	5

Table 1 shows that both male and female athletes in the U.K. attach great importance to the competitive nature of interscholastic sport: both groups ranked it as the second most important component motivation, behind health and fitness, for their participation in interscholastic sport. A considerable difference in the ranking of the recreative aspect of interscholastic sport between male and female athletes in the U.K. was evident, however, as females ranked it as the third most important component motivation, while the male athletes ranked it only fifth. A further discrepancy was evident in the ranking of the ascetic experience as the sixth most important component motivation by the female athletes, and the third most important by male athletes. Such a divergence could suggest that while both males and females attach equal status to the competitive nature of school sport, male students tend to be more highly dedicated to their interscholastic sports performances. Correspondingly, the ranking of the recreative experience as the third most important component motivation by female athletes could suggest that they are not as dedicated to their interscholastic sports performances and attach a greater emphasis to the recreative function of the activity.

Table 2.
The principal component motivation for involvement in interscholastic sport of male and female athletes in the U.S.A.

Component	Male (n=30) (Ranking)	Female (n=30) (Ranking)
Health and fitness	1	1
Competitive experience	2	2
Recreative experience	3	4
Social experience	7	5
Aesthetic experience	6	7
Ascetic experience	4	3
Pursuit of vertigo	5	6

The findings shown in table 2 also highlight the importance attached to the competitive aspect of interscholastic sport by male and female athletes in the U.S. The ranking by both groups of health and fitness as the most important component motivation for their involvement in interscholastic sport was identical to those obtained from the U.K. sample. The recreation component was ranked by the females as the fourth most important component motivation for their participation in inter-school sport, and the third most important, by male athletes. The ranking of the component motivations by gender in the American sample, in contrast to that of the U.K., was much more uniform in nature.

Discussion

Although sport has been described as a microcosm of society in that it reflects society's values, social stratification, organisation and problems (NIXON, 1984; MCPHERSON, CURTIS and LOY, 1989; FIGLER and WHITAKER, 1991; LEONARD, 1993; EITZEN and SAGE, 1994), the relationship between sport and society is an interdependent one. Thus, through socialisation and the reinforcement of certain values, sport is a powerful force in shaping beliefs about appropriate male and female attitudes and behaviours (SAGE, 1990). As one result, the competitive emphasis placed on interscholastic sport in the U.S. can be largely explained by the predominant values held in American culture, where a deal of emphasis is placed on competitive success. Indeed, research indicates that many Americans have internalised (through the process of socialisation) values that predispose them to be interested in the outcome of competitive situations (FIGLER & WHITAKER, 1991; LEONARD, 1993; COAKLEY, 1994). To suggest that sports should emphasise co-operative or individualised reward structures would be considered by many Americans as a distortion of what they believe is the natural essence of sport (COAKLEY, 1994). The findings of the study, in relation to the high ranking afforded to the competitive category in terms of participant motivation by U. S. athletes in interscholastic sport, therefore, supports the stated hypothesis in the American context.

In contrast to the expected finding, the U.K. athletes also placed a high premium on competition as opposed to recreation in relation to their involvement in interscholastic sport. Although opposed to earlier findings of JONES (1984) and GLAMSER (1986), it agreed with the more recent conclusions of HARDMAN and NAUL, (1992). Indeed, as stated earlier, concern has recently been expressed in this context by British physical educators regarding the advent of the competitive ethos within school programmes (HARDMAN and NAUL, 1992; KIRK, 1992). However, an explanation for such emphasis could well lie with the prevailing political climate of the day.

During the 1980s, the incumbent Conservative government, through introducing a system of parental (consumer) choice in schooling, simultaneously created a competitive educational system, culminating in the establishment of national league tables related directly to pupil's examination results. Such an ethos found a natural expression within physical education and particularly inter-school sport, where success was exploited in terms of a school's general achievements.

A school's sporting success was made additionally significant following the association of school sport teams with the fate of elite international sporting teams. Although the public debate surrounding the relationship between school physical education and elite sport had begun in the 1970s, it was during the following decade that forceful official representations were made that the traditional values of excellence in games within schools were being undermined by "ideologically motivated teachers, who wished to promote equality by dispensing with failure" (KIRK, 1992, p.4). Consequently, greater emphasis was placed on individual achievement and excellence within teams thus, bolstering a strong competitive element within school sport. Returning to the data presented in table 1, a noticeable difference between the participatory motivations of males and females noted there, was the significantly higher ranking given to recreation by females (3) as opposed to males (5). Such results are in broad agreement with the earlier findings of COHEN (1993) and SAGE (1990), who wrote in the context of sport generally that the emphasis of female attitudes is on performance rather than outcome.   Similarly, HARDMAN et al., (1988) also concluded that female athletes place a greater emphasis with interscholastic sport participation on the development of self esteem, support for the school and the establishment of social contacts than do their male counterparts. Although some scholars have contended that such differences can be explained in terms of socially constructed role expectation (FIGLER and WHITAKER, 1991), such gender differences are not universally borne out from the present study, due to the very similar findings in this context evident from the American sample.

Although the principal emphasis of this study was to examine the relative importance attached to the competitive as opposed to the recreative motivations for participation in interscholastic sport, it would be remiss not to comment on the high ranking given to the health component. This was ranked by both gender groups in both countries as the most influential motivation component for participation in inter-school sport.

The emergence of health-based physical education programmes in the U.K. during the 1980s combined concerns for physical fitness with concerns for the individual learner. It can be seen as indicative of a broader cultural shift from "public to individual and external to internal forces of social control" expressed as individual responsibility to keep fit and healthy (KIRK, 1992, p.6). Such social developments were already well under way in the U.S., as growing concern and awareness regarding the increased sedentary life-style and associated disease of persons from all socio-economic strata had stimulated mass participation in sport and exercise (EITZEN and SAGE, 1994).

Within the British context, such an accentuation can further be seen to support the ethos of individuality and corresponding reduction of external (state) controls ushered in by the Thatcher government and a number of other social groups in the 1980s, thus bringing it closer to the American model. As a result, this emphasis, as manifested by the study's sample, can also be expressed in terms of physical education and school sport as a social process, subject to considerable political, social and cultural forces.

Conclusion

The similarity in attitudes held by British and American high school athletes toward their involvement in interscholastic sport can be seen as symptomatic of the adoption by British society of the largely American tenets of the importance of competition, individual effort and initiative in the 1980s. These findings illustrate the beliefs of HARDMAN and NAUL (1994) that the shrinking global village and the collapsing of trans-national borders are leading to convergence rather than divergence in the educational and sport delivery systems of nations.
Although it might well be inevitable that the imminent international merging of educational and sports processes will impact on the delivery

and structure of physical education and sports programmes, the findings of the study, albeit from relatively small samples, do provide further food for thought concerning the social construction of the subject, and the role of powerful groups within society in shaping the aims and content of physical education within our schools.

References

BLAIR, P.F., KROTEE, M.L., NAUL, R., NEUHAUS, H-W., and HARDMAN, K.: A cross cultural study of youths attitudes concerning the role of sport in the educational process. In: *International Journal of Comparative Physical Education and Sport*, XIV(1), 1992, pp.4-15.

COAKLEY, J.J.: Sport and socialisation. In: *Exercise and Sports-Science Reviews*, 21, 1993, pp.169-200.

COAKLEY, J.J.: *Sport and society: issues and controversies* (5th ed.). St Louis, MO, C.V. Mosby, 1994.

COHEN, G.L.: *Women in sport*. Newbury Park, CA, Sage Publications, 1993.

EITZEN, D.S., and SAGE, G.H.: *Sociology of American sport*. (5th ed.). Dubuque, IA, Brown and Benchmark, 1994.

FIGLER, S.K., and WHITAKER, G.: *Sport and play in American life*. (2nd ed.). Dubuque, IA, W.C. Brown, 1991.

FREY, J.H., and EITZEN, D.S.: Sport and society. In: *Annual Review of the Sociology of Sport*, 17, 1991, pp.503-522.

FREY, J.H., and MASSENGALE, J.D.: American school sports: Enhancing social values through restructuring. In: *Journal of Physical Education, Recreation and Dance*. August, 1988, pp.41-44.

GLAMSER, F.: School sport in England: A comparative view. *Journal of Sport Behaviour*, 11(4), 1986, pp.193-203.

HARDMAN, K., KROTEE, M., and CHRISSANTHOPOULOS, A.: A comparative study of inter- school competition in England, Greece, and the United States of America. In: BROOM, E.F., CLUMPNER, R., PENDLETON, B., and POOLEY, C.A., (Eds.), *Comparative Physical Education and Sport*, (vol.5). Champaign, IL, Human Kinetics Publishers, 1988, pp. 91-102.

HARDMAN, K., and NAUL, R.: Inter-school sports competition: historical-cultural antecedents in England and Germany. In: *International Journal of Comparative Physical Education and Sport*, 14(1), 1992, pp.15-31.

HARDMAN, K., and NAUL, R.: The development of sporting excellence in England and Germany: an historical comparison. In: WILCOX, R., (Ed.), *Sport in the global village*. Morgantown, WV, Fitness Information Technology Inc., 1994, pp. 449-458.

JONES, R.L.: *A comparative study of the structure and organisation of university sport in the United States of America and the United Kingdom*. Unpublished Masters thesis, University College of North Wales, Bangor, Wales, 1984.

KENYON, G. S.: A conceptual model for characterising physical activity. *The Research Quarterly*, 19(1), 1968, pp.96-105.

KIRK, D.: *Defining physical education: the social construction of a school subject in post-war Britain*. London, Falmer Press, 1992.

LEONARD, W.M.: *A sociological perspective of sport* (4th ed.). New York, MacMillan Publishing, 1993.

MCPHERSON, B.D., CURTIS, J.E., and LOY, J.W.: *The social significance of sport*. Champaign, IL, Human Kinetics Publishers, 1989.
NIXON, H.L.: *Sport and the American dream*. New York, Leisure Press, 1984.

SAGE, G.H.: *Power and ideology in American sport*. Champaign, IL, Human Kinetics Publishers, 1990.

Chapter 9

Assessment of Psychological Stress Conditions amongst German and Japanese Soccer Players

*Dieter Teipel, Soichi Ichimura, Mitsuhiro Matsumoto,
Yoshio Sugiyama, Kanshi Uemukai and Akihiko Kondo*

Introduction

According to LAZARUS and LAUNER's (1981) fundamental concept, the perception and evaluation of psychological stress can be described in a three phase model: (i) primary appraisal; (ii) secondary appraisal; and (iii) reappraisal of a specific situation. **Primary appraisal** means the subjective evaluation of the threat of a situation, which is determined by the concept of individual abilities and motives. **Secondary appraisal** refers to the applicability of coping strategies in the specific situation. **Reappraisal** is related to the new assessment of the situation after a specific time.

Soccer players are required to deal with several kinds of stressors in the club, in the team, in training and as well as before, during and after games. Thus, the education of soccer players implicitly incorporates primary and secondary appraisal of various stressful conditions. In many cases, primary and secondary appraisal result in performance decreasing effects rather than in performance increasing effects.

BAUER and UEBERLE (1984) have emphasised that the coach has to enable soccer players to make adequate appraisals of stressful situations and apply specific coping strategies. Accordingly, the task of the coach in training is to guide, direct and observe the players' various activities. Before the game, the coach should motivate players individually and regulate their activation levels. After the game, the coach should conduct a general causal attribution of the win, draw or defeat and an individual performance evaluation.

TEIPEL (1992) investigated the attitudes of 230 German male and female soccer players concerning specific situations in training, before and after games. High levels of stress were found during training in situations where teammates were lacking in motivation, where conflicts between players and coaches and between players and teammates existed, and where there was evidence of inadequate team preparation for the next game. Before the game, the highest levels of stress were detected in conditions of substitution shortly before the start of the game and of feeling unfit during warm-up. After the game, highly stressful situations occurred when defeat was caused by player error and/or an injury was worse than expected. Female soccer players rated most of the conditions in training, before, and after the game, as more stressful than male soccer players. These higher stress ratings appeared to be directly related to the lower degree of soccer experience amongst the female than amongst the male players.

MATSUMOTO et al., (1994) analysed the assessed levels of the specific stress conditions in male and female Japanese soccer players. The 154 female Japanese players rated the perceived stress in 18 of the 35 conditions in training, before, and after the game, far higher than in the 246 male Japanese players. Among other variables, female Japanese players regarded the conditions of overly high performance expectations and aggressive behaviour in training, information about playing against the best of the opponents and spectator insults during pre-match warm-up, as well as the attribution of a defeat to misconduct and negative spectator reactions after the game, as more stressful than did male Japanese players.

In the study reported here, primary appraisals of specific stress conditions in training, before, and after the game of a group of German and Japanese soccer players were analysed. Comparisons were made of the German and Japanese players comprising the group, the male German and Japanese players and the female German and Japanese players.

Method

A specific questionnaire was applied for the assessment of stress conditions in training, before and after the game. The situations in training consisted of 15 items and the conditions before, as well as after, the game each comprised 10 items. The 35 situations were answered on a 7-point scale from "1 = not stressful" to "7 = very stressful". In total, 630 male and female German and Japanese soccer players participated in the study. The 230 German soccer players (130 males and 100 females) were active in leagues from professional to amateur level; the 400 Japanese soccer players (246 males and 154 females) played at various performance levels. The group of 246 male players consisted of 70 players from the professional league and 176 players from university teams representing high to low levels of performance. The 154 female played with university teams ranging from high to low levels of performance.

The average age of the 230 male and female German players was 24.30 years, the males were 24.96 years and females 23.40 years old. In contrast, the 400 Japanese players had an average age of 20.99 years, i.e. more than 3 years younger than the German players. The average age of the Japanese male soccer players was 21.53 years and of the female soccer players 20.12 years. Thus, the male players were about 1.4 years older than the female players.

The German soccer players had an average period of soccer experience of 14.62 years, males had 17.44 years and the females 10.94 years. In comparison, the Japanese players had only 8.87 years of experience. The Japanese male soccer players had an average of 11.23 years experience and so were by far more experienced than the female soccer players with only 5.16 years.

Statistical analysis of assessments was by means of descriptive and inferential procedures. The comparison of the evaluations of the stress conditions between the various groups of the male and female German and Japanese players was made by analysis of variance.

Results

Evaluations of the specific stress conditions are reported for the whole group (630), comparatively for the 230 German and the 400 Japanese soccer players, 130 male German and 246 male Japanese soccer players, as well as the 100 female German and 154 female Japanese soccer players.

1. In training

The whole group (n=630) German and Japanese male and female soccer players considered the 15 situations during training to be in the medium to highly stressful range. The relatively highest stress level was found when tedious exercises were engaged in. The second highest stress level occurred when a player's ability was not challenged. The third highest stress level was detected when teammates' attitudes were seen to be negative. Additionally, stress occurred in the following situations: tense atmosphere during training; adverse field conditions; conflicts between the player and teammates; inadequate coach-directed preparation of the team for the next game; and conflicts between the player and the coach. In contrast, the situation when coach expectation of performance level was too high produced the lowest level of stress. Moreover, in the situation when training was considered to be too demanding, stress level was low.

Comparison of the assessments of the stress levels revealed that the Japanese soccer players had, in 14 of the 15 conditions, higher stress levels (in 12 of these 14 conditions significantly higher levels: $p < .01$) than the German players.

The Japanese players regarded the situation, when tedious activities were practised, as by far more stressful than did the German players. The Japanese players showed higher levels of stress than the German players, when their abilities were insufficiently challenged. Furthermore, the Japanese soccer players had higher stress levels, in situations of adverse pitch conditions, training too prolonged, teammates playing aggressively, ineffectively regarded exercises, and final training too intensive. In addition, when the atmosphere in training was tense, when there was insufficient training and when the coach did not prepare the team adequately for the next game, the Japanese players found these conditions more burdensome than did the German players. The situations, when there were conflicts between players and teammates, when there were arguments between a player and a coach, and when

Teipel et al

157

team-mates showed inadequate attitude, were also seen to be rather stressful more by the Japanese and the German players.

Comparison between the male German and Japanese soccer players clearly revealed that the male Japanese players showed, in 14 of the 15 conditions (in 11 0f these 14 significantly so) higher levels of stress evaluation than the German male players. The male Japanese players considered the situations when tedious exercises were practised, when the player was not challenged in accordance with his abilities, and when the pitch conditions were adverse much more stressful than did the male German players.

Analysis of the female German and Japanese soccer players showed that in 14 of the 15 situations (in 13 of these 14, significantly so) there were higher stress levels amongst the female Japanese players than amongst the female German players. The female Japanese players adjudged conditions practise of tedious exercises, inadequate challenge to ability and too intensive final training as by far more burdensome than did the female German players.

2. Before the game

The whole group of the 630 soccer players regarded being dropped from the team shortly before a game as the most stressful situation. The second most stressful situation was related to late arrival because of traffic congestion. The third highest level of stress was recorded when the player did not feel fit during warm-up.

On the contrary, the situations, when the player had to play against the best of the opponents, when the opponents were known for hard and physical play, and when the expectations of the club presidency were unrealistically high, were rated low in stress level.

Comparison of the 230 German and the 400 Japanese soccer players revealed in 9 out of 10 conditions, statistical differences. In all 9 cases, Japanese players' assessments were significantly higher than those of the German players. The Japanese players regarded the situations of a referee's actions (particularly when a player had experienced earlier problems with the referee), verbal abuse from opponents' spectator supporters during warm-up and unrealistically high club presidency expectations as being much more stressful than did the German players. Moreover, the Japanese players, more than their German counterparts, considered the situations of facing the best opposing player, renowned opposition hard, physical play, playing out of position, and late team arrival prior to a game because of traffic congestion as more stressful. The effect of a player being dropped from the team shortly before the game did not reveal any differences between the German and the Japanese players.

Analysis of the responses of male German and Japanese players showed very significant differences in all 10 conditions. The male Japanese players assessed 9 out of the 10 conditions as being far more stressful than the male German players. The male Japanese players viewed the situations of opponent spectator supporter verbal abuse during warm-up, facing the best opposing player, and renowned opponent hard, physical play, as more stressful than the male German players.

In 8 of the 10 conditions, the female Japanese players manifested significantly higher stress than the German female players. The female Japanese players displayed, in situations of unrealistically high expectations of the club presidency, a referee's actions when there had been earlier problems experienced by the player, and verbal abuse from opponents' supporters during warm-up, far higher stress levels than the female German players.

3. After the game

The whole group of players regarded the most stressful condition as being defeat stemming from player misconduct. The second highest stress level occurred when an injury turned out to be worse than expected. The third highest stress level was found when team cohesion dissipated after a defeat. Furthermore, high stress levels were detected when the coach gave no explanation for a player substitution and when a player was criticised despite a good performance. In contrast, the stress rating was rather low when the spectators whistled because of the team's poor performance and when the press reported inadequate and negative performance.

Comparison showed in 7 out of 10 situations (in 5 of these 7 significantly so) higher stress levels amongst the Japanese players, but in 3 of the 10 situations (in 2 of these very significantly so) there were higher levels amongst the German players. The Japanese players manifested higher stress rates than the German players in situations of teammate criticism despite a good performance, negative press reports on inadequate performance, and lack of coach explanation for a player substitution. Moreover, the Japanese players displayed higher stress perceptions than the German players when an injury turned out to be worse than expected and when a defeat stemmed from personal misconduct. On the other hand, the German players revealed higher stress assessments than the Japanese players when the injury turned out to be worse than expected and when the poor performance was caused by lack of effort by some teammates.

The analysis of the stress evaluation by male German and Japanese players showed that the male Japanese player had, in 7 out of 10 conditions (in 4 of these 7 very significantly so), higher rates than the male German players. In the situations of teammate criticism despite a good performance and the lack of explanation for the substitution of a player, the male Japanese experienced higher stress rates than the male German players. The male German players, however, adjudged the situations of an injury turning out worse than expected and poor performance caused by lack of effort by some teammates, as producing higher rates of stress than did the Japanese players.

In respect of the comparison between the female German and Japanese players, the female Japanese players manifested, in 9 out of 10 situations (in 6 of these 9 very significantly so), higher stress perceptions than the female German players. The female Japanese players, more than their German counterparts, felt that in conditions, when a player was criticised by team-mates despite a good performance, and the spectators whistled because of a poor performance, higher amounts of stress were experienced.

The marked differences of stress evaluations between male and female German and Japanese soccer players were apparently caused by large differences in experiences as soccer players at high and lower league levels and in the tendencies of causal attribution of failure. It can be hypothesised that the much longer experience of various situations in training, as well as before, during and after games, and the tendency of external attribution of failure of the German players, resulted, in most conditions, in significantly lower stress level assessments than were produced by the shorter experience and the tendency of internal attribution of failure of the Japanese players.

The findings of this investigation demonstrated a high degree of similarity with the results of the studies of TEIPEL (1992) and MATSUMOTO et al., (1994). In TEIPEL's (1992) study, the group of 230 German male and female soccer players regarded most of the conditions related to high degrees of personal responsibility in training, before, and after, the game as highly stressful. The female players showed higher stress level assessments in most of the conditions than the male soccer players. In MATSUMOTO et al's (1994) investigation, the female Japanese soccer players regarded most of the situations as more stressful than did the male Japanese players.

Concluding Comments

This study was concerned with analysis of specific stress conditions in training, before, and after, games of 230 male and female German and 400 male and female Japanese soccer players ranging from high to low levels of performance.

The whole group (n=630) of players regarded tedious exercises practised during training and insufficient challenge to ability as rather stressful. Before the game, the highest stress levels were found in the situations of a player dropped from the team, shortly before the match, and late team arrival shortly before the start of a game. After the game, the highest stress perceptions were detected when defeat was attributed to player misconduct and when an injury turned out to be worse than expected.

The 400 Japanese players regarded 26 conditions in training, before, and after, the game, as very significantly more stressful and 2 conditions as less stressful than did the 230 German players. In 25 conditions, the 246 male Japanese players manifested very significantly higher, and in 2 situations lower, stress assessments than did the 130 male German players. The 154 female Japanese players rated 26 conditions in training, before, and after, the game, as very significantly more stressful than did the 100 female German players.

It seems reasonable to conclude that the apparently higher stress levels experienced amongst the male and female Japanese players in comparison with the male and female German players were caused by the differences in the experience of soccer players and in the causal attributions of failure. The longer experience of the German soccer players and the more external causal attribution of failure led to a lower appraisal of stress in most of the conditions in training, before, and after, the game than the shorter experience and the more internal attribution of the Japanese players.

References

BAUER, G., and UEBERLE, H.: *Fussball. Faktoren der Leistung, Spieler- und Mannschaftsführung.* München, BLV, 1984.

LAZARUS, R.S., and LAUNIER, R.: Stressbezogene Transaktionen zwischen Person und Umwelt. In: NITSCH, J.R., (Ed.), *Stress. Theorien, Untersuchungen, Massnahmen.* Bern, Huber, pp.213-259.

MATSUMOTO, N., TEIPEL, D., SUGIYAMA, Y., and UEMUKAI, K.: Evaluation of stress conditions in training, before and after games in Japanese male and female soccer players. In: *Bulletin of Sport and Physical Education Centre of the University of Tsukuba*, 16, 1994, pp.35-42.

TEIPEL, D.: *Beanspruchung von Spielern und Trainern im Fussball.* Köln, Sport und Buch Strauss.

Chapter 10

A Comparison of Australian and Japanese Judo Practitioners' Values and Attitudes towards Sport

Kosuke Nagaki

Introduction

The worldwide diffusion of western sports assisted by their inherent value of rationalism (GUTTMANN, 1978) has been accompanied by the spread of oriental cultural sports such as the martial arts of Karate, Aikido and Judo to the western world. Of the latter, judo in particular has come to enjoy international federation status with standardised rules and has been recognised as an Olympic sport since 1964.

Jigoro Kano established judo at the beginning of the Meiji Era (1882). It was based on Jujutu, a martial art practised by the Samurais during the Edo Era. The spiritual aspect of Judo was influenced by the value of *Shugyo* (KANO, 1899; 1915), "discipline" in Samurai thought. Shugyo was directly related to values connected with several Japanese religions, (mainly Taoism, Zen of Buddhism, and Mikkyo) and is characterised as the relation between the process of acquiring technique and the formation of personality. It seems that all Japanese traditional Arts share these same sorts of values.

Jigoro Kano, a Japanese educational leader at the time, defined these traditional values of Judo from an educational view and promoted it as a means of bringing a sense of Japanese identity to the common people. Thus, he named it *Kodokan-Judo*: "Ko-do" meaning to teach the way of life. Largely because of this historical context, Judo has been included within the secondary school physical education programme in Japan.

Judo spread throughout Europe at an early stage and the International Judo Federation had 177 national members world-wide by 1995, which is testimony to its attraction to the 'West' as a universal sport. Generally, sports are accepted according to social and cultural backgrounds. In the case of Judo, it is evident that there have been periods of both slow and rapid change during its transition to international recognition. Rapid changes occurred with the influence of western values, which have occasionally produced conflicts (e.g. uniforms and traditional Japanese rules).

The spread and acceptance of sport from a fusion of oriental and western values can be analysed through a cross-cultural study of attitudes and values and attitudes toward sport among judo practitioners. It is also possible to highlight the universality and diversity of oriental and occidental values in relation to sport.

Methods

Two surveys were conducted in Australia: in Perth, 1995 and in Brisbane, 1996. The choice of Australia for the study was influenced by apparent Australian enthusiasm for Sport (CALDWELL, 1972), which implies distinctive values and attitudes towards sport. Australian culture has been strongly influenced by British culture, particularly in the area of sport. This influence is important because the British were leaders in the formation of modern sport and diffusion to the rest of the world. Yet, Australians seem to have no particular prejudice and to be positive in accepting Japanese culture, studies on which have been remarkably well developed in the country.

The males' only sample was made up of practitioners in Perth, who usually practised at the University of Western Australia and who belonged to the Judo Federation of Western Australia, and practitioners in Brisbane, who were associated with the Judo Federation of Queensland. Many of the practitioners in both groups were Anglo-Saxon so their attitudes and values toward sport could be assumed to be Western. Compared with other main sports, the Australian judo practitioners were in a minority. Hence, it was difficult to gather data. Nevertheless, the data have significance as a minority representation. The Japanese sample group was made up of university Judo club members; it included some 40 practitioners, who practised with the Australian group.

From participant observations, there seemed to be no particular difference in level of technique and each group had well-experienced practitioners (see table 1). Table 1 also shows the mean age and Judo experience in years of both groups. Practitioners with more than 5 years of experience in judo formed the largest group.

Table 1.

Survey samples

Number		Australian Judo Praticioners		Japanese Judo Practitioners	
		1st Survey (1995: Perth)	2nd Survey (1996: Perth, Brisbane)	1st Survey (1995)	2nd Survey (1996)
Age (mean)		42	48	111	118
Experience		22.9	27.9	19.9	20.4
More than	1 year-3year	7 (16.7%)	4 (8.3%)	19 (17.1%)	5 (4.2%)
	2 year-5 year	7 (16.7%)	5 (10.4%)	24 (21.6%)	25 (21.2%)
	5 year	28 (66.&%)	39 (81.3%)	68 (61.3%)	88 (74.6%)

A questionnaire survey was used to determine Australian and Japanese Judo practitioners' values and attitudes toward sport considered. Two points were considered to be important in determining the scales as measures:

- the scales should accord with international comparative studies of sport

- the scales should include the perspective of particular Japanese values and attitudes toward sport

Three types of scales were adopted and were based upon these two points.

Results

1. Sport Orientations

WEBB (1969) proposed a trichotomy to characterise three possible orientations in sport: the scale was constructed as "play fairly, play well, play to win". Webb explained that this scale showed the professionalisation of attitudes toward sport and the achievement criteria in western industrialised society was reflected in it. Some researchers adopted this scale and modified it. For example, KIDD and WOODMAN (1975) devised a phenomenological model: their scale was "to have fun, to play well, and to win". TATANO's study also indicated that "to have fun" scale was a significant aspect of sport. YAMAGUCHI (1984) added "self-discipline" to the Webb scale as "self-discipline" is thought to be a traditional Japanese value in sport: his study indicated it was significant. He also indicated that the "fair" scale was not suitable as a Japanese value in sport.

Based on these points of view and results, the scale of orientations toward sport in this survey was constructed as "to enjoy the exercise, to win, to play it for self-discipline". The question in the survey was "What do you think is most important in playing sport?" The responses were ranked in order of importance.

The Australian group indicated that "to enjoy" had the highest ranking, "self-discipline" was second, and "to win" had the lowest ranking. The Japanese group indicated that "self-discipline" had the highest ranking, "enjoy" the second, and "to win" had the lowest ranking. There was a significant difference between the two groups (X=14.3, p<0.001).

With regard to the enjoyment aspect of sport, a fundamental orientation in sport for Westerners, the Australian group seemed to value it in the same manner as other Westerners. The self-discipline aspect of sport has been emphasised ever since the establishment of Judo by Jigoro Kano. The finding in this study confirmed its continuing importance.

Figure 1.

Orientations toward sport

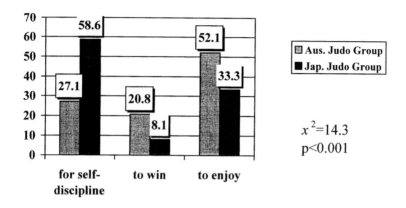

$x^2=14.3$
$p<0.001$

"To win" had the lowest ranking in the both groups: amongst the Japanese group, it was ranked extremely low. It is possible here that the Japanese group members were inclined to value the process of acquiring self-discipline or enjoyment rather than victory as an achievement result. On the other hand, as more than one-third of the Japanese group responded to enjoyment and about one-third of the Australian group responded to self-discipline, it seems possible to fuse the Western and Japanese orientations in sport among Judo practitioners.

2. Attitude towards Physical Activity

KENYON (1968) proposed conceptual dimensions of physical activity and constructed a scale of attitude toward physical activity. For this study, 6 scales were adopted: social experience, health and fitness, the pursuit of vertigo, an aesthetic experience, catharsis, and an ascetic experience. The scales were divided according to present sporting activities and to future activities. Practitioners were asked to choose the most important scale.

Figure 2.
Kenyon's attitude towards physical activity scale

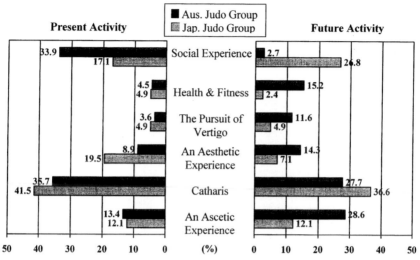

The scale of health and fitness was chosen highly by both groups in the present survey. Judo seems to be well matched to their views of sport because it demands strenuous exercise and is useful for improving health and fitness. In the Australian group, the pursuit of vertigo, an ascetic experience and a social experience had a reasonable response, while an aesthetic experience and catharsis had almost no response. With regard to the future activity of the Australian group, only the ascetic experience showed an increase and the other scales ratings were unchanged. The ascetic experience of the Japanese group was about twice that of the Australian group in present activity, but for the future, it was only about one tenth of the Australian figure. These figures seem to depend on the traditional Japanese attitude that sport is only suitable for young people. Indeed, the number of people who engage in sport is inclined to noticeably decrease after graduation from university in Japan. This may be because Japanese businessmen are too busy with work to engage in sporting activities. The Australian group members, on the other hand, were inclined to value an ascetic experience as a long-term orientation compared with the Japanese group.

Figure 3.
Japanese attitudes and values toward sport

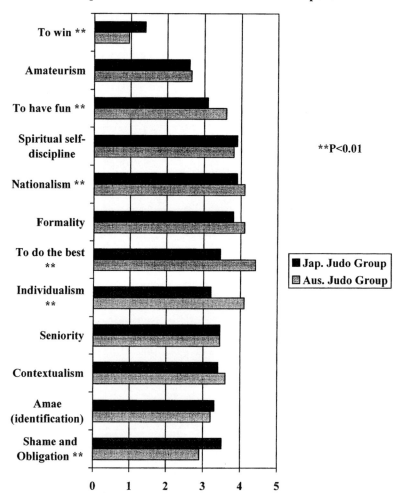

KENYON's (1970) research, using sample adolescent populations in Canada, America, Australia and England, indicated that all of the countries were negative towards an ascetic experience and Australians had the lowest ranking. However, the present survey results are more recent than Kenyon's data. In the Australian group, it should be noted that the ascetic value of future sporting activities received more than 25% of the responses, and as such might be said to have considerable importance in Australian sporting attitudes.

3. Japanese Values and Attitudes toward Sport

TATANO (1984) constructed a scale of Japanese values and attitudes toward sport to differentiate Japanese attitudes when compared with Westerners. The questionnaire factors were based on the kind of valid references, which have been proposed concerning Japanese characteristics. Figure 3 indicates the mean score of each factor on an esteem scale of 1-5.

The Japanese group was positive to "spiritual self-discipline" and "formality", although ratings were not high. These factors were held to be traditional and well matched in the context of Judo. The Australian group was positive in responses to "to do the best", "formality", "nationalism" and "spiritual self-discipline". Seemingly, "formality", and "spiritual self-discipline" had approximately the same importance with the Japanese group. The Australian group was positive in its orientation to "individualism", but the Japanese group was disposed toward "groupism". Such difference seemed to reflect Western and Japanese values of human relations. In contrast with the Japanese group, the Australian group was negative towards "shame and obligations". Perhaps, individual social and cultural backgrounds have an influence on these emotional differences.

Concluding Comments

The three scales used to measure values and attitudes towards sport in this study seem to have overlapped various points of view and suggest that in future care will have to be devoted to develop a more precise means of measurement for comparison of Judo practitioners.

An interesting feature of the survey's findings is that Judo appears to increase the value of self-discipline amongst Australian participants. Certainly, this is the case when comparisons are made with other

Australian sports participants or with Judo practitioners in other countries. It might be reasonable to expect the development of a new value through the fusion of enjoyment (a western value) and self-discipline (a Japanese value). That is to say, the value of self-discipline is based on enjoyment. Finally, it seems that "groupism" as the Japanese attitude of human relations and "shame and obligations" as Japanese emotions in sport were unacceptable even to Judo practitioners in Australia. In this regard, the findings of this study provide supportive evidence that values and attitudes toward sport reflect cultural viewpoints.

Future further research should focus on female Judo practitioners to clarify and determine whether there are sex differences in attitudes and values in Judo.

References

CALDWELL, G.: Sport and Australian identity. In: *Hemisphere*, 16(6), 1972.

GUTTMANN, A.: *From ritual to record: the nature of modern sports.* New York, Columbia University Press, 1978.

KANO, J.: Shugyo Tanren. In: *Kokushi*, 5, 1899, pp.1-5.

KANO, J.: Shuyo and Judo. In: *Judo*, 6, 1915, pp.1-7.

KENYON, G.S.: A conceptual model for characterizing physical activity. *The Research Quarterly*, 39(1), 1968, pp.96-105.

KENYON, G.S.: Attitudes toward sport and physical activity among adolescents from four English speaking countries. In: LUSCHEN, G. (Ed.), *Cross-cultural analysis of sports and games.* Champaign, IL, Stipes, 1970, pp.138-155.

KIDD, T., and WOODMAN, W.: Sex and orientations toward winning in sport In: *The Research Quarterly*, 46(4), 1975, pp.476-483.

TATANO, H. (Ed.): *A cross-cultural study on attitudes and values toward sport*. The report in Science Research to the Japanese Ministry of Education, 1984.

WEBB, H.: Professionalization of attitudes toward play among adolescents. In: KENYON, G.S. (Ed.), *Aspects of contempory sport sociology*. North Palm Beach, FL, The Athletic Institute, 1969.

YAMAGUCHI, Y.: *Socialization into physical activity in corporate settings: a comparison of Japan and Canada*. Doctoral Dissertation, Department of Kinesiology, University of Waterloo, Ontario, Canada, 1984.

Chapter 11

A Cross-cultural Comparison of Body Image among Australian and Thai University Students

Jennifer O'Dea, Catherine O'Brien and Supranee Kuanboonchen

Introduction

Research into body image has investigated gender differences but very few studies have looked at body image differences between ethnic groups or cross-cultural differences. Gender differences have been observed in nearly all body image studies of young adults (O'DEA, 1995). Women tend to overestimate their body size and specific body parts, whereas men tend to perceive themselves as being generally underweight and they report wanting to be bigger, taller and more muscular (BOOTH, 1990; FALLON and ROZIN, 1985; HARMATZ, GROENENDYKE and THOMAS, 1985; MISHKIND et al., 1986; TUCKER, 1984). Preliminary research into ethnic differences in body image has looked at a comparison of Australians, Samoans (WILKINSON, BEN-TOVIM and WALKER, 1992) and Cook Islanders (CRAIG et al., 1992). The results of these studies suggest that Pacific Islanders may not be as pre-occupied with slimming as Australians are. The study reported here was designed to investigate cross-cultural differences between a group of young Australian and Thai University students.

Methods

The sample comprised 660 students from two Australian and one Thai University. Students were enrolled in various degree programmes. The body perception questionnaire (STUNKARD, SORENSON and SCHUISINGER, 1980) was administered to the students during normal lecture times. The Thai students were given a copy of the questionnaire in the English language, which was verbally translated into Thai at the time by their lecturer. Students were asked to report their gender, age, ethnic background, height and weight. They were presented with nine female and nine male adult figure drawings, which ranged from emaciated (1) to very obese (9). Students were asked to "select the figure, which looks most like you" (Self-Score) and the figure which you would like to look like (Ideal Self-Score). In addition, students were asked to select "which female figure looks best" (Ideal Female Score) and "which male figure looks best" (Ideal Male Score). From the student selections, a mean score and standard deviation were calculated.

Results

A total of 455 Australian students (24.7% Male, 75.3% Female) and 205 Thai students (66.8% Male, 33.2% Female) participated. The mean, (standard deviation) age of the Australian students was 21.8 (4.5) years and that of the Thai students was 27.3 (7.9) years. Results are presented in table 1.

Table 1.

Comparison of the body image of male and female students

	Males			Females		
	Australian (n=112) Mean (SD)	Thai (n=137) Mean (SD)	F Value	Australian (n=343) Mean (SD)	Thai (n=68) Mean (SD)	F Value
Self Score	4.07 (1.16)	4.45 (1.43)	4.89*	3.72 (0.99)	3.59 (1.04)	0.94
Ideal Self Score	4.22 (0.92)	4.12 (0.89)	0.82	3.03 (0.63)	3.26 (0.74)	5.63*
Ideal Female Score	3.74 (0.98)	3.40 (0.71)	9.52**	3.07 (0.64)	3.39 (1.04)	11.64**
Ideal Male Score	4.45 (1.28)	4.00 (0.96)	9.82**	3.95 (0.63)	3.89 (0.65)	0.35

* $p<0.05$ ** $p<0.01$ *** $p<0.0001$

Self Score

There was no statistically significant difference in the way female students perceived their body weight ($p > 0.05$). Male Thai students perceived themselves as significantly heavier than the male Australian students ($p < 0.05$).

Ideal Self Score

There was no significant difference between male students for the body shape that they would most like to have ($p > 0.05$), but among females, the Australian students desired the slimmest body shape ($p < 0.05$).

Ideal Female Score

Male Thai students were significantly more likely to select a slimmer ideal female figure than that selected by the Australian males ($p < 0.01$). Female Australian students selected a very slim ideal female figure compared with Thai females ($p < 0.01$).

Ideal Male Score

Australian males selected a larger ideal male figure compared with Thai students ($p < 0.01$), but there was no difference in the selection of female students ($p > 0.05$). The slimmest figure of all (mean = 3.05 (0.63)) was selected by female Australian students and that figure was the ideal to which they aspired.

Gender Differences within Groups

Table 2 contains the gender differences among Australian and Thai students.

Table 2.

Gender differences in body image in Australian and Thai students

	Australian			Thai		
	Males (n=112) Mean (SD)	**Females (n=343) Mean (SD)**	**F Value**	**Males (n=137) Mean (SD)**	**Females (n=68) Mean (SD)**	**F Value**
Self Score	4.07 (1.16)	3.72 (0.97)	9.74**	4.45 (1.43)	3.59 (1.04)	19.34***
Ideal Self Score	4.22 (0.92)	3.06 (0.63)	214.17 ***	4.12 (0.89)	3.27 (0.75)	46.08***
Ideal Female Score	3.74 (0.98)	3.07 (0.64)	66.97 ***	3.40 (0.71)	3.40 (1.04)	0.00
Ideal Male Score	4.45 (1.28)	3.95 (0.63)	29.48 ***	4.00 (0.96)	3.90 (0.65)	0.64

* p<0.05   ** p<0.01   ***p<0.0001

There were similar gender differences between Australian and Thai students for the Self-Score (males perceived themselves as larger than females) and the Ideal Self-Score (males desired a larger figure than the females). The trend in gender differences continued among the Australian students for the Ideal Female Score (males preferred a larger female figure than the females who preferred a smaller ideal female figure) and the Ideal Male score (males preferred a larger male figure than the females). These gender differences did not exist among the male and female Thai students whose ideal male and female figures were almost identical.

Discussion

The body image of Australian and Thai males was different for their perceptions of the ideal male and female figure with Australian males perceiving a larger male and female ideal to be desirable. The opposite was apparent among Australian and Thai females with the Australian females desiring a much slimmer female ideal than the Thai females. It appears that the Australian males desire a larger body than that of their current figure and the Thai males desire the opposite. However, both the

Australian and the Thai females appear to desire a slimmer figure than their current shape. Of particular interest is the lack of gender differences among the Thai students when it comes to the ideal male and female figure. The clear agreement on these ideals is in contrast to the differences between male and female Thais for the discrepancy between their current shape and their ideal shape. Both male and female Thais perceived themselves to be significantly larger than they would like to be and significantly larger than their ideal figure.

The gender differences among the Australian students are similar to those found by FALLON and ROZIN (1985) in a group of 475 undergraduates from the United States. That study found that the male students considered themselves to be too thin and that the females considered themselves too fat. In the current study, the ideal female figure desired by the Australian female students was very close to becoming underweight and hence, may reflect an unhealthy and unrealistic body image. The ideals of other students appeared to be reasonably healthy and attainable. The results of this study suggest that there may be a cultural ideal for both male and female slimness among Thais and that pursuit of weight loss may have a more traditional origin than currently believed. It may be that the pursuit of thinness among Western women may not necessarily be the main influencing factor among Thai women and that Thais have always desired a slim figure. The agreement between the sexes suggests that there may be a cultural "norm" for the slim ideal of both the female and male figure in Thailand. It is also possible that Western products and habits as propagandised on television and through the 'Information Superhighway' are now influencing cultural norms. Further research among greater numbers of Thai people may confirm these findings.

References

BOOTH, N.: The relationship between height and self-esteem and the mediating effect of self-consciousness. In: *Journal of Social Psychology*, 130, 1990, pp.609-617.

CRAIG, P., SWINBURN, B., MATANGI, H., and MATENGA-SMITH, T.: Body size perception in Cook Islanders and Australians (Abstract). *Proceedings of the Australian Society for the Study of Obesity*. Sydney, NSW, July 1992, p.49.

FALLON, A., and ROZIN, P.: Sex differences in perceptions of desirable body shape. In: *Journal of Abstracts in Psychology*, 94, 1985, pp.102-105.

HARMATZ, M., GRONENDYKE, J., and THOMAS, T.: The underweight male: the unrecognized problems of body image research. In: *Journal of Obese Weight Reduction*, 4, 1985, pp.258-267.

MISHKIND, M., RODIN, J., SILBERSTEIN, L., and STRIGEL-MOORE, R.: The embodiment of masculinity in cultural, psychological and behavioural dimensions. In: *American Behavioural Scientist*, 29, 1986, pp.545-562.

O'DEA, J.: Body image and nutritional status among adolescents and adults - a review of the literature. In: *Australian Journal of Nutrition and Diet*, 52, 1995, pp.56-57.

STUNKARD, A., SORENSON, T., and SCHUISINGER, F.: Use of the Danish adoption register for the study of obesity and thinness. In: KETY, S., et al., (Eds.), *The genetics of neurological and psychiatric disorders*. New York, Raven Press, 1980, pp.115-120.

TUCKER, L.: Physical attractiveness, somatotype and the male personality: a dynamic interactional perspective. In: *Journal of Clinical Psychology*, 40, 1984, pp.1226-1234.

WILKINSON, J., BEN-TOVIM, D., and WALKER, M.: An insight into the personal and cultural significance of weight and shape in large Samoan women (Abstract). *Proceedings of the Australian Society for the Study of Obesity. Sydney.* NSW, July 1992, p.23.

PART 3

PHYSICAL EDUCATION AND SPORT PEDAGOGY

Chapter 12

Sex Differences in Motor Co-ordination among Primary School Children in Japan and the U.S.A.

Motohide Miyahara, Tadayuki Hanai, Masatsugu Tsujii,
Marian Jongmans, Sheila E. Henderson, Anna Barnett,
Miwako Hori, Kazunori Nakanishi and Hidenori Kageyama

Introduction

For many years, physical educators have acknowledged the needs of children with developmental co-ordination problems. In countries such as Australia, United Kingdom (UK), United States of America (U.S.A.), the Netherlands, and Finland research has been conducted to investigate the cause, the prevalence and the management of children with poor motor co-ordination. In some of these countries, systematic educational placement and re-mediation procedures have been established to meet the needs of these children. In contrast, the problems of such children are often overlooked in Japan. Although the status of health and fitness has been assessed as part of an annual nation-wide primary and secondary school programme for three decades, **motor co-ordination** has not been specifically evaluated.

Investigation has been conducted on only experimental and sporadic bases. A few articles have been written on motor co-ordination, but most are at the descriptive level and lack empirical support. This present study was part of a comprehensive study of movement difficulties among Japanese children designed to supplement the information regarding the children's motor co-ordination. Sex differences in motor co-ordination were compared between Japan and the U.S.A.

Methods

The motor competence of 159 Japanese children (77 boys, 82 girls) in a primary school affiliated with the Gifu University of Education was evaluated, using the Movement Assessment Battery for Children (HENDERSON and SUGDEN, 1992). This test battery was standardised in the U.S.A. with a representative sample population with respect to geographic region, gender, ethnic origin and the family's educational level. In contrast, the Japanese students' sample was from one primary school only. The school is located in a medium-sized city in the central part of Japan where the students enjoy a mixture of urban and rural lifestyles. In addition, physical education is taught on the basis of the Japanese national standard curriculum, and little variation is expected between different schools all over Japan. The sampling bias of the Japanese subjects may in part be justified by these two factors.

Of the 158 Japanese pupils, 6 year olds and 12 year olds were excluded from the data analysis, because the 6 year olds born before April were enrolled in the kindergarten, and the 12 year olds born after April in the junior high school. Hence, the data of these age groups was not complete. The total of 133 Japanese students (66 boys, 67 girls) was compared with 638 American children (283 boys, 355 girls) with respect to eight sub-tests of the Movement ABC: three manual dexterity tasks (pegboard, bi-manual task, drawing); two ball skill tasks (throwing, catching); and three balance tasks (static balance, two dynamic balances).

Results

Because of the difference in sample size and corollary variance between Japan and the U.S.A., no multivariate analysis was suitable to perform on the data. Instead, a series of t-tests was conducted in order to examine the sex difference in each country on the raw data of each sub-test. There were significant sex differences on manual dexterity, throwing, catching and statistic balance tasks.

On the manual dexterity tasks, significant sex differences existed among the 7, 9, 10 and 11 year old American students, whereas there was no sex difference among the Japanese students across all the age groups. Seven year-old American girls threaded a lace more quickly than did the American boys of the same age. However, 9 and 10-year-old American boys threaded nuts on a bolt more quickly than the American girls of the same age. Among 11-year old American children, girls cut out an elephant shape from a paper with a pair of scissors more accurately than boys. In the throwing tasks, the American boys threw a beanbag or a tennis ball at the target more accurately and precisely than the American girls across all age groups, whereas no sex difference was found among the Japanese children.

Both in Japan and the U.S.A., boys excelled in catching tasks. Such differences existed from 8 through to 11 year olds in the U.S.A., whereas only among 8 and 10 year olds in Japan. On static balance tasks, however, girls performed better than boys both in Japan and the U.S.A. This difference in static balance existed among 11 year olds in Japan and among 9 and 10 year olds in the U.S.A. No sex difference was revealed on the pegboard, drawing, and dynamic balance tasks in both nations.

Discussion

The study examined sex differences in motor co-ordination between Japanese and American children. The differences between boys and girls were less pronounced in the Japanese sample than the American standardisation sample on manual dexterity and throwing tasks.

The sex differences in manual dexterity among the American children were task-specific. Because threading lace is traditionally considered a feminine chore, while threading nuts on a bolt is often associated with masculine labour, the sex difference could be attributed to the gender stereotype in the American culture. On the throwing tasks, sex differences were revealed throughout all age groups in the American sample. It is of interest to examine whether a consistent sex difference, such as in throwing, exists on the various gender-biased manual tasks across all age groups in the U. S. A.

A question remains as to why the sex differences in motor co-ordination are less evident, and less influenced, by gender stereotypes among Japanese than among the American children. One possible answer is the difference in sample size in Japan and the U.S.A. Since the US sample is consistently numerically larger than the Japanese sample, the statistical power to yield the sex difference within the American sample is stronger than in the Japanese sample. If the same number of Japanese and American subjects are sampled, the same sex differences may be found among the Japanese sample as among the American sample. On the other hand, with reference to the results, Japanese boys and girls may be equally exposed to opportunities to learn motor skills. While gender stereotypes of various motor tasks do exist in Japan, both boys and girls are equally encouraged in physical education, arts and crafts, and home economics classes in primary schools. In the U.S.A., physical education has been disappearing from the elementary school curriculum in many states, and the opportunities for American children to learn motor skills depend heavily on the family and extra-curricular youth sports. Under such circumstances, it is difficult to foster equal opportunities for both boys and girls.

In both Japan and the U.S.A., boys are often better at ball skills than girls, and girls are better at static balance than boys. These tendencies may be ascribed to genetic difference or learning environment, or both. Further research should be carefully designed to determine the influential determinants. It is clear that more data on the motor co-ordination of Japanese children needs to be systematically collected in Japan with respect to geographical region and socio-economic status.

Reference

HENDERSON, S.E., and SUGDEN, D.: *Movement Assessment Battery for Children*. London, Psychological Corporation, 1992.

Chapter 13

An International Comparison of the Tasks and Historical Trends in Selective-Learning Instruction in Physical Education in Japan

Koichi Kiku

Introduction

The purpose of this study is to determine special features and problems of selective-learning instruction in physical education in Japan from comparisons of summaries of concept, curriculum and method of selective-learning instruction in three countries: the United States (U.S.), the United Kingdom (U.K.) and Germany. Discussion embraces the special requirements of teachers of health and physical education in the future, by identifying common problems observed in these three countries in selective-learning instruction from the viewpoint of the teachers who planned the curriculum and those who arrange it.

Selective-learning instruction in Physical Education is defined as classes of physical education as a compulsory subject in junior high and high schools, where a student selects the item of sports. The spread of selective-learning classes is an international trend in the promotion of curriculum individualisation, sports diversity and respect for the individual (TAKAHASHI, 1992:131). In Japan, selective-learning classes were officially introduced at the same time as the revisions of Course of Study in 1989, actually enforced in Junior high schools in 1994 and in High Schools in 1995.

There are two considerations to the theme concerning selective-learning classes of Physical Education. The first is to assess which selective-learning classes are widely introduced as part of the New Course of Study in Japan as compared with the aims of the selective-learning classes already introduced in foreign countries. The second is to find a means to estimate what problems to expect in the future, how to solve these problems and to understand the problems already encountered in the selective-learning classes in foreign countries. Generally speaking, there is some difficulty in making comparison because of differences in the educational systems and the social structure in each country. Also, it is difficult to assess common trends in the U.K., U.S. and Germany even if the situation regarding selective-learning classes and curriculum trends are correctly understood. The influences on the Physical Education curriculum are unpredictable due to the dramatic changes in political and economic systems in Western countries, e.g. the end of the ideological battle between East and West, and the effects of a sluggish economy on the education systems.

The Background and Content of the Introduction of Selective-learning Classes to Japan

The spread of selective-learning classes is a world trend centred mainly in western countries. The common aims listed immediately below are evident and provide a background to the introduction of selective-learning classes in Japan (TAKAHASHI, 1992:131). Selective-learning classes are considered to:

- provide opportunities to have experience in various kinds of sport, corresponding to individual interests and talent

- have a greater educational effect because they promote the learning of a sport selected by the student personally

- facilitate sport-specialised talent and competence through prolonged study of sport

- develop high quality classes because of the teachers' ability to teach a sport, in which students enjoy participating

Post-industrial society sluggish economies and widespread information orientation mean that the developed nations, including Japan, need to make changes in their education systems. International Education, Individual Education and Diverse Education have been promoted as the key concepts. In this context, it is useful to understand the introduction and promotion of selective-learning classes as a strategy of curriculum development and a concrete method of education. It is also considered important to promote life-long sports through individual interest in and talent for sport, especially in high schools, with the educational target to develop the habit of intentional exercise. Developing an attitude of willingly and intentionally learning a sport achieves the target of practising life-long sports. Curriculum and unit plans are devised accordingly.

Table 1 shows the sequence of areas of exercise and its study method in Japanese elementary, junior high and high schools.

In elementary school in Japan, a class studies one aspect of sport; thus, it may be regarded as a compulsory class. In junior high school, 1st year students can select martial arts or dance. Beginning with the 2nd year, they are allowed to select individual sports such as apparatus gymnastics, athletic activities, swimming and team sports (as ball games), martial arts and dance. In high schools, students are permitted to choose any sport from the area of exercise except gymnastics regardless of their school year. Teaching documents issued by the Ministry of Education reveal the respective aims of the selective-learning classes in three stages of development. In Stage I, the selective-learning class aims to achieve general enjoyment and pleasure from exercise in spite of individual differences in body character and attitudes; students choose activities from apparatus gymnastics and athletics (individual sport domain). In Stage II, the aim is to develop ability and talent in a student's favourite sport and allow the student to concentrate on a sport in accordance with individual aptitude and preferences; students choose the domain and activity from individual and team sports. In Stage III, the aim is to develop and maintain voluntary group organisation, collect study information, prepare a suitable environment in response to various demands, while at the same time developing an attitude of enjoyment of sport throughout the life-span; students choose the domain and activity from individual and team sports, martial arts, and dance. Unit scale (middle to large), learning group (single sex/mixed classes, single/multi-classes), unit time (up to one hour/two successive hours, flexible schedules) and teacher's activities (team teaching opportunities) are variously selected within the spread of choice in the three stages.

Table 1.
The sequence of exercise areas and learning method in Japanese elementary, junior high and high schools

Elementary School

1st and 2nd year	3rd and 4th year	5th and 6th year
A Basic movements B Games	A Basic movements B Games C Apparatus gymnastics D Swimming E Dance	A Gymnastics B Apparatus gymnastics C Athletic activities D Swimming E Ball games F Dance (G Health education)

*All areas are compulsory

Junior High School

	1st year	2nd year	3rd year
A Gymnastics B Apparatus gymnastics C Athletic activities D Swimming E Ball games F Martial arts G Dance	A ⌐ B C ⊢ Compulsory D E ⌐ F ⌐ One G ⌐ Choice	A ─ Compulsory B ⌐ C ⊢ Two choices D ⌐ E ⌐ F ⊢ Two choices G ⌐	A ─Compulsory B ⌐ C ⊢One or two D ⌐ Choices E ⌐ F ⊢Two choices G ⌐
H Knowledge of Physical Education	This area is compulsory mainly in 1st and 2nd grade.		

High School

	1st year	2nd year	3rd year
A Gymnastics	Gymnastics is compulsory at all grades		
B Apparatus gymnastics C Athletic activities D Swimming E Ball games F Martial arts G Dance	Three or four Choices Including F Or G	The same with 1st grade	The same with 1st grade
H Theory of Physical Education	This area is compulsory in all grades.		

On the whole, selective-learning classes are intended to be part of life-long sport from the Japanese junior high school upwards by establishing a self-oriented learning system with a spread of choices in sports items that follows the progress of the school year. So emphasis is placed upon the students recognising their own talent and interest and how to train. It is important to know the processes ('how to learn' and 'how to develop') of the sport as well as improving skills and physical strength. Hence, it is considered an important motivation for individual students to continue with the sport throughout life as a result of their studies.

Curriculum Trends in Western Countries and Selective-Learning Classes

a. The Case in the U.S.

According to SIEDENTOP (1992), in America recently, a number of Physical Education curriculum models have been introduced e.g. various items activity model, movement education model, social ability development model, special scientific approach model, adventure education model, and sport education model. Many schools have a mixed physical education curriculum, which combines these models. However, a major influence, especially in the Junior High and High School stages, were recreational sports which were started by introduced by returning soldiers after World War II, and which make up a significant part of life-long sports activity. For example, a variety of recreational sports activities which can easily be pursued after leaving school such as tennis, archery, bowling, golf etc. were provided as choice opportunities within the study of physical education.

As a general rule, at the Junior High School stage, the programme requires selection from a group of compulsory sports. In other words, encouragement is given to study a limited selection of sports in short units. Moving on to the High School stage, the target is a selective system, whereby any unit may be studied to the exclusion of others. Such a development process in selective-learning is nearly the same as that in Japan as shown in the Course of Study for Junior and High Schools. Also, the concept of popularisation of mixed education, especially through the introduction of the 'big-unit' system in High school, is very similar to Japan.

However, in the case of the U.S., there is the historical background of initiation into life-long sports through the introduction of recreational sports activities. Thus, there is a tendency to consider in the first instance the relationship between life-long sports and physical education from the viewpoint of experience of 'sports activities'. In this regard in the Japanese selective-learning system, there is a tendency that the 'characteristics of exercise' and 'how to study' from the point of view of students are given more consideration than life-long sports as a 'sports item'.

b. The Case in Germany

According to KRUGER (1992), the concept of a course for school sports was fixed in the *Action Plan for School Sports* in 1972 and the *Second Action Plan for School Sports* in 1985 in West Germany, clearly demonstrating its educational significance. The former plan emphasises the study of sport itself. As is often the case in Japan, the course of study for the state of Northrhine-Westphalia calls for students in the Primary stage (lst-4th school years) to study under the traditional compulsory type, separate classes, many subjects system. In the Middle stage I (5th-10th school years), selective classes are introduced with the range of selection increasing with progress through the school years. In the Middle stage II (11th-13th school years), equivalent to High school in Japan, selective classes are introduced in every course. At the same time the range of choice in each subject increases with the possibility for the student to develop his/her own curriculum stage by stage (according to level of ability) in a single subject, because the principle of selective-learning classes is based upon interest and ability to cope. There is also a basic requirement in the large unit system, whereby at least one individual and one team sport is studied over a three-year period.

In the *Second Action Plan* of 1985, the educational aspect of sport was re-emphasised while the aim of the sports class was directed at nurturing the individual talents of the students and encouraging participation in sports outside school. From the importance placed on the latter aspect, the relationship between school and regional sports clubs was improved, and accentuated the importance of the 'open sports class' which guaranteed thematic-seeking learning based on independent self-motivation making much of a student's own interests.

The relationships between selective-learning classes and extra curricular sports, and selective-learning classes and regional sports are worthy of note as being similar to the introduction of 'contract teaching" in the US beyond the frame of school education. However, in Japan, the emphasis remains only on the regional characteristic of sports that are taken as the learning subject for physical education.

c. The Case in the U.K.

The Education Reform Act of 1988 brought control of the education system (originally administratively controlled by Local Education Authorities) under the autonomous control of a national body. Subsequently, DEPARTMENT OF EDUCATION AND SCIENCE (DES) published *Physical Education from 5 to 16, Curriculum Matters* in 1989 while the DES and WELSH OFFICE published *Physical Education in the National Curriculum* in 1992. These two publications outlined the main points of the curriculum for physical education in compulsory education for students between 5 and 16 years of age.

The general education model, which drives the national curriculum, is obviously affected by the concept of movement education. It is especially strong in the Primary School stage but continues to influence the contents of study after 12-14 years (so-called 'Key Stage 3) when selective-learning classes are partially introduced. At Key Stage 3, selective-learning provides choice of 3 out of 4 physical activity areas: Athletic activities, Gymnastic activities, Dance and Outdoor Adventurous activities (Games are compulsory and choice has to be made within a set range). In Key Stage 4 (14-16 years), the students are free to choose activity areas in each school year (the choice can be made from within or without the offered range). Compared with Japan, the number of activity areas from which to choose in Key Stage 4 is fewer, therefore, it may be presumed to carry 'Big Unit' weighting. In the UK model, consideration is given to inclusion of local and regional traditions in sports activities and these may have implications for selective-learning classes. The emphasis on Games (notably, Games is the only activity area within the physical education curriculum which is compulsory from age 5 to 16), and especially traditional team games such as cricket, hockey, netball, rugby and soccer, reflects the advocacy interests of a significant politician, the then Prime Minister, John Major. This provides an example of political influence and intervention.

Common Problems and Future Issues

According to the earlier comments of SIEDENTOP (1992) and KRUGER (1992), there is a fundamental gap between the aim, contents and value intention and the organisation and actual guidance methods of the teachers who are responsible for the curriculum. In the UK, there is a relationship between the education movement and selective-learning as well as the influence of the General Certificate of Secondary Education (GCSE) on the method of guidance and contents of study in selective-learning classes (that is, the influence of the hidden curriculum). For example, at Babington Community College, Leicestershire in the Midlands region of England, a school institution that took the opportunity of 'opting out' from local education authority control to receive direct funding support from central government, there has been an attempt to standardise the contents and methods of study. One outcome has been a specially orientated examinations-driven curriculum for selective-learning classes to obtain improved GCSE examination results. In this situation, the teachers who are specialists in education mediate the changes influenced by the national education system's approach to selective learning. Therefore, consideration is given to the 'speciality' of the subject (in this case physical education) based upon the sound education background and individual talent of the teacher.

In Japan, there is much misunderstanding and confusion amongst groups of teachers because of a failure to be free from existing curriculum and methods constraints and not being open to acceptance of the idea of selective-learning classes and appropriate methods of learning. Research before the introduction of selective-learning classes in Junior and Senior high schools (through enforcement of the *New Course of Study* in 1991) showed the most important problem in non-introduction schools was the common understanding among teachers about selective-learning classes. Schools which did introduce the system did not share the problems that arose in the 'non-introduction' schools (YAMASAKI, 1991).

In countries (including Japan) that have introduced selective-learning, the 'speciality' of the teachers is a matter for consideration given the all-round application of the curriculum including the relationship with out-of-school sports. It is expected that the selective-learning of sports will play a role as a stage in life-long sports activity, or might at least be a basis for it. The major reforms in education systems that we see being introduced in economically advanced countries is in response to a new social demand and is aimed at improving competitiveness of education through individual education, separate education and variety of education. On the other hand, at the same time there is an attempt to increase the amount of selection and to streamline the content of selection. It is, therefore, pointed out in Japan that the promotion of selective-learning classes makes the current physical education classes meaningless with regard to the type of class. To counter these misgivings, there is a need to examine the quality of demand for sports in society as a whole in the future and clearly establish the role of school physical education in this era of life-long sports participation. Originality of the sport and the speciality of the teacher involved in selective-learning classes should also be given consideration.

There is need to reform the University Teacher's Training Course with regard to selective-learning classes in Physical Education and to establish a new teachers' training system. If the practice of selective-learning is to acquire all-round enjoyment of the sport culture, then it becomes important for the teachers themselves to participate in the sport culture outside of school. The American Educational Research Association (AERA) promotes various studies to establish teachers' general education and their specialisation [SATO, 1996:146). Now is the time for countries that have introduced a selective-learning curriculum to re-consider the new speciality and the guidance of study for physical education teachers in selective-learning classes for now and the future.

Concluding Comments

The purpose of this study was to determine special features and problems of selective-learning instruction in Japan from comparisons of summaries of concept, curriculum and method of selective-learning instruction in three countries: the United States, the United Kingdom and Germany.

Regular selective-learning instruction was introduced into Junior High and High schools in Japan in 1989. Under this method, students are free to choose a sport from within the range offered in the curriculum for physical education where previously there had been no choice. In the case of Japan, the target was part of the life-long sports philosophy aimed at low economic growth and ageing society and was intended to develop habitual attitudes towards practising sports and exercise as part of an individual's personal interest.

In the three countries under consideration, the introduction of selective-learning came earlier than in Japan. The target was similar in Japan but there are differences in the historical developments, the contents and the subjects of selective-learning instruction. For example, in the United States, there is a tendency to increase the number of choices in the sports class because of an emphasis on sports as an area of activity. In what was formerly West Germany, there was a tendency towards thematic-seeking learning, emphasising the role of education in schools because of the attention devoted to the relationship between schools and community sport. In the United Kingdom, the national curriculum of physical education in schools was introduced as a result of the Education Reform Act of 1988, but selective-learning instruction in physical education had been operating before then in many regions. In the United Kingdom, as in Germany, an increasing emphasis has been placed on the relation between schools and community sports. Study content has to some extent been influenced by the requirement for examination in the GCSE structure within the general education reforms.

Apart from the subtle differences stated above, it is possible to identify a common problem at the practical level of the selective-learning curriculum: misunderstanding and confusion in actual class organisation and the method of teaching associated with the gap in concept, contents and intention of the teachers responsible for delivery. It is also possible to point to the common subject of training in new 'specialities' and 'special abilities' in countries that have introduced selective-learning instruction. These subjects are not confined to achieving superiority of technique or method of teaching but connect to the macro theory of physical education and the actual class.

The overall indication is that it is necessary in Japan to reform the University training course for teachers and to establish a course programme for teachers responsible for selective-learning instruction in physical education.

References

DEPARTMENT OF EDUCATION and SCIENCE: *Physical education from 5 to 16. Curriculum matters.* London, HMSO, 1989.

DEPARTMENT OF EDUCATION and SCIENCE and the WELSH OFFICE: *Physical education in the national curriculum.* London, HMSO, 1992.

DEPARTMENT FOR EDUCATION: *Physical education in the national curriculum.* London: HMSO, 1995.

KIKU, K: The trends of sports and physical education curriculum and selective-learning instruction in some foreign countries. In: *Sports to Kenko*, 1994, 26(3), pp. 9-11 (in Japanese).

KIKU, K: An international comparison of selective-learning instruction in physical education: the case of Great Britain and Japan. In: *Taiikuka Kyouiku*, 1994, 42(4), pp.34-36 (in Japanese).

KIHARA, S: A revision of the national curriculum for physical education in England and Wales. In: *Taiikuka Kyouiku*, 1996, 44(3), pp.72-73 (in Japanese).

KRUGER, M: Modern development of school sport in Germany. In: *Gakko Taiiku*, 1992, 45(1), pp.28-32 (in Japanese, translated by Nagashiza).

MONBUSHO: *The making of instruction plan and method of teaching. Teaching materials of health and physical education in high school.* Tokyo, Japanese Ministry of Education, 1992 (in Japanese).

OFFICE FOR STANDARDS IN EDUCATION: *Physical education: a review of inspection findings* 1993/94. London, HMSO, 1995.

OKADE, Y: On the theory of Siedentop's sport education. In: *Aichi Kyoiku Daigaku Kiyo*, 20, 1995, pp.1-32 (in Japanese).

SATO, G: The latest education theory in the U.S.: In: *Kyoikugaku ga wakaru*, 1996, pp.144-146 (in Japanese).

SIEDENTOP, D: Physical education curriculum in the U.S. In: *Gakko Taiiku*, 45(1), 1992, pp.14-21 (in Japanese, translated by Takahashi et al.).

TAKAHASHI, T: Physical education curriculum and selective-learning instruction in the U.S. In: *Kenko to Tairyoku*, 23(7), 1991, pp.9-14 (in Japanese).

TAKAHASHI, T: Problems and trends of physical education curriculum in the world. In: *Gakko Taiiku*, 45(1), 1992, pp.10-13 (in Japanese).

YAMASAKI, S: *A study on selective-learning instruction in school physical education: on practical problems and teacher's consciousness.* Thesis, Nara Women's University, 1991 (in Japanese).

Chapter 14

Achievement Motivation in Physical Education in Japan and Norway: a Lesson on Semantic Differences

Motohide Miyahara, Jan Hoff, Geir Espnes and Tamotsu Nishida

Introduction

Cross-cultural comparison is a powerful tool in the study of achievement motivation. If differences are found through the process, they may afford opportunities to examine the interaction between environmental and individual factors influencing achievement motivation (MAEHR, 1974). To compare differences across cultures, researchers may use either the same or different psychometric tools to gather data in different socio-cultural contexts. Those who administer the same instrument take an etic approach, assuming universal communality in item content, whereas those based on an emic approach employ different psychological measurements (BERRY, 1969). Etic measures require the evidence for factorial invariance before quantitative mean comparisons can be made across cultures. On the other hand, although such a direct comparison is not applicable with emic measures, it is possible to compare the equivalence of constructs derived from emic measures. KAMEOKA (1985) states that the application of confirmatory factor analysis is a promising procedure to evaluate the equivalence of etic measurement and emic construct. The contribution attempts to examine the internal reliability and the factorial communality of an etic measure in Japan and Norway using confirmatory factor analysis.

Method

The Achievement Motivation in Physical Education Test (AMPET) (NISHIDA, 1989) was chosen as an etic measure in an attempt to achieve the ultimate goal of comparing achievement motivation in physical education between Japan and Norway. The AMPET is a self-report questionnaire, originally developed in the Japanese language, consisting of an 8-item x 7 categories (learning strategy; overcoming obstacles; diligence and seriousness; competence of motor ability; value of learning; anxiety about stress-causing situations; failure anxiety) and an 8-item lie scale. The test is standardised with 10,055 representative Japanese students from the 4th graders in primary schools (9 and 10 year olds) through to third-year senior high school students (14 and 15 year olds) stratified with respect to geographic region and population density. The reliability of the test was examined by Chronbach's alpha of each category and varied between .797 and .950, and the internal consistency ranged from .600 to .883. The external validity of AMPET was confirmed by the significant correlations with the scores of a motor ability test, school mark in physical education, teachers' rating of students' behaviours in physical education classes, the sub-scores from the Motive of Academic Achievement Test, the level of athletic competition, participation in sports clubs, and the results of a self-report survey regarding the frequency, duration, interest, and enjoyment of physical activity. The 7-factor construct was demonstrated by an exploratory factor analysis. The English version of AMPET is available (NISHIDA, 1988), and it has been used for cross-cultural comparisons (NISHIDA, 1991).

The second and third authors, who use English as a second language, translated the English version of AMPET into the Norwegian language. The first draft was administered to 70 university students, and their comments were sought. Based upon the students' feedback, minor changes were made. Then, a cross translation from Norwegian into English was conducted by a sports psychologist fluent in both English and Norwegian languages. As a result of cross-translation, the Norwegian translation was judged appropriate.

The final Norwegian version of AMPET was administered to 670 Norwegian high school students (369 males, 301 females), ranging from 12 to 18 years of age. The students attend one of 6 high schools: 3 high schools located in the city of Trondheim (pop. 150,000); and 3 high schools in local villages in central Norway. The central areas of Norway are considered representative of the nation in terms of the cultural, economic and political environment. Since the school system and curriculum are consistent throughout Norway, it is reasonable to assume that the sample is representative of Norwegian high school students.

Results

1. Reliability

Chronbach's alpha was used to examine the reliability of each category, which varied between .583 and .705. The internal consistency in terms of item-sub-scale correlation coefficients ranged from .150 to .712.

2. Validity

The construct validity of the higher-order 7-factor model (NISHIDA, 1988) was tested by a confirmatory factor analysis with LISREL8 (JÖRESKOG and SÖRBOM, 1993) on the basis of the co-variance matrix. The goodness-of-fit was poor (c^2 [1463, N=592] = 6,216.70, p <. 01, CFI =. 74). An exploratory factor analysis was performed in order to identify the factor structure of the Norwegian AMPET.

A 4-factor solution was considered to be the best after Kaiser's varimax rotation. Four factors are labelled as "commitment and self-monitoring", "performance anxiety and fear of failure", "perceived competence and value of learning", and "learning from models". The original Factor 1 (*learning strategy*), Factor 2 (*overcoming obstacles*), and Factor 3 (*diligence and seriousness*) are reduced to the first factor (*commitment and self-monitoring*). The original Factor 6 (*anxiety about stress-causing situations*) and Factor 7 (*failure anxiety*) were fused into the second factor (*performance anxiety and fear of failure*). The original Factor 4 (*competence of motor ability*) and Factor 5 (*value of learning*) correspond to the third factor (*perceived competence and value of learning*). The 3 items concerning "learning from models" from Factor 1 made an independent fourth factor. This 4-factor model was submitted to a confirmatory factor analysis, which still evidenced a poor goodness-of-fit (C^2 [1478, N=592] = 6,760.42, p < .01, CFI = .71).

Discussion

The Norwegian version of AMPET demonstrated a lower internal consistency and reliability than the original Japanese version. The reason for lower inter-correlations is explained by the results from the following analysis to examine construct validity. The higher order 7-factor model was not verified by the confirmatory factor analysis based on the co-variance matrix of the Norwegian AMPET.

However, an exploratory factor analysis on the Norwegian AMPET revealed 4 factors. Most interestingly, the 3 items on "learning from models" constituted an independent factor. This indicated that the Japanese students perceived modelling as a learning strategy, whereas the Norwegian students did not. In the Japanese language, the word referring to learning, manabu has its derivation from the classic word, manebu, which means to imitate. It is the traditional Japanese learning method to copy exactly what teachers do. In the Norwegian language, on the other hand, the word "å imitere" literally means mimicking. In Norway, "ape-methoden" or the monkey-method of imitation is used only when a new skill is first introduced, but it is not generally considered as a learning strategy. Such a difference in the perception of imitation partially explains why the 3 items regarding "learning from models" were extracted as an independent factor from the Norwegian AMPET.

The Norwegian data fitted into neither the 7-factor nor the 4-factor models as results of confirmatory factor analysis. This indicates that the Norwegian version of AMPET is not applicable for cross-cultural comparison with the Japanese AMPET as an etic measure. In future research, it is necessary to develop an emic measure of achievement motivation in physical education in Norway, and the construct equivalence of the emic measures ought to be compared between Japan and Norway.

References

BERRY, J.W.: On cross-cultural comparability. In: *International Journal of Psychology*, 4, 1969, pp.119-128.

JÖRESKOG, K.G., and SÖRBOM, D.: LISREL8: *Structural Equation Modeling with the SIMPLIS Command Language*. Hillsdale, NJ, SSI Scientific Software, 1993.

KAMEOKA, V.A.: Construct validation of psychological measures in cross-cultural research: analysis of linear structural relationship. In: GUERRO, R.D., (Ed.), *Crosscultural and national studies*. North-Holland, Elsevier Science Publisher B.V., 1985, pp.57-68.

MAEHR, M.L.: Culture and achievement motivation. In: *American Psychologist*, 29(12), 1974, pp.887-896.

NISHIDA, T.: Reliability and factor structure of the achievement motivation in physical education test. In: *Journal of Sport and Exercise Psychology*, 10(4), 1988, pp. 418-430.

NISHIDA, T.: A study on standardization of the Achievement Motivation in Physical Education Test. In: *Japanese Journal of Physical Education*, 34(1), 1989, pp.45-62.

NISHIDA, T.: Achievement motivation for learning in physical education class: a cross-cultural study in four countries. In: *Perceptual and Motor Skills*, 73(3/Part 2), 1991, pp.1183-1186.

PART 4

SPORT FOR ALL

Chapter 15

Development of Leisure Sport and Structural Changes of the Sports Systems in Germany and Great Britain

Ilse Hartmann-Tews

Introduction

The aim of many studies within the field of the sociology of sport and leisure has been to identify national as well as cross-cultural trends. As research traditions differ from country to country, it is difficult to directly compare national studies on structural changes. Nevertheless, KAMPHORST and ROBERTS (1989, p.383 ff.), in comparing 15 country reports, have identified some general cross-cultural trends in sport. Amongst others, these general trends include: increasing participation rates up to the early 1980s, accompanied by greater democratisation; individualisation and a broader range of sports engaged in; and a growth in organisational settings, which provide diversified kinds of physical activities and sport.

By and large, these developments have been characterised in sociological analyses as a part of social change, continuous and unfolding naturally through time. For the most part, sport sociologists have followed INGLEHARDT'S (1977) notion on changing values among western populations and BECK'S (1992) outline of global social change towards a new modernity. Although these analyses are stimulating, sociologists should be aware that their potential to explain structural change is limited. With these references, theories of modernisation are adduced to explain changes in demand and supply of recreational physical activities and sport, whereas agency and political factors are considered as derivative matters of secondary concern. Merely to describe pluralisation and differentiation as a general process makes it appear an automatic equlibrating mechanism, something that occurs as cultural reflection or quite naturally as a "free market" process. A comparison of historical analysis suggests that this is not the case: structural formation and modification of the sporting systems proceeded at different rates and in different directions. If general causes or mechanisms - like individualisation, growing demands - create the potential for differentiation, they do not seem to adequately explain the extent to which, and the particular way in which, that potential is realised.

To gain a better understanding of the structural changes and their ideological underpinnings, the social processes that produce differentiation must be described in specific concrete terms and agency must be incorporated into explanations. When they are, the contingency of differentiation will be more clearly understood, therefore too, its responsiveness to historical variation. Comparative analyses drawing on recent theoretical work on differentiation seem to be the most promising strategy to achieve this aim as they address the organisational agents which determine path and pace of differentiation.

Following these theoretical perspectives, the focus of this study is on the role of voluntary associations in the process of differentiation. As the nucleus of the sports system, it is supposed that voluntary sports associations are interested in maintaining and broadening the autonomy of their action, in including a growing number of people into their organisations and in expanding their structural fabric in order to meet the demands of their membership more adequately. This supposition is based on research in the sociology of organisations which reveals that increase of membership, expansion and structural growth are likely to raise the significance of organisations and to broaden the latitude and autonomy of their action. Thus, it can be assumed that structural expansion of organised voluntary sport will provide their central agents with an opportunity to acquire more influence within the organisational fabric and on state bodies that oversee and support the voluntary sector.

In order to identify some central aspects of the structural developments of the German and British sports systems, their prerequisites, potential and realisation, two questions are addressed here: i) whether there has been increasing inclusion in to the sports systems over the last 25 years; and ii) if so, the extent to which voluntary associations have expanded their positions as the backbone of the sports system.

Inclusion into the Sports System

There are two indications for the measurement of inclusion in sport: the most often used indication is self-reported participation rates in recreational physical activities and sport as they are documented in survey data; and the other is membership in voluntary associations in sport.

1. Self-reported participation in sport

Self-reported participation rates in physical activities and sport provide inaccurate information (BOOTHBY, 1987). This central finding of social research has been realised by many social scientists and professional information gatherers but does not prevent them from carrying out surveys about whether, why, when and how often people take part in recreational physical activities and sport. Discussions on the validity and reliability of survey data have a long tradition and comparative research especially should be highly receptive to the theoretical and empirical findings evolved.

Against these methodological reservations and without any genuine comparative dataset, it seems impossible to compare participation rates in the countries focused on here. Nevertheless, most recent comparative analyses on single country studies of participation in sport allow for some empirically based assumptions that more or less confirm the trends summed up by KAMPHORST and ROBERTS (see HARTMANN-TEWS, 1996; ANDREFF, BOURG, HALBA and NYS, 1994):

- participation in recreational physical acivities and sport has been rising through the past 25 years in Germany and Great Britain

- a process of democratisation in participation can be witnessed, although at different paces and levels

- the global participation rate in recreational physical activities and sport in these countries seems to be about 60% of the population aged 16 and over and seems to be more or less the same in Germany and Great Britain.

2. Membership in sports clubs

Although Great Britain can be said to be the 'trailblazer' of the development of voluntary organsations in sport, there are few systematically collected data on voluntary sector sport in Britain today. The most recent official statitics estimate that there are about 150,000 clubs and associations with a membership of about 6.3 million people (SPORTS COUNCIL, 1991). In contrast, detailed statistics about the voluntary sector are found in Germany, where the German Sports Federation (Deutscher Sportbund - DSB) regularly publishes data on its club and individual membership, the latter being differentiated by sport, age-groups and gender.

Table 1.
Membership in sports clubs in Germany and Great Britain 1950-1990

Year	Germany club membership	Great Britain club membership
1950	3,219,000	?
1960	5,329,500	?
1970	10,139,200	?
1980	16,953,500	?
1990	21,567,600	6,315,000
1995	25,985,500	?

DEUTSCHER SPORTBUND (1990); SPORTS COUNCIL (1991)

With reference to 1990, there are two notable differences. First, it is evident that the voluntary associations in Germany include many more people than those in Great Britain. In order to derive a comparative rate of inclusion in the voluntary sector of sport, multiple memberships have to be considered i.e. the fact that membership statistics of the national governing bodies of sport are generally aggregated data on the basis that the individual member can be registered with several clubs. A comparative rate of inclusion should be based on the ratio of net members of sports clubs to the population of the respective country. On the basis of these figures, it can be estimated that in Germany about 30% of the population is in membership of at least one sports club compared with about 12% of the population in Great Britain. The second notable finding concerns the number and size of voluntary associations. Contrary to the findings of membership figures, it turns out that the number of sports clubs in Germany is lower than in Great Britain. On average there are 300 members in German sports clubs and about 40 in British clubs. Nevertheless, the size of the clubs varies enormously. The majority of German sport clubs (70%) is small in size with less than 300 members and only 6% are big clubs with more than 1,000 members (HEINEMANN and SCHUBERT, 1994). Assumptions about the structure of British clubs are that the large majority of all clubs is small in size (SPORTS COUNCIL, 1991).

Together these two findings show a marked difference in the development of the sports systems in Germany and Great Britain. Increasing participation rates in physical activities and sport in Germany have been strongly linked with a growing voluntary sector, whereas in Great Britain, the growing number of people active in physical recreation and sport has been far more attracted by commercial enterprises and the public sector. To indicate these major structural developments and changes in the sports system in Great Britain, COLLINS (1990) used the metaphor of "Shifting Icebergs". Taking up this metaphor, the following section serves to shed light on some major forces of change with a focus on organisational agents, which (as indicated earlier) determine path and pace of differentiation. Initially the configuration of central agents and major structural features of the respective sporting systems are introduced, then attention is drawn to strategies and interactions between the State and the voluntary sector that had been favoured by these configurations and which in turn have favoured specific structural developments and configurations.

Structural Features of the Sports Systems

1. Germany

The federal structure of Germany - consisting of sixteen constituent states (Länder) - is reflected by the structure, organisation and division of responsibilities in the field of sport (refer figure 1).

Figure 1.

Structural features of the German sports system

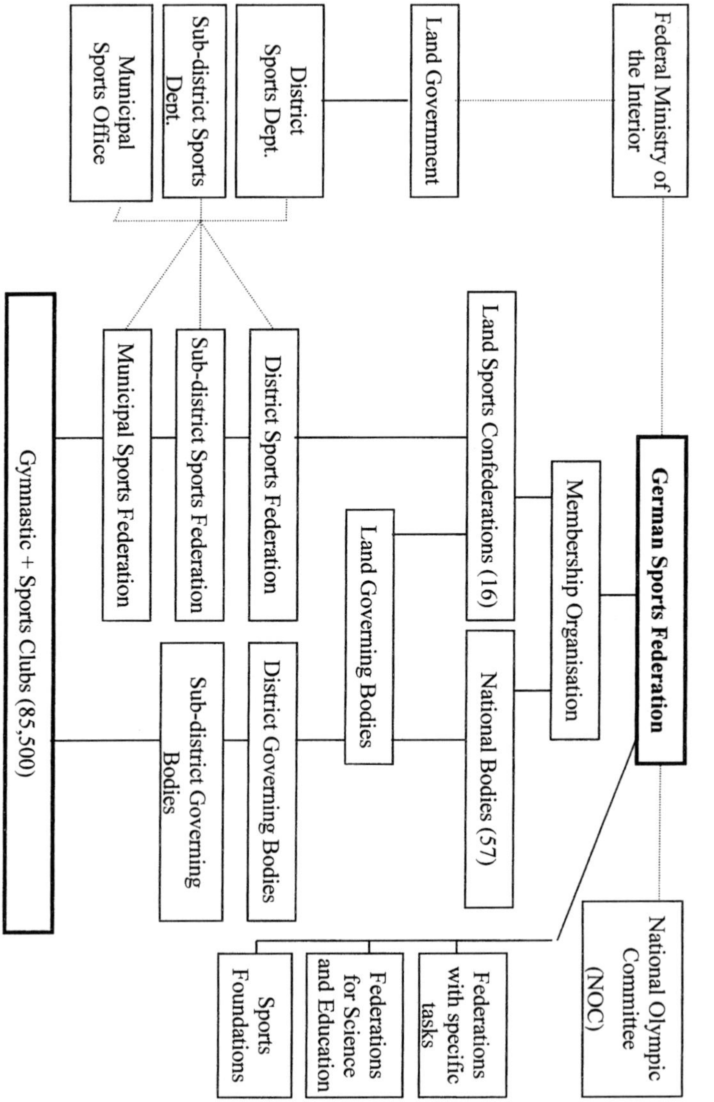

The Federal Government, the Länder and local authorities provide the legal and material basis for the development of sport. They support the activities of sports organisations in those cases where the latter's staffing and financial resources are inadequate. All public promotion is in accordance with this principle of subsidiarity.

The structural features of the sports system in Germany are characterised by a highly organised voluntary sector. The DSB is the umbrella organisation of voluntary associations in sport. It was founded in 1950 albeit when there was still a strong mistrust of organised interests. Its aim was, and still is, to coordinate all necessary joint measures for the promotion of sport and physical recreation, and to represent the mutual interests of its member organisations at all governmental levels and the general public. The National Olympic Committee (NOC) for Germany is an independent and autonomous non-governmental sports organisation. It promotes the Olympic idea and carries out the tasks entrusted by the IOC to the NOCs.

The DSB represents 5 groups of members: 57 National Governing Bodies for single sports); 16 Sports Confederations of the constituent states; 12 federations with particular tasks; 6 federations for science and education and 2 promoting federations. All members are independent as far as their organisation, finance and activities are concerned and the DSB has no right of interference in these matters.

The National Governing Bodies represent and organise the activities of their respective sports. They are responsible for the coaching and care of their top-level athletes and their main task is to organise championships and select teams for participation in international competitions. To pursue these tasks, they have Federal Training Centres at their disposal as well as Federal coaches employed by the DSB.

In each of the 16 constituent states of Germany, all sports clubs are additionally registered at the Land Sports Confederation, which represents their interests at the levels of the federal states and the general public. Their main characteristic is that they represent gymnastic and sports clubs beyond the interests of individual disciplines. Thus, their activities in the area of top-level and the development of mass sport are multifarious.

Figure 2.

Structural features of the British sports system

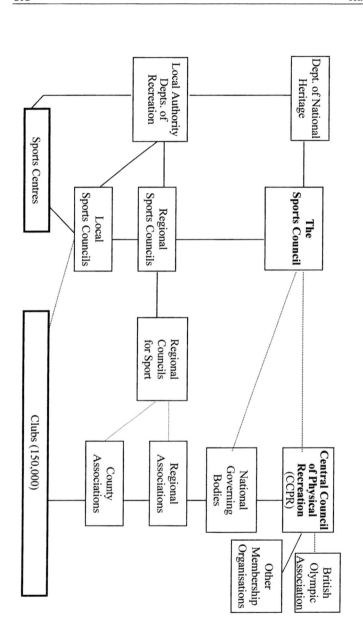

The voluntary sector of sport is financed from various sources. These mainly comprise: subscriptions and donations from members (at club, federation and confederation level); subsidies from the public that are granted at all administrative levels; proceeds of the National Lottery (Glücksspirale) of which 50% are donated to the sports bodies; indirect financial support by the recognition of charitable status which involves tax relief of all clubs affiliated to the DSB; sponsorship; and catering trade profits at club level.

2. Great Britain

The structure of the British sports system is characterised by fragmentation and "confused roles and responsibilities" (SPORTS COUNCIL, 1991). This reflects not only political differentiation but substantial social differentiation as well. Although the United Kingdom is a unitary and not a federal state, most sports set up individual governing bodies for each of the Home Countries - England, Wales, Scotland and Northern Ireland. The fragmentation also not only reflects the historical development of particular sports, especially social differentiation into separate organisations for men and women, but also the fact that sub-disciplines of sports evolved and established their own specialist organisations (e.g.bowls: crown green, flat green, indoor).

The Central Council of Physical Recreation (CCPR) is the umbrella organisation of the voluntary associations in sport. It was founded in 1935 as the Central Council for Recreative Physical Training (CCRPT) largely as a result of confluent interests of voluntary sector and state agencies based on a widespread concern about the physical and moral deterioration of youth in a period of high unemployment rates (COALTER, LONG and DUFFIELD, 1986, p.25). Today it embraces some 270 organisations directly or indirectly related to sport and physical activities, of which about 200 are Governing Bodies of Sport. The work of the CCPR is well summed up in its slogan to be: "The independent Voice of Sport and Recreation" (CCPR, 1991, p.6). The membership organisations are grouped into six divisions: Major Spectator Sports, Games and Sport, Movement and Dance, Outdoor Pursuits, Water Recreation, Interested Organisations.

At central government level, sport and physical recreation have variously been mainly identified with Ministries/Departments for Housing and Local Government, the Environment, Education and, until very recently, the Department of National Heritage[1], although there is no one national Government department or agency wholly designated and responsible for sport and physical recreation; instead a number of government departments have areas of responsibility.

The Sports Council[2] is a particular and typical institution for the political culture of Britain in so far as it acts as a quasi-non-governmental body (Quango). Established by Royal Charter in 1972, since when its objectives have been to foster the knowledge and practice of sport and physical recreation among the public at large and the provision of associated facilities, and to encourage the attainment of high performance standards in conjunction with the governing bodies of sport and physical recreation. It is an independent body but financed by the government and in the exercise of its functions "shall have regard to any general statements on the policy of the Government" (COGHLAN and WEBB, 1990, p.268). In addition there are Regional Councils for Sport and Recreation (established from 1975 onwards), composed of representatives of local authorities and of sports interests in each region and ready to advise on investments and the promotion of sport. It is noteworthy, according to Coghlan and Webb (1990), that sometimes the geographical radius of action of the various councils and regional governing bodies differs, thus being an obstruction to effective organisation and cooperation. The Regional and Local Sports Councils were established to facilitate the regional coordination and provision of facilities and recreation.

As in Germany, the voluntary sector of sport is financed by various sources. In addition to some minor variations in the source of finances, there are two major differences: first, a National Lottery and respective proceeds for the voluntary sector of sport have only recently been established in Great Britain; and second there is no indirect public financial support of the sports clubs and governing bodies via the recognition of charitable status.

A summary of the analysis at this stage reveals two central findings:

1. The voluntary associations of sport in post-war Germany have
   included a growing number of people: the net membership rate rose
   from 7% in 1950 to 30% in 1990, whereas in Great Britain - the
   'trailblazer' of the development of clubs - only 12% of the population
   aged 16 years and over are registered in a club[3]. Taking into
   consideration that participation rates are presumably more or less the
   same, it is evident that a growing number of people has joined
   commercial and public sector organisations to take part in physical
   activities and sport (refer COLLINS, 1990).

2. The structural fabric of the German sporting system builds upon a
   highly organised voluntary sector. Expansion and growth have been
   successfully used to broaden the latitude of its action and to gain more
   influence on state bodies - the granting of charitable status is only one
   example.

Structural Changes as (Un-)intended Consequences of Action

The explanation of structural changes has to take into consideration not
only a broad fabric of individual and organisational agents but also
effects of their actions regardless of whether the outcomes are intended or
unintended. Hence, a focus on the voluntary sector illuminates only a
small part of social development and concentration on major aspects of
actions results in some neglect of various effects which may have helped
or hindered developments. Nevertheless, a comparative analysis reveals
some marked differences in structural developments, three of which
seem to be most characteristic.

i) Different historical settings

The DSB was founded in 1950 as the one and only umbrella organisation
for voluntary associations. After World War II, organised sports
structures were destroyed and the moral bases of sports organisations
broken. Organised sport in Germany had to regain recognition and
acceptance. Thus, the foundation of the DSB was celebrated as a new
beginning with new organisational structures, which in turn became a

breeding ground for the development of Sport for All initiatives. The two pillars of organised sport - Governing Bodies and Sports Confederation at state level - have the potential for a division of labour: the Governing Bodies can concentrate on competitive and elite sport, whereas the Sports Confederations, representing the interests of the clubs beyond their activities, can devote more attention to the promotion of recreational physical activities for all. They have often been labelled as a 'steering machine' in promoting Sport for All, i.e. in providing courses and facilities for recreational physical activities and sport for everyone.

The Central Council of Physical Recreation on the other hand was founded in 1935 (as the CCRPT) as an encompassing organisation of which member organisations had confluent interests. Different from the post-1945 situation in Germany, the CCPR in Britain was not confronted with the problem of restructuring its central social units. It continued its work through the 1950s and 1960s without any significant organisational changes, still having to deal with,or even face up to, the jealously safeguarded autonomy of member organisations. In contrast to the DSB, the CCPR was neither urged to regain recognition nor were its member organisations willing to think about a joint policy nor establish working groups or committees to tackle problems such as finance, youth work, sport for all, women and sport etc.

ii) Sport for all - the role of institutional entrepreneurs

Different historical settings may be seen as predisposing elements for the organisation and expansion of the structural fabric of the voluntary associations. In explaining the differences of path and pace of structural developments of the sports systems, the concept of institutional entrepreneurs who act as catalysts seems to be of additional explanatory value here (EISENSTADT, 1990).

Already in 1959, the DSB had started a campaign to promote the idea of recreational sport. Its motto "Second Way" to sport was chosen to indicate that beside the traditional understanding of sport, (i.e. competitive and elite sport), new models and ways were to be developed broadening the definition of sport by encompassing recreational sport for all (Freizeitsport). A variety of programmes were initiated that would cater for everyone - children, women, unemployed, old people. Willi

Daume, President of the DSB for more than 15 years, succesfully played the role of an 'institutional image maker' and promoted the idea of sport for all with vast numbers of campaigns and by initiating structural changes within the sports clubs.

The strategy of Daume - and later on of the DSB - to implement sport for all was twofold. It was directed on the one hand to governmental agencies and the population and, on the other hand, to its member organisations, which had to be convinced about the integration of leisure sport activities. Central aspects of this campaign were:

- elaboration of central values of sport and effects of participation in recreational physical activities and sport as there are educational values, health-related positive effects (prevention and rehabilitation) and social integrative effects;

- public campaigns to attract people who had not (regularly) taken part in sport (adults, women, older people);

- lobbying at governmental level and initiating a huge state-supported building programme for recreational and sporting facilities (the 'Golden Plan');

- professionalisation of internal structures by establishing specialised committees for sport for all at all administrative levels[4].

With this dual strategy and the inclusion of millions of people, the DSB and its member associations gained recognition as proactive organisations in public welfare. This in turn led to recognition as charitable non-profit organisations which helped to secure a range of tax reliefs.

iii) Sport for all - the development of a social service

The CCPR was unsuccessful in bringing together the heterogenous interests and acting as a pressure group for the benefit of the voluntary organisations. Instead it seems that one of the functions of the CCPR was "'to work itself out of a job' - or rather a series of jobs" (EVANS, 1974, p.231). For example, the CCPR, in line with government policy, drew back from youth work in the early 1960s, although this grass roots work had been a central field of action. Some 20 years later, when some Governing Bodies applied to be granted charity status, the Charity Commission refused the application on the ground of lack of youth work and service for public welfare.

Many observers characterise the developments in the 1970s and 1980s as a process of marginalisation of the CCPR, which was closely connected to the establishment of the Sports Council as an executive body. The changing social conditions of the 1950s and growing concern about a new climate of crime and male juvenile delinquency led to a range of government sponsored inquiries which concentrated on the role of the education and youth services. The CCPR inspired Wolfenden Report amongst others identified a nation-wide shortage of all types of recreational and sporting facilities and especially a 'gap' in provision for physical recreation when young people left school (COALTER et al, 1986, p.27). This led to the establishment of an Advisory Sports Council in 1965 that was the forerunner of the Sports Council with executive powers in 1972.

At the outset, the CCPR was effectively incorporated into the new state-appointed organisation. The Advisory Sports Council was administered largely by sportsmen and physical educationists who retained close links with the CCPR and the sports associations. The relative independence of the Sports Council was eventually secured, when it could act as "honest broker" between government bodies, local authorities and voluntary associations. From the mid-1970s onwards, a growing number of tasks made professionalisation necessary and inevitably led to the replacement of physical educationalists and sport generalists. In addition, judicious use of government appointees accelerated the processes of organisational growth and bureaucratisation. More and more emphasis was placed on managerial efficiency and accountability with the attendant shift from providing a framework for voluntarism to a more interventionist and directive approach. Many commentators (e.g. COGHLAN and WEBB, 1990; COALTER et al. 1986) have remarked that there has been a parallel movement of marginalisation of the CCPR and growing congruence between the politics of government and those of the Sports Council.

The processes underlying the emergence and development of the Sports Council are similar to the classic model of the development of a social service. Needs are defined (from the voluntary sector or public sector), provision for it is sought on a voluntary basis, limitations of voluntary effort are acknowledged, state assistance is sought with the effect that increased aid leads to increasing state interest and intervention, and the point may be reached where voluntary effort is subordinated to state direction and control. In line with this general process, government involvement increasingly shifted to an instrumental use of sports policy, and in order to promote social integration, vast amounts of money were invested in public sport and leisure facilities.

Concluding Remarks

One of the intentions of this study was to acquire a better understanding of the structural changes of the sports systems by incorporating socio-structural configurations, agency and political factors into the analysis. Although this extract from a far more complex piece of research can only provide a glimpse of the social processes that produce differentiation, it draws attention to variables that help to explain different paths and paces of structural changes.

Notes

1. Since changes introduced by the Labour Government, the Minister with the portfolio for Sport has been located in a newly created ministerial department for Culture, Media and Sport.

2. In late 1996, a new structure for Sport was created at central level: UK Sports Council and National Councils for England, Scotland, Wales and N. Ireland.

3. There is a traditional assumption in the study of voluntary associations that Germany is a 'nation of joiners'. This is a comparative statement, yet surprisingly, there has been little comparative research about sport association membership. From a recent comparative study of voluntary association membership in fifteen countries, membership levels in Germany and Great Britain are almost identical and range in the middle of the countries analysed (CURTIS, GRABB and BAER, 1992).

4. A research project conducted by the DSB indicates that today about two thirds of all NGBs are also involved in recreational physical activities; 57% have special committees; and 61% have their own professional staff for such activities (WEDEKIND and KUHLMANN, 1993, p.5).

References

ANDREFF, W., BOURG, J.-F., HALBA, B., and NYS, J.-F.: *The economic importance of sport in Europe: financing and economic impact.* Brussels, CDDS, 1994.

BECK, U.: *Risk society - towards a new modernity.* London, Sage Publications, 1992.

BOOTHBY, J.: Research note. Self-reported participation rates: further comment. In: *Leisure Studies*, 6, 1987, pp.99-104.

CENTRAL COUNCIL OF PHYSICAL RECREATION: *The organisation of sport and recreation in Britain.* London, CCPR, 1991.

COALTER, F., LONG J., and DUFFIELD, B.: *Rationale for public sector investment in leisure.* London, Sports Council, ESRA, 1986.

COGHLAN, J.F., and WEBB, I.M.: *Sport and British politics since 1960.* London, Falmer Press, 1990.

COLLINS, M.: (1990). Shifting icebergs: the public, private and voluntary sectors in British sport. In: TOMLINSON, A., (ED.). *Sport in society: policy, politics and culture.* Brighton, CSRS, 1990, pp.1-12.

CURTIS, J.E., GRABB, E.G., and BAER, D.E.: Voluntary association membership in fifteen countries: a comparative analysis. In: *American Sociological Review*, 57, 1992, pp.139-152.

DEUTSCHER SPORTBUND: *Deutscher Sportbund 1986-1990. Bericht des Präsidiums.* Frankfurt am Main, DSB, 1990.

EISENSTADT, S.N.: Modes of structural differentiation, elite structure, and cultural visions. In: ALEXANDER, J.C., and COLOMY, P., (Eds.): *Differentiation theory: problems and prospects.* New York, Columbia University Press, 1990, pp.19-51.

EVANS, J.: *Service to sport: the story of the CCPR*, 1935-1972. London, Pelham Books, 1974.

HARTMANN-TEWS, I.: *Sport für alle!?* - Strukturwandel des Sports in internationaler Perspektive. Cologne, 1996.

HEINEMANN, K., and SCHUBERT, M.: *Der Sportverein.* Schorndorf, Hofmann, 1994.

INGLEHARDT, R.: *The silent revolution. Changing values and political styles among western publics.* Princeton, University Press, 1977.

KAMPHORST, T., and ROBERTS, K., (Eds.): *Trends in sports - a multi-national perspective.* Enschede, Giordano Bruno,1989.

SPORTS COUNCIL: *A digest of sports statistics for the UK.* 3rd Edition. London, The Sports Council, 1991.

WEDEKIND, S., and KUHLMANN, D.: *Breitensport-Profile von Mitgliedsorganisationen*

Chapter 16

Changes in Sport in Thailand: Traditional to Modern

Tetsuya Sagawa

Introduction

Thailand is a south-east Asian country, which is generally replete with traditional culture. At the same time, Bangkok, the metropolis of Thailand, has grown into a modern city in accordance with the recent rapid economic development. In the local areas, urban life patterns have gradually superseded traditional life patterns, the decline of which has produced the threat of disappearance of traditional cultural activities. This study considers reasons for changes by focusing on children's sport in the north-eastern Thai province of Ubon Ratchathani, selected because the pace of modernisation there is relatively slow and many traditional cultural activities continue to exist. Change in children's sport is considered from the perspectives of region and time.

Regional Changes in Sport

Sample areas

Three areas were selected for regional analysis:

- Provincial - Amphoe-muang Ubon Ratchathani

- District - Amphoe Phibun Mangsaharn

- Agricultural Village - Ban Nong Goenhoi (Dej Udom district)

Population sample

For each of three areas the sample population included boys and girls in the fifth grade (year), and contextual details were collected showing the percentage of farmers, number of siblings and average monthly pocket money (see table 1.).

Table 1.

Sample characteristics

	Ban	Amphoe	Amphoe-muang
Samples	45	40	50
Boys	21	20	25
Girls	24	20	25
The number of brothers (person)	4.5	3.7	3.2
Farmers' percentage (%)	100.0	27.5	16.0
Monthly pocket money (Baht)	11.8	84.9	165.2

Data collection

Questionnaires to solicit information from the school children on participation in games and other sports activities on weekdays and weekends were administered in December 1988. The games and sports activities listed in the three areas numbered 617, comprising 79 different kinds of activities.

The activities were classified by area, sex and experience in participation. The dispersion of games' and sports' items is explained by using an amount of information, which is the relative entropy. This scale is suited to measure dispersion of nominal data. A higher score of relative entropy indicates larger dispersion of items; conversely a lower score indicates smaller dispersion.

Table 2.

Relative entropy of the three areas

		Ban		Amphoe		Amphoe-muang	
		Items	Relative entrophy	Items	Relative entrophy	Items	Relative entropy
Boy	Weekdays	17	.7732	13	.7782	17	.7757
	Weekend	12	.8341	18	.8839	26	.8816
Girl	Weekdays	14	.7906	14	.8930	16	.9154
	Weekend	20	.8556	14	.8266	26	.9239
Total		**37**	**.7636**	**31**	**.8219**	**51**	**.8512**

Results

In rural areas the relative entropy is low: the number of games and sports is small and is becoming centralised. In urban areas the relative entropy is high: the number of games and sports is large and is becoming dispersed. A comparison between weekdays and weekend participation showed that weekdays have relatively low entropy (activities are concentrated in just a few highly popular sports), and relative high entropy is evident at the weekend, when the activity range increases and disperses. Furthermore, in a comparison by sex, boys' relative entropy is lower than that of girls. It seems that boys prefer specific sports, for example, soccer.

For the regional areas, the rates of children's participation were divided into three categories. In Category A, the participation rates in each sport in Amphoe-muang were higher than the rate in Amphoe and the rate in Ban was lower than in Amphoe. In Category B, the participation rates in each sport in the three areas were the same. In Category C, the participation rates in ban were higher than Amphoe, and those of Amphoe-muang lower than Amphoe. The activities were classified in accordance with these three categories.

Table 3.

Examples of categorised activities by regional area

Category A	Bicycle, soccer, takraw, badminton, ping pong
Category B	Jump rope, jump over rubber-bands, chase and tag, foot racing
Category C	Hide and seek, kite flying, Tii Cap, Mai Khit, Mak Kaeng, Kii Chang

Category A is composed of many modern sports (see table 3), which mainly emanate from Europe. This suggests that modern sports are dominant in urban areas. Because of its popularity throughout Asia, sepaktakraw is regarded as a modern competitive sport. In Thailand, it is one of the most popular sports, ranking in television broadcasts alongside soccer and Muai Thai (Thai Boxing). Category B is composed of activities (see table 3.), which are regarded as traditional. They also feature as popular activities in physical education. Category B sports are deemed to be stable because they manifest both traditional and modern characteristics. Traditional games and sports, which have strong native characteristics, feature in Category C (refer table 3.): 'Tii Cap' is a game of chase and tag much like 'Kabaddi'; 'Mai-khit' is a complex strategic game of hit and catch, using short and long sticks; and 'Mark Kaeng Kii Chang' is a kind of beanbag game using small sticks. An analysis of the regional area patterns of activity participation suggests that modern sports are likely to spread throughout urban areas and that traditional activities remaining in rural areas will gradually disappear.

Changes by Generation in Sport

Prior to analysis of sport participation by generation, a list of 72 sports, which were practised in north-eastern Thailand, was compiled from a literature survey and field observation. The resultant inventory served as a basis for a questionnaire survey administered to people resident in the Ubon Ratchathani province. The survey was conducted in February 1990 and September 1991 and was made up of a sample of 104 in the age range of 10-64. The sample was made up of three age groups:

- Group A 10-13 years
- Group B 15-29 years
- Group C 30-64 years

Group A comprised the generation which attended primary school in the 1990s, group B was in primary school in the period 1970-85, and group C was in the period 1940-70. Comparative studies of the three groups were made by examining the rate of participation in each sport.

Table 4.

Samples and the period of primary schooling

Group	A	B	C
Samples	36	32	35
Boys	16	17	24
Girls	20	15	11
Age	10-13	15-29	30-64
Period	1990's	1970-85	1940-70

A comparison of the participation rate in sport of higher than 70% was made. For boys, there were 32 items in groups B and C, but there were only half (15 items) in group A. In the case of girls, group C had 27 items, group B 28 items, and group A 17 items. For both boys and girls, the number of group A's items was much lower than groups B and C.

Table 5.

The number of items higher than 70%

Group	A	B	C
Boys	15	32	32
Girls	17	28	27

These findings suggest that there is a change by generation in children's sports activities between group A and groups B and C. Notably, group A comprised then current primary school pupils. A pertinent issue here is whether members of groups B and C accurately reported past experience. This issue notwithstanding, the difference is noteworthy. By inference, children's sport experiences in the 1990's are decreasing in comparison with past generations. Based on this finding, an analysis of both modern and traditional sports scoring more than 70% was conducted. Group A boys showed a higher percentage participated in modern sports than the older generations represented in groups B and C, but these older generations also have participation rates of higher than 70% in modern sports with the one exception of volleyball for group C (refer table 6).

Table 6.

Percentage of modern sports by age group

Group A		Group B		Group C	
Sepaktakraw	95%	Ping Pong	88%	Soccer	92%
Soccer	90%	Soccer	82%	Sepaktakraw	88%
Muai Thai	90%	Volleyball	82%	Muai Thai	88%
Volleyball	85%	Sepaktakraw	82%	Ping Pong	75%
Ping Pong	85%	Muai Thai	76%	Volleyball	63%

Significantly, the rather high percentage of engagement in modern sports for the 30-64 age group was for males. For females, the rates of participation in modern sports were low in every generation group. It seems that until the beginning of 1990's modern sports were less popular for girls in north-eastern Thailand.

A comparison of the three groups was undertaken of the participation rate in traditional sports, which was indicated by more than 80% of group C. In the case of males, there were 15 items in group C, 11 items in B group but in group A only 1 item. For females, there were 18 items in group C, 13 items in group B, and only 6 items in group A (see table 7). The same tendency is revealed in both male and female groupings with marked reductions from group B to A.

Table 7.

The number of traditional sports items higher than 80%

Group	A	B	C
Boys	1	11	15
Girls	6	13	18

This finding indicates the decrease in frequency in participation in traditional sports in recent years. Throwing rings, kicking stones and flying kites showed less than 30% participation. It is clear that engagement in traditional sports is on the decrease in north-eastern Thailand.

Concluding Comments

It is clear from the two surveys conducted that participation by children in sports is changing from generation to generation in Ubon Ratchathani province. In particular, the frequency in the rate of engagement in traditional sports is decreasing. For males, there is no difference in modern sports' participation between generations. Amongst females, until the beginning of the 1990s, modern sports were not commonly engaged in. As modern sports have come to predominate in urban settings, it has become difficult to find traditional sports in these areas.

This study demonstrates that traditional indigenous sports in north-eastern Thailand face the threat of disappearance and with it the possibility of native culture. In order to retain local cultural identities, efforts should be made to re-discover the inherent values of traditional sports-related activities and to uncover the reasons for the changes taking place.

Chapter 17

Sport in Developing Countries: the Role of Physical Education as part of Sport for All

Robert Chappell

Introduction

According to COGHLAN (1992) developing countries may be defined as: "a range of sovereign states that are to a greater or lesser extent in a process of social and economic change needing co-operation and assistance from others better placed" (p.1). Of course, the co-operation and assistance referred to in this definition is in relation to economic and social conditions, as this directly affects the role of physical education and sport in a country. Paradoxically some developed countries could be termed 'developing' in terms of their participation in certain sports, as is the case of Holland which participated in the 1996 Cricket World Cup. Holland did not have much success against well-known cricketing nations which are 'developing' countries such as India, Pakistan and the West Indies. In this instance, Holland, although a developed country, is clearly in need of co-operation and assistance from others that are better placed in terms of playing cricket! The reverse is also true in the case of Brazil - a 'developing' country but the world football champions.

Authors such as ANTHONY (1979) and COGHLAN (1985, 1992) have attempted to categorise developing countries. The most important point to raise is that made by COGHLAN (1986) in a UNESCO Report on the reduction of disparities between developed and developing countries in sport and physical education:

> ... there is no such homogeneous group as developing countries for sport and physical education; virtually every country that is formally defined thus for economic reasons is different in its progress to date in sport and physical education and its needs. There are wealthy developing

countries, indeed some of the richest countries in the world are classed as developing countries, and there are poor developing countries. In between in terms of wealth there is virtually every possible situation.

Of significance, however, are the United Nations two broad categories of developing countries:

• developing countries which are post-industrial

• developing countries which are largely non-industrial

The significance of these categories is that developing countries, which are post-industrial, might be in a better position to support the growth of programmes in physical education and sport.

It is also erroneous to assume that all developing countries have the same culture, the same problems, and that there is a need for common solutions. Indeed, some developing countries might not wish to be helped in terms of developing physical education and sport programmes. As LILLIS (1977) noted in relation to Africa:

> Africa is not a homogeneous region. There may be distinctive similarities in the problems experienced by each nation but the collection of nations that is Africa varies considerably in wealth, tradition, historical circumstances, socio-economic development, cultural awareness and political outlook. There are common problems but no universal needs.

Furthermore, as COGHLAN (1996) notes, Africa is black, brown and white. It is Christian, Muslim and Marxist, and speaks a variety of languages, depending on which mother country colonised it. Hence, English, French, Portuguese and Arabic are spoken along with the languages of its own country.

A further problem, which affects the role and importance of physical education and sport in a country is its political orientation. Developing countries encompass socialist countries, democratic countries and military dictatorships. For example, in Niger, Lieutenant-Colonel Ibrahim Bare Mainassara, the leader of the military coup in January 1996, told foreign diplomats that the army had no plans to retain power, but wished to make some constitutional changes before returning the nation to democracy. Similarly, the Commonwealth informed Nigeria that it faced expulsion if democracy was not restored within two years and that economic sanctions would be applied if General Sani Abacha, its military leader, refused to meet a Commonwealth Mediation group. Of great concern is a number of conflicts in developing countries as in Sierra Leone, where there has been a four year civil war between government forces and 1,000 revolutionaries, in which 10,000 people have been killed, and children have been fighting in the front line. Clearly, these difficult political situations are not conducive to the development of physical education, nor will it be a main priority.

Of course, it must be emphasised that there are developing countries that excel in certain sports, and do not need help and co-operation from other countries in order to improve. For example: a) Brazil and Nigeria - Soccer; b) India and Pakistan - Hockey; c) Kenya -Middle and Long Distance Running including Cross Country; d) Malaysia - Badminton; e) China - Diving, Gymnastics, Track and Field and Swimming and f) West Indies, India and Pakistan - Cricket.

In fact, taking into account that African nations, as an example, only really started to compete in the Olympic Games in 1968, when 27 African countries competed, they have achieved great success. At the 1992 Olympic Games in Barcelona, seven African countries won a total of 24 medals.

Furthermore, some developing countries have good sports facilities and are able to host major international sports competitions, as is the case with the Indian sub-continent, which hosted the 1996 Cricket World Cup. However, it could be assumed that most developing countries do not have good or even fair facilities across a full range of international sports.

It must also be understood that developing countries were not devoid of sport prior to colonisation, as many traditional games and contests have always existed. The traditional games and dances of western African nations have been articulated by CHESKA (1987) and indicate the importance of these traditional activities. It was following the Pheips-Stroke (1920-1925) report on education in Africa that native activities were suppressed, especially in urban areas. As a consequence sports such as athletics, football, cricket, table-tennis and netball were introduced to African schools (IKULAYO, 1994). It should be possible to introduce new sports into a developing country, but the right balance must be struck between the development of elite athletes in international sports and participation in indigenous activities. To some people, especially the young, Western sports like Western dress represent progress, civilisation, a means of international communion, and a path to fortune (RIORDAN, 1986). Western sports do have a role to play in developing countries but it must be a responsible one.

Another error that is made in relation to the development of physical education and sport in developing countries is that not all countries have the same values in relation to participation in sport. So, the values and norms considered to be important in western ideology are not necessarily valid in developing countries. According to RIORDAN (1986), western sports are neither 'natural' nor 'right' for other peoples and may be looked upon as indecent and irrelevant to the needs of developing countries. But, having made this comment, taking into account the number of developing countries participating in the Olympic Games, the Soccer World Cup, the Cricket World Cup and the I.A.A.F. World Championships, it would seem that many are slowly accepting the norms and values of Western ideology in relation to sport.

The Way Ahead

Some authors (DUBBERKE, 1986; COGHLAN, 1992) maintain that the development of physical education and sport can be justified on the basis of improving health and the quality of life. Many believe that physical education and sport are values in themselves, and think that even poor people have the right to play sport and improve their performance. However, in answer to the dilemma as to which, sport-for-all or elite sport, should be given the main priority, perhaps it could be suggested that they could be of mutual benefit, as success at elite sports can influence participation in sport-for-all.

Sport for all, and in particular school physical education, should be recognised as the base of the participation pyramid. Physical education in schools should be seen, therefore, as the most important aspect of the development of sport in developing countries, as the broader the base of participation, the higher the pyramid can be built. At the top of the pyramid would be elite sport with performances at international competitions. So, even if high level sport is supported by national governments, greater attention should be given to sport-for-all, especially school physical education.

The term 'Sport for All' was adopted by the Council of Europe in 1966 in an attempt to define the sport for all concept as something quite different from the traditional concept of sport. Sport for all embraces all forms of physical activity from organised games to a minimum of physical exercise performed regularly. The member states of Western Europe backed the sport for all concept, and resources and policies were established in order to develop this philosophy. In 1978, UNESCO followed with the International Charter of Physical Education and Sport. Article 1 of the charter stated:

> ... every human being has a fundamental right to access to physical education and sport which are essential for the development of his personality. The freedom to develop physical, intellectual and moral powers through physical education and sport must be guaranteed both within the educational system and in other aspects of social life

Both Charters, the Council of Europe, 1976 and UNESCO, 1978, had a great effect globally, although dissatisfaction has been expressed at the inability of UNESCO to provide adequate finance to promote sport-for-all in developing countries over recent years (COGHLAN, 1986).

Physical Education as part of Sport for All

As COGHLAN (1981) rightly commented "... children are children the world over, so they will play and demand activity, they will run, chase, kick anything and throw anything" (p.30). The task of the providers then is to harness and develop this energy by providing facilities, even basic facilities, and safe environments so that this may be done. In India, for example, there is a distinct lack of facilities for even basic physical education. According to KUMAR (1982), only 2% of the schools at that time, and there are over one million junior and senior schools, have a playground. The rest of the schools are housed in small rooms, usually in residential areas, where there are no facilities for physical education. The same is true in many other countries in Asia, Africa and South America.

In 1971, the International Council of Sport and Physical Education with the support of UNESCO, and in collaboration with the Supreme Council of Sport in Africa, issued the *Rabat Declaration on Sport in Africa.* This Declaration made important points in relation to the development of physical education, which perhaps need to be re-addressed.

In the area of physical education in schools, it was suggested that model educational programmes should be elaborated to include:

- better school sports facilities
- sports facilities for use out of school
- an improvement in teacher training facilities
- curriculum development

There were also some recommendations in relation to education for coaches, specialist overseas training, and the development of regional institutes of physical education and sport. All of these objectives are commendable but there must be the political will to improve physical education programmes by all governments in developing countries. As COGHLAN (1986) noted, although physical education as a subject is included in educational curricula, it is often given the lowest priority in terms of financial and human resources. An easy and useful undertaking would be to guarantee physical education lessons in schools, and this is a serious challenge to respective governments. Even if governments approve of regular lessons in physical education, it takes a long time to implement this approval, but it should be done. To compound matters, specialist physical education teachers are generally in short supply at secondary level. At primary (elementary) level, the teaching of physical education in the training courses for intending teachers is virtually non-existent, thus, denying children at the formative age any experience of sport and physical education in preparation for later years (COGHLAN, 1986).

If traditions of physical activity were developed in schools, children would then be better disposed to take part in sports activities in the post-school situation. The importance of school physical education and organised post-school activities in relation to the resultant health and well-being of the community cannot be over emphasised. Therefore, more resources should be made available in developing countries for physical education as a health factor, to improve the quality of life, and in order to develop a broad range of participation from which elite athletes may develop.

The first stage of this development must be the realisation of existing inadequacies in that there is an enthusiasm for the ideal of physical education, but an acceptable status, equipment and facilities do not exist in most schools (COGHLAN, 1986). In order that the quality of physical education and sport be improved, both governmental and non-governmental aid needs to be expanded (COGHLAN, 1994, 1996). Great importance should be attached to organisations such as the *Supreme Council for Sport in Africa* as its members know the local conditions, and what steps need to be taken in order to improve the situation. It is re-assuring to know that the *Voluntary Services Overseas* (VSO) agency in Britain has started a scheme employing young people to assist in various sports programmes overseas.

Whatever, the development of physical education needs to be wanted by interested developing countries. Developed countries cannot merely decide what is wanted by a developing country, so support for physical education should only be granted if it is requested by the host country. There is a need for true partnership if there is to be co-operation in the field of physical education. For developing countries that wish to co-operate with aid programmes there must be:

- the will to promote sport and physical education as statements are not enough; there has to be a clear statement of policy by governments

- a 'shopping list' of needs and priorities indicated

- a policy development which embraces 'sport for all' as well as elite sport

- a commitment to long term programmes

Bi-lateral arrangements between developed and developing countries in the area of physical education and sport are of great importance. Aid programmes have been in place for a number of years, but the recession in the West and the break-up of the so-called 'Socialist Bloc' have curtailed progress. In order to address this problem, in 1988 the Commonwealth Heads of Government set up a working party to examine how sport might contribute to strengthening the Commonwealth. It called upon the developed countries of the Commonwealth such as the U.K., Canada, New Zealand, Australia and South Africa to play a major role in helping the rest of the Commonwealth countries, as they are virtually all developing countries.

In Canada, $5million has been allocated by the federal government, channelled through the Commonwealth Games Association of Canada, to be spent on the improvement of coaching, administration, physical education, curriculum development, and sport for the disabled, in developing countries. This is to be commended, especially in relation to the development of physical education programmes, and it is hoped that such programmes will be expanded in the near future.

It is clear that many governments in developing countries are eager to promote physical education and sport for the masses, but the problems faced by such countries are immense and in some cases overwhelming. This does not mean that those respective governments from developing countries and international organisations in the developed world should not try to improve the situation. But the scale of the task is daunting and at present, the development of physical education and sport may not be a high priority. From a western viewpoint, there might be a problem in that an agenda can be set and a programme outlined to address these issues. However, the reality of the situation in developing countries is complex and may not be appreciated by 'outsiders'. Therefore, it is difficult to offer advice from afar, as for many in the developing world, sport and physical education are an irrelevance. Nevertheless, in a civilised world, there is a moral obligation to address situations, to make suggestions and offer financial help where appropriate.

References

ANTHONY, D.: The analysis of sport and physical education in developing countries. In: HOWELL, R., *Methodology in comparative physical education and sport.* Champaign, IL, Stipes Publishing Co., 1979.

CHESKA, A.T.: Traditional names and dances in western African nations. In: *ICSSPE Sports Science Studies*, 1, 1987.

COGHLAN, J.: Physical education needs in Africa. In: *FIEP Bulletin*, 51(2), 1981, pp.28-31.

COGHLAN, J.: Sport for all in developing countries. In: *FIEP Bulletin*, 55(1), 1985, pp.27-31.

COGHLAN, J.: *Ways and means of reducing current disparities between developed and developing countries in the field of physical education and sport.* ICSSPE/UNESCO, 1986.

COGHLAN, J.: *An overview of the issues, problems and programmes that concern bridging the gap between developed and developing countries in sport and physical education.* Paper presented at pre-Olympic Scientific Conference, Malaga, 1992.

COGHLAN, J.: *Towards more equal opportunities in sport and physical recreation-issues, problems and programmes in developing countries.* Paper presented at International Sports Congress and Trade Fair. Bangalore, India, January 1996

DUBBERKE, H.: Critical remarks regarding sports for developing countries. In: MANGAN, J., and SMALL, R., *Sport, culture and society.* London, E. and F. Spon, 1986.

IKULAYO, P.: Competitive sports in Africa with particular reference to Nigeria. In: DUFFY, P., and DUGDALE, L., *HPER - moving towards the 21st century*. Champaign, IL, Human Kinetics, 1994, pp. 149-161.

KUMAR, A.: Difficulties in sports advancement in developing countries. In: *FIEP Bulletin*, 52(2), 1982, pp.25-27.

LILLIS, K.: *Assessment of needs in physical education and sport in Africa and proposals for implementation of the first conference of ministers and senior officials responsible for physical education and sport in the education of youth*. UNESCO, November 1977.

RIORDAN, J.: State and sport in developing countries. In: *International Review for Sociology of Sport*, 21(4), 1986, pp.287-301.

Chapter 18

Public Accountability: Federal Government Initiatives in Canadian Amateur Sport

Darwin M. Semotiuk

Introduction

In sport, fitness and recreation, Canada has been held in high regard by the international community for its important contributions. However, since the publication of the DUBIN *Report* in 1989, public accountability as it relates to federal government involvement in Canadian amateur sport has been under some scrutiny. Additionally, there has been an introspective analysis of the structure, function and future of those organisations and agencies presently operating within the Canadian sport system. The parameters of the Government of Canada's *Sport Funding Accountability Framework* (1995) and a *Business Plan for Sport in Canada* (1996) demonstrate the high priority that has been assigned towards successful participation in international sport and highlight the need for the Canadian sport system to move towards greater self-sufficiency. Here, the future of Canadian amateur sport programming is assessed within the context of selected political and economic factors.

Motives underlying National Government Involvement in Sport

In trying to develop a more complete understanding of the relationships that exist between the National Government and the system of sport, several penetrating questions arise concerning the nature of this connection: why and for what purposes are national governments involved in sponsoring sports programmes?; why are some national systems more involved than others?; and is their degree of involvement dictated by a philosophical orientation of individualism or collectivism? The fact that there are no easy responses to these queries suggests the need for a scheme to determine reasons for involvement. Isolation of the numerous motives for governmental participation reveals that some of the reasons are openly proclaimed and obvious, whereas, some are more subtle, and consequently more difficult to detect.

A perusal of the literature providing an historical perspective on the role of national government involvement as well as scrutiny of contemporary documents obtained from different countries resulted in the exposure of several functional motives underlying the commitment to support sport. National governments are motivated to participate in programmes of sport for specific reasons. The motives that are outlined here are those which explain or justify a permanent intervention by the government into the domain of sport. MEYNAUD (1966) isolates three major reasons for government involvement: concern for the maintenance of public order; concern for physical condition; and affirmation of national prestige. Using an expanded version of MEYNAUD's classification scheme, the motives underlying government involvement in sport can be further divided. It should be emphasised that each of these functions is not exclusive of the others, but rather they are often closely aligned and interrelated. In all, nine motives/functions can be identified: individualising (individual health and well-being); socialising or nationalising (social order and control); international goodwill; national prestige (success in international competition; military (defence of the country); labour productivity; economic (source of income); political indoctrination; and legislative (laws - maintain social order) (SEMOTIUK, 1981a, 1981b). In Canada, an analysis of the budgetary expenditures over the last three decades leads to the conclusion that success in international sport remains the most important motive and priority for government sports officials, politicians and decision-makers.

Historical Considerations - Government of Canada and Sport

The name Ben Johnson and his positive doping test at the 1988 Seoul Summer Olympic Games continues to be a Canadian embarrassment of the highest order and also continues to have relevance in discussions on Canadian federal sports policy. No one single event has had as much impact on Canadian amateur sport as this. The tainted 9.79 seconds one hundred metre sprint in Seoul gave rise to an open trial of Canada's national sport systems, a trial, which continues through today.

Over the last eight years, a number of important studies, reports, reviews, and policy statements have been undertaken. The significant efforts include:

- *Commission of Inquiry into the Use of Drugs and Banned Practices Intended to Increase Athletic Performance* (DUBIN, 1990)
- *Minister's Task Force on Federal Sport Policy, Sport: The Way Ahead* (BEST, BLACKHURST and MAKOSKY, 1992)
- *Federal Directions in Sport* (CADIEUX, 1993)
- *Report of the Core Sports Commissioner* (BEST, 1994).

In June 1993 the Government of Canada undertook a major restructuring of its ministries. With the reorganisation, the Department of Fitness and Amateur Sport (along with a junior ministerial appointment) ceased to exist with the sport responsibilities (Sport Canada specifically) being transferred to the Department of Canadian Heritage and fitness going to the Department of National Health and Welfare. At this time, the Minister's response to *Sport: The Way Ahead* (BEST et al., 1992), was contained in *Federal Directions in Sport* (CADIEUX, 1993). Despite the change in government in September 1993, this statement continues to provide the foundation for Canadian sports policy. The vision for change in the sport system is contained within the eight themes proposed by the government:

- A Sport Plan for Canada

- An Athlete Centred Sport System

- Equitable and Accessible Sport

- Development of Volunteer and Professional Sport Leaders

- New and Innovative Partnerships and Strategic Alliances

- The Pursuit of High Performance Athletic Excellence

- Values, Ethics and Fair Play in Sport

- New Economic Models for Sport

(CADIEUX, 1993)

It is significant to note that in order to attain world class levels of excellence, Canadian athletes and coaches must have access to the most up-to-date technical, financial and social support services. It is also significant to point out that it will be necessary to develop innovative strategies to define a new economic model for sport development delivery. Of particular importance is the need to look at further diversification of funding for sport.

It was out of this latter suggestion that initiatives were undertaken to address the issue of declining government financial resources and to establish criteria for how the monies might be more effectively allocated (BEST, 1994). The changing economic climate has hastened the decision to selectively fund certain sports, reduce, and, in some cases, eliminate the funding support for others. This new approach has been implemented with considerable speed (by normal government standards) and with predictable results.

Funding Support for Canadian Amateur Sport

Since 1961, the Government of Canada has directly contributed in excess of one billion dollars (Canadian) in support of Fitness and Amateur Sport. It would be relatively safe to claim that approximately 80% of that amount has been directed towards high performance sport objectives. On an annual basis, the Federal Government spends approximately ninety (90) million dollars on fitness and amateur sport programmes. With the Government of Canada's global budget for 1996-97 set at $159.3 billion, this represents .057 of one per cent of that total. Of particular concern to the Government and all Canadians is the matter of a $578.4 billion public debt and a budgeted deficit of $24.3 billion (3% of GDP) for 1996-97 (MARTIN, 1996,). Expenditure control and expense reduction strategies are beginning to have immediate impact on the funding levels for amateur sport. Everyone in sport is being affected, and all organisations have embarked on courses leading to fiscal self-sufficiency. Those sports organisations, which have established strong ties with the corporate sector, will be well positioned to deal with the significant reductions in Federal Government funding support.

Sport Funding Accountability Framework (SFAF)

Recent reports on sport policy expressed the generally unanimous view that fundamental adjustments had to be made to the sport funding system in Canada. No fundamental changes to the funding system had been made since the federal government first began directly supporting amateur sport development more than thirty years ago. As a result, the Department of Canadian Heritage (Sport Canada), in consultation with the sport community, developed the Sport Funding and Accountability Framework (SFAF). It was piloted and refined in 1995, for full implementation as of April 1, 1996. The Canadian Government's objective in its support of amateur sport is the achievement of high performance excellence through fair and ethical means. It is clear that federal funding flows predominantly (but not exclusively) to high performance sport with attention being focused on the following policy priorities:

• Canada's high performance athletes and programmes

• coaches and coaching development

• delivery of services

• increased access for women, athletes with a disability and aboriginal persons

• initiatives contributing to the achievement of broad social and economic policy objectives

It is held that sport contributes to the achievement of federal policy objectives: Canadian identity; national unity; social development; youth integration and economic growth and prosperity.

The SFAF is a comprehensive objective tool to ensure that federal funds are allocated to National Sport Organisations (NS0's), that contribute to federal sport objectives and priorities. The notion of accountability is fundamental to the framework and its application. It encompasses three main components: eligibility, funding determination and accountability.

Specifically, the objectives of the SFAF are to:

- rationalise Sport Canada's funding contributions to NSOs

- provide a more objective system of allocating funding to NSOs based on merit

- ensure accountability as part of the federal government and NSO relationship

(SPORT CANADA, 1996a)

To be eligible for funding consideration for the period 1996-2001, NSOs must first meet established prerequisites and, following a detailed assessment by Sport Canada, achieve a score above the eligibility threshold. In January 1996, NSOs provided information to Sport Canada via their responses to a thorough assessment questionnaire. Using a detailed rating guide, Sport Canada then evaluated the responses to determine which NSOs were eligible to receive federal support and to what extent. The assessment is based on evaluation criteria organised in three key categories: high performance, sport development and management practices. The 1996 assessment took into account data from January 1, 1988 to December 31, 1996 and is largely based on quantitative criteria, with some consideration given to qualitative criteria.

In the high performance category (60%), an organisation's score is based on athlete results and the NSOs high performance system. The score for athlete results is arrived at by weighting World Championships and Olympic results by factors that reflect the competitive profile for each sport. An NSO's score for its high performance system takes into account how an NSO operates its national team and support programmes. For example, factors relating to coaching, training, athlete monitoring, and athlete involvement in decision-making are used to determine this part of an NSO's score.

Sport development (30%) considers athlete development, coach development and officiating. These in turn are scored according to the NSO's membership, participation in national and provincial championships and the Canada Games, technical resources, and the certification of coaches and officials. Technical resources in this case

refer to the extent of leadership provided by the NSO in the development
of resource materials and programmes for athletes, coaches and officials.
The management category (10%) assesses an NSO's financial operations,
service capacity in both official languages and the opportunities provided
for women in sport.

From April 1, 1996 thirty-six NSO's continue to receive federal
government funding support. With accountability being an integral
component of the SFAF the federal government has made a statement:
tax dollars are to be used for intended purposes and to achieve desired
results. NSOs receiving funding in 1996 must negotiate and sign an
'Accountability Agreement' with Sport Canada based on key objectives
from the NSO's multi-year plan. Clearly, the existence of such an
agreement is to ensure that public funding contributes to the achievement
of federal priorities and policy objectives for sport.

**Business Plan for Sport in Canada: Strategies for Continued
Growth and Self-sufficiency**

In January 1996, the development of a *Business Plan for Sport in Canada*
(SPORT CANADA, 1996b) was launched. At that time the federal
government distributed the *Business Plan Think Piece* (December, 1995)
and draft *Work Plan* (December, 1995) to stakeholders in the sport
community. Factors in the current environment, such as declining
resources for sport from traditional sources, have motivated the federal
government to provide leadership to the development of a Business Plan
for Sport. This is a consultative, co-operative public policy exercise
undertaken in conjunction with partners in sport to enhance the self-
sufficiency of the sport system and sustain the development of sport in
Canada.

The results of the Business Plan project will focus on recommendations
and strategies leading to new sources of funding for sport, increased self-
sufficiency and effectiveness of sport organisations and delivery
mechanisms, the financing of high performance sport, and the closer
linking of sport with other government priorities.

Participating with Sport Canada in the certain aspects of the Business Plan are the provincial and territorial governments, NSOs, Municipal Sport Organisations (MSO'S), the corporate sector, other units within the Department of Canadian Heritage and other federal departments (Finance/Revenue).

In addition to re-configuring the Sport Canada funding system by creating the Sport Funding and Accountability Framework, the Government has recently taken a number of additional actions:

- implementation of changes to the Athlete Assistance Program (AAP) by increasing the amount of monthly stipends to carded athletes and making additional policy revisions in line with the recognition high performance athletes and athlete support programs are the foremost priority for federal funding

- shifting away from funding for administration through elimination of funding reductions to multi-sport and service organisations on the basis of their relative contribution to the policy objectives and priorities, and gradual elimination of funding, over the next few years, to the Canadian Sport and Fitness Administration Centre

- discussion by the federal government with their provincial/territorial counterparts regarding the need to address respective roles and responsibilities for support the Canadian sport system
                                                              (SPORT CANADA, 1996c)

It is significant to note that the re-focused federal directions and actions have highlighted the presence of policy fragmentation between the federal and provincial/territorial governments. Since the federal government is focusing its funding on high performance sport, there is now a potential for gaps in the system and the issue has been raised of how to ensure the development of athletes for the future.

There are a number of realities in the current environment, which challenge the continued development of the sport system in Canada. Indeed, there are some who question whether the sport community will be able to maintain the advances made over the last 25 years. The issues include the following:

- the rapidly decreasing level of public sector funding for sport at both the federal and provincial/territorial levels

- the increasing cost of sport programming; while these escalating costs affect sport at all levels, they have a potentially greater impact at the high performance level, which has significantly higher costs for travel, facility rental, equipment etc.

- the corporate sector is also under financial pressure and, as a result, it is becoming increasingly difficult for many sports to generate significant sponsorship revenue; there is also more competition with other non-profit sectors for corporate support

The decision by the Government of Canada to focus its resources on the high performance end of the sport continuum has raised a number of substantive policy issues:

1. With insufficient federal and provincial/territorial sport budgets to maintain the continued development of the sport system (programmes and infrastructure) in Canada, strategies must be developed to attract increased financial support from other sources such as corporate sector support, self-generated revenue by sport organisations, professional sport leagues and teams, television revenues, lotteries and so on.

2. Notwithstanding this, there is a social and economic rationale for some level of continued public support for sport. Given the limited size of the Canadian market and hence, the limited ability of the private sector to fully support sport, there will always be a need for state involvement. There is also a need to address whether government support for sport in the form of direct contributions is most efficient and effective or whether it should be provided indirectly in some other form such as through the tax system.

3. There is a need to ensure that the essential elements are in place to support a process of athlete development from the early stages through to the high performance level, if Canada hopes to have high performance athletes in the future. High performance excellence can

be achieved consistently only if there is a strong developmental system to support athletes with the talent and dedication.

4. The changing role of governments in Canadian society is also reflected in sport. Governments need to work in partnership with key leaders in the sport community but will no longer play the primary leadership role. There is, therefore, a need to identify these key sport leaders and establish strategic alliances to ensure the continued development and self-sufficiency of the sport system.

5. The current sport system is characterised by gaps and inconsistencies in public sector financial support. There is, therefore, a need to enhance the communication and co-operation between the federal government and those of the provinces and the territories, as well as a need for a more co-ordinated inter-sectoral approach with government departments at the federal level. Horizontal and vertical alliances within the public sector will be vital to the health of the Canadian sport system.

In order to address these important policy issues, the *Business Plan* is collaborating with and soliciting input from the following stakeholder groups: provincial/territorial governments; a Corporate Advisory Committee; the national sport community; the Minister's Athletes' Advisory Committee; the Canadian Olympic Association; and other federal government departments. Data collection, including international comparative data, in areas such as the economic impact of sport and the value of sport, will provide supporting rationale for the recommendations arising from the Business Plan. A business case will be presented to all partners, including the public sector, as a central justification for continued public support, as well as enhanced private support, to the sport system.

A number of Business Plan "Working Groups" have already been established both within and outside Sport Canada and are well into their work. December 1996 was identified as the target date to have these groups submit their reports (SPORT CANADA, 1996c). It was expected the collation and analysis of the data, along with the development of strategies and recommendations would take place early in 1997. No doubt, the desired end product will be a blueprint of discrete strategies/recommendations, specifically tailored to governments and sport system partners and designed to both ensure the continued development of sport and to render the sport community more self-sufficient and less dependent on direct government funding in the longer term.

Concluding Comments

A new reality must be faced by Canada's sport system. With conscious government decisions to reduce programme funding in all sectors due to the high public debt and annual budget deficit, fewer resources are being made available for amateur sport. New funding will have to be identified and it is inevitable that some of the present costs will have to be absorbed by the user i.e. athlete, coach and administrator.

The new report card is now in and Canadian sport is faced with the prospect of finding new and different ways of doing business. Sport will be obliged to become more self-sufficient and less dependent on government. Sport, like many other taxpayer-supported activities, will have to be able to account for the resources it receives. Accountability, self-sufficiency and strategic alliances will be the terms that guide amateur sport in Canada as it moves towards the 21st century.

References

BEST, J.C., BLACKHURST, M., and MAKOSKY, L.: *Minister's task force on federal sport policy. Sport: the way ahead.* Ottawa, Ontario, Ministry of State, Fitness and Amateur Sport, 1992.

BEST, J.C.: *Report of the core sports commissioner.* Ottawa, Ontario, Department of Canadian Heritage, May 19, 1994.

CADIEUX, P.: *Federal directions in sport. Response to the Minister's task force on federal sport policy.* Ottawa, Ontario, Ministry of State, Fitness and Amateur Sport, 1993.

DUBIN, C.L.: *Commission of inquiry into the use of drugs and banned practices intended to increase athletic performance.* Ottawa, Ontario, Minister of Supply and Services, 1990.

MARTIN, P.: *Budget in brief.* Ottawa, Ontario, Department of Finance, 1996.

MEYNAUD, J.: *Sport et politique.* Paris, Payot Publishers, 1966.

SEMOTIUK, D.: Motives for national government involvement in sport. In: *International Journal of Physical Education*, XVIII (1), 1981a, pp.23-28.

SEMOTIUK, D.: Motives for national government involvement in sport. In: *Comparative Physical Education and Sport*, 7(2), 1981b, pp.13-23.

SEMOTIUK, D.: *Federal government sport policy in transition: new directions for Canadian amateur sport.* Paper presented at the 9th Biennial Conference of the International Society for Comparative Physical Education and Sport, Prague, Czech Republic, July 2-7, 1994.

SPORT CANADA: *Sport funding and accountability framework (SFAF) - overview.* Ottawa, Ontario, Sport Canada, Department of Canadian Heritage, 1996a.

SPORT CANADA: *Business plan for sport in Canada - strategies for continued growth and self-sufficiency. A Sport Canada Think Piece.* Ottawa, Ontario, Sport Canada, Department of Canadian Heritage, 1996b.

SPORT CANADA: *Business plan for sport in Canada - an update.* Ottawa, Ontario, Sport Canada, Department of Canadian Heritage, 1996c.

PART 5

SPORT-BUSINESS AND MANAGEMENT

Chapter 19

Physical Education, Sport, and the Global Political Economy: Human Considerations

George H. Sage

Introduction

The ecology of physical education and sport is concerned with the relationships between sport and the larger world. Every day in every way, this wider environment impacts on, and influences, our professional lives as well as our broader social relations. Unfortunately our professional habits tend to lead us to focus on the immediate and the local and hence, we typically give little attention to how physical education and sports are linked to the political, economic, and social relations which underlie various forms of oppression and social injustice. Consequently, we remain largely oblivious to issues about political and economic power and ideology, and their linkages to sporting activities. Indeed, sport culture has actually been an effective social practice for diverting attention away from issues of political economy and ideological forces.

The intention here is to map out several crucial global issues and connect them to physical education and sport with a view to making a contribution to an understanding of the political economy of physical education and sport. It will also help to promote a greater awareness of the ways in which sports goods are manufactured and to form a social consciousness that may serve as an impetus for action toward constructing a better future for those who are involved in making the sporting goods and equipment we all use. In this context, as one illustration, is the paradox that exists between the imagery of patriotism that American professional sports teams shamelessly construct and the fact that much of their licensed merchandise is manufactured in foreign countries by exploited labour.

Wealth, Sports Goods and Equipment Production

When we are involved in sports (as fans, athletes, coaches, physical educators etc.), there are two ingredients that are indispensable. Regardless of where physical education takes place or where sport is played, there are two essentials: one is the participants; the other is the apparel that is worn and the equipment that is used - uniforms, T-shirts, footwear; balls, bats, gloves, and so forth. They make playing sports more comfortable, attractive, and efficient. But there is one aspect of sporting goods and equipment about which most of us involved in PE and sport know very little. It is about who makes those sporting goods and equipment, and under what conditions?

This production process is a great void, a mystery, an unknown, and of little interest to most people associated with sport. It did not ought to be because sporting goods and equipment are not gifts of nature; all sporting goods and equipment are made by people, who, except for a random chance of nature that has put them where they are and us where we are, are just like us. It is their labour that allows all of us to play, watch, coach, and administer sports. Their labour, in effect, is the very foundation of our sporting experience.

In sport, we go to great lengths to assure that athletes have the very best uniforms and equipment to wear and use. Moreover, the health and welfare of athletes are attended to with great care. Coaches' and administrators' needs are met with high salaries and pleasant working conditions. But what about those who toil in factories all over the world to make sporting experiences satisfying and pleasant for athletes, fans, coaches, and administrators?

Despite the dedicated work of human rights' and workers rights activists, religious organisations, and critical sports scholars, little success has been achieved in obtaining media coverage about the conditions of manufacturing in 'Third World' countries. There is little public awareness of the plight of the workers, and thus little in the way of improved wages and working conditions. In recent months, there has been mixed news with respect to sporting goods manufacturing. First the good news: a major breakthrough came in Spring, 1996, when labour activist, Charles Kernaghan (National Labor Committee), informed a U.S. Congressional

Committee about child labour and atrocious working conditions at a Honduran factory making sportswear (sold by Wal-Mart) for TV talk show host Kathie Lee Gifford. Initially, Gifford verbally attacked Kernaghan, claiming his was merely "a vicious attack" on her, but as evidence mounted linking her sportswear to child labour and sweatshops, she moved from denial to acceptance, and then to a crusade against child labour and sweat-shops (ASSOCIATED PRESS, 1996; GREENHOUSE, 1996).

The issues of appalling working conditions, poverty wages, and child labour have recently been a major focus in all of the United States' media. A number of Gifford's shows have been devoted to this topic, and several TV magazine programmes in the United States have devoted segments to it. The June 1996 issue of *Life* magazine contained a lengthy article about child labour in Pakistan, where children stitch soccer balls and make badminton shuttlecocks for 60 cents a day.

In brief, significant public attention has been focused on the oppressive conditions of workers in various industries in developing countries. One of the industries highlighted is the sporting goods manufacturing industry. A very public worldwide attention has begun to focus on the callous exploitation of men, women, and children in Third World countries who use up their lives making sporting goods and equipment that people in First World countries wear and use to play sports. Recently, a Bill has been introduced into the U.S. Congress that will prohibit U.S. companies from importing goods made by child labour and prohibit loans from the U.S. to agencies that use child labour (THOMAS, 1996a; THOMAS, 1996b; SALEN-FITZGERALD, 1996; STROM, 1996). Other developed countries are considering similar laws.

The revelations about working conditions and child labour where Kathie Lee Gifford's sportswear is made are not isolated to those factories, nor are they something new. Furthermore, they represent only one aspect of the central political, economic, and social phenomenon of our day - the global economy. This global economy involves the most fundamental redesign and centralisation of the world's political and economic structure since the Industrial Revolution, and it is driven by some 500 trans-national companies, which now control about 80% of the world's trade.

Of the world's one hundred largest economies, fifty are now corporations KORTEN, 1995; MANDER, 1996; BARNET and CAVANAGH, 1996).

A key aspect of economic globalisation is a capital system and division of labour known as the "export processing system." In this system, product research, development, and design take place in developed countries while the labour-intensive, assembly line phases of product manufacture are relegated to 'Third World' nations. The finished product is then exported for distribution in developed countries of the world (BARNET and CAVANAGH, 1996; BERBEROGLU, 1992; BROWNE AND SIMS, 1993; KORTEN, 1995).

The strategy of shifting production from developed to developing countries has been used by trans-national corporations for several reasons. In 'Third World' countries wages are lower and worker benefits fewer. The work force is not likely to be organised, and if it is organised, it is less likely to be assertive. Management can exert total control over the work process, with few or no restrictions on hiring, firing, or re-assigning workers. Work-place health and safety regulations are less stringent or poorly enforced. The cost of protecting the environment and community health and safety are lower due to weak or poorly enforced regulations (SCHAEFFER, 1996; CRAYPO and NISSEN, 1993; KORTEN, 1995).

As the export processing system has developed, trans-national corporations have closed down factories in their own countries and exported work to people earning wages that keep them in poverty in places like Indonesia, China, India, Thailand, Sri Lanka, the Caribbean and Latin America. The Fortune 500 firms in the U.S. eliminated 4.6 million manufacturing jobs between 1980 and 1995. Today, corporate layoffs in the U. S. are at a pace approaching half a million jobs per year. Layoffs due to the export processing system are not just an American phenomenon. From 1992 to 1993, the top 1,000 British corporations reduced their total work force by 1.6 million workers. This pattern is the same in other developed countries. Consequently, 12% of France's workforce is unemployed; 11% of the European Union workforce is unemployed. Corporate downsizing is the order of the day and extreme economic insecurity, unknown except in periods of deep economic depression, is now the norm in developed countries (GORDON, 1996;

HARRISON, 1994; FRANK AND COOK, 1995; MCFATE, LAWSON
AND WILSON, 1995; SWEENEY, 1996; KUTTNER, 1996).

Trans-national corporate publicity conveys the impression that economic
globalisation has been an earnings boom for everyone around the world.
But the reality is that a major consequence of the export processing
system has been a massive redistribution of wealth - steeply downward
for the vast majority of the world's population, and steeply upward for a
tiny minority at the top. The *Human Development Report* by the United
Nations is a sobering story of extreme economic inequality. Some 20%
of the world's population who live in the richest nations receive
approximately 82% of the world's income. At the other end, the poorest
20% barely survive on 1.4% of the total income. Moreover, this gap has
more than doubled since 1960; so the gap between the poor and the rich
of the world is widening (OMICINSKI, 1996). According to THE
WORLD BANK (1995) in a sample of 117 countries, the ratio of per
capita income in the richest to that in the poorest countries increased
from eleven in 1870 to fifty-two in 1985. In the United States between
1980 and 1995, the richest 1% of American families gained 91% in
average inflation-adjusted income after taxes; the poorest 20% lost 17%
of inflation-adjusted income. Today, the top 1% of families has 42% of
American wealth (SKLAR, 1996; BYRNE, 1996; NELSON, 1995;
WOLFF, 1995).

Hidden Injuries of the Global Economy

Moving plants and operations to 'Third World' countries is a way for
trans-national corporations to boost profits, but for workers in those
countries the consequences have been grim: wages are so low that
workers cannot provide for their basic needs, unjust and inhuman
working conditions, sexual exploitation, social disruption, and distorted
economic development. Moreover, attempts to organise labour unions are
often violently suppressed by government 'soldiers'. Work-place
democracy and worker rights are non-existent. Health and safety in the
work place are often unregulated, as are pollution and other
environmental protections (ESTES, 1996; KOPINAK, 1996)

The cheapest labour of all is child labour and millions of children under 14 years old work full-time in export processing factories. India has some 55 million child labourers and in Pakistan, an estimated 10 to 12 million child workers toil in slave-like conditions of bonded servitude. One Pakistani factory owner, when asked why he employs children, said: "Children are cheaper to run than tractors and smarter than oxen" (SCHANBERG, 1996).

In factories all over the 'Third World', women under the age of 25 from rural areas make up two-thirds of the total work force. They do because manufacturers perceive women as being docile and obedient (making them less likely to protest against poor working condition) and willing to work for low pay.

Economic Realities of Sports Good Manufacture

Sporting goods manufacturing is not dislocated from other forms of global capitalist production; indeed, it is one of the most flourishing export processing industries. Sporting goods manufacturers who produce all of their products domestically are now a minority because many of them have relocated to numerous low-wage export-processing countries across the world.

Nowhere is this phenomenon more tangible than in Asia. The products of hundreds of sporting goods corporations are made in various countries of Asia. Nike, Reebok, and Adidas are the world's largest suppliers of sport footwear and apparel; and Nike is the market leader with a 32% market share (JOSEPH, 1996; BROOKES and MADDEN; 1995; ENLOE, 1995). Today, although Nike is legally registered as an American corporation, none of its footwear is manufactured within the U.S.; everything is sub-contracted from elsewhere. Actually, 99% of all branded sports footwear production is in low cost labour nations of Asia.

In order to lower labour costs, Nike closed its U. S. factories in New Hampshire and Maine in the 1980s and began sub-contracting its work to factories in Korea and Taiwan, where workers were poorly paid and denied basic rights. Reebok, L.A. Gear, Adidas, and others quickly followed that lead. However, as minimum wages increased and unions spread in these countries, Nike and the other sports apparel and footwear corporations shifted their production sites to Indonesia, China, Thailand, and the Philippines in their relentless drive for the lowest-cost labour.

A network of human rights' workers, labour activists, and religious organisations has reported on child labourers making soccer balls in Pakistan for Nike, Adidas, and Umbro. More than half of the 9 million soccer balls imported into the U.S. each year are made in Pakistan by children who toil 10 hours a day in sub-human conditions. All baseballs used by MLB are made by workers earning $3(US) per day; and similar productive operations exist for other sporting goods products.

When reports first began to surface in the popular and scholarly literature in the early 1990s about the dismal wages, adverse working conditions, and violations of basic human rights that were common in the export processing zones, including sporting goods factories, many, who were studying this form of capitalist enterprise and reporting about it, expected that some positive steps would be taken in light of the revelations. Six years on, studies of their productive operations clearly show there has been little progress. The most recent data reveal that there is a yawning gap between the image being marketed by Nike, Reebok, Adidas and other sporting goods firms and the reality of their production operations. Wages and working conditions remain abominable (BROOKES and MADDEN, 1995; ENLOE, 1995).

Nike posted a record annual revenue of $4.7 billion in 1995 and spent an estimated $260 million on athletes to endorse its products. Michael Jordan alone was paid more than the combined yearly income of 30,000 Indonesia women who toil under horrible conditions to make the Nike footwear he endorses. A typical worker in the Asian plants that make Nike, Reebok, and Adidas products works for a monthly wage that is 30% below what is needed to buy goods and services to meet the minimal physical needs for a married person with one child. Workers in their plants (mostly women under the age of 22) routinely put in ten and a half hour days, six days a week, with forced overtime two to three times per week (BROOKES and MADDEN, 1995; ENLOE, 1995). It is their low wages and long hours which make Nike, Reebok, and Adidas commercially successful.

Low wages and long hours are the main ingredients of the success of these sporting goods makers, but the contribution of another cost-saving measure cannot be underestimated: minimal investment in safe working conditions. The typical worker labours in poorly ventilated buildings in stifling heat. Laws requiring industrial safety are almost useless in practice because employers do not follow the rules and regulations set out in the laws. There is a lack of proper knowledge of work-induced health hazards, and there is a lack of trained professionals and proper equipment to prevent and to treat work-related injuries. Not surprisingly, the results of cutting costs on safety and workers' health have been dreadful BROOKES and MADDEN, 1995; ENLOE, 1995).

The record on workers' rights is also. Independent unions are not permitted, and labour organisers are routinely attacked, beaten, and fired from their jobs. Nike worker protests have been met with on-the-spot dismissals and managerial indifference (BROOKES and MADDEN, 1995; ENLOE, 1995; BALLINGER, 1992; INGI LABOR WORKING GROUP, 1991). Moreover, Nike has the audacity to run advertisements showing pre-adolescent and adolescent girls with this text alongside the girls:

> If you let me play, I will like myself more. I will have more self-confidence. I will suffer less depression. I will be 60% less likely to get breast cancer. I will be more likely to leave a man who beats me. I will be less likely to get pregnant before I want to. I will learn what it means to be strong if you let me play sports.

Given the wages and working conditions of Asian girls who work in Nike's plants, there is a blatant inconsistency with those advertisements.

Many United States, Canadian and western European sporting goods firms have moved their production operations to the Caribbean and Latin American countries during the past 20 years. To use Rawlings' Sporting Goods Company as an example, all of the balls used by Major League Baseball are Rawlings' baseballs. Prior to the mid-1950s, all Rawlings' baseballs were manufactured in St. Louis with unionised labour. In order to reduce labour costs, Rawlings shifted its baseball manufacturing to a non-union plant in Missouri. When that plant was organised by a union,

Rawlings moved its baseball manufacturing to an offshore location in Puerto Rico. But when the initial tax 'holidays' for foreign investors ran out and minimum wage laws were implemented in Puerto Rico, Rawlings left to exploit even cheaper labour in Haiti, the poorest country in the Western hemisphere and one of the 25 poorest in the world.

Haiti was the ideal setting for Rawlings' offshore baseball assembly operation. There were generous tax holidays, a franchise granting tariff exemption and the only legal trade unions were administered by the government. Strikes were illegal, and the minimum wage was so low that a majority of Haitians could not derive anything that might reasonably be called a 'living' from the assembly plants. "Far from creating a way out of poverty, the [Rawlings'] wages provided the basis for only an impoverished standard of living" (DEWIND and KINLEY, 1988, p.118).

In 1990, due to the political situation in the country, the Rawlings' plant in Haiti was suddenly closed. All baseball manufacturing was moved to a Rawlings' plant in Costa Rica, where it remains today. Most of the workers are women who must stitch 30 to 35 baseballs each day to earn $5 to $6 in the day (WIRPSA, 1990).

These are only a few of the many examples of the sporting goods' export processing system. The sporting goods operations have indeed achieved commercial success, but they have been built by following a model which places profits over worker needs, a labour policy that violates the human rights of workers, and that results in pervasive and often cruel suppression of those workers. Thus, for workers in sporting goods and equipment manufacturing in the 'Third World' trans-national investment in assembly production carries with it some heavy burdens.

The inevitable question is do we have role in all of this, and if so, what is it? Well, we could adopt the response of Michael Jordan, that worldwide idol of millions of people, that icon of sporting excellence. Jordan brushes off disclosures that Nike footwear is made under appalling conditions in Asian factories by saying, "I don't know the situation; why should I? I'm just trying to do my job. Hopefully, Nike will do the right thing" (KRIEGER, 1996, p.2C; BAUM, 1996, p.4B). The appropriate reply to Jordan was supplied by labour rights leader Charles Kernaghan, who said, "If you are selling your name to a product and making millions of dollars doing it, you're responsible for asking some very serious questions" about how it is made. Jordan might have been excused when he was unaware of the plight of Nike workers in Asia, but he knows quite well now, and because of who he is he could help those exploited workers enormously. Despicably, Jordan continues to ignore them. Worse yet, Shaquille O'Neal, Andre Agassi, Pete Sampras, and other athletes and celebrities who have multi-million dollar endorsement contracts remain silent.

Such irresponsibility is unworthy of anyone involved in physical education and sport. Certainly, those involved as academics have a responsibility to examine closely what effects political, economic, and social policies are having on the overall well-being of workers throughout the world who make sporting goods and equipment. A concerned attention is desperately needed if the world is to be built on humane considerations. Efficacy can only be achieved by looking beyond personal and professional lives and becoming a part of the millions of individuals and hundreds of groups who are confronting, resisting, opposing corporate decisions that bring exploitation and injustice upon those who make our sporting goods and equipment. The slogan of organised labour is apt: "an injury to one is an injury to all."
One of the main challenges is simply convincing ourselves that the adverse effects of globalisation can be successfully fought and that current practices are not inevitable. In reality, specific policies imposed by politicians and corporate decision-makers result from the corporatisation of the world (THE NATION, 1996).

We can begin by renouncing our content with sporting goods and equipment made by children, and by men and women earning sub-poverty wages working in inhumane conditions. The role for caring and compassionate people in the physical education and sport professions is finding ways to join the struggle for the betterment of other humankind, to intervene in, and help shape the future of, our own life, but also the lives of exploited workers. Social justice must be valued more than personal gain, and it must be realised that our own personal gain comes in the struggle for social justice. After all, we are most in touch with our own individual humanity when we stand close to all of humanity (HOUCK and WILLIAMS, 1996).

We can employ the strategies against the exploitation and social injustices of the export processing system that were so effective against apartheid in South Africa. We can be the conscience of what is going on. We can take that which is unconscionable and make it unprofitable. We can "Just Do It" (WHYE, 1996, p.7B). The needs of working people can only be met through a worldwide coalition of labour and other movements. "Efforts to rein in the runaway global economy need to be international. But long-term solutions to today's social problems will also require a range of small, local initiatives that are as diverse as the cultures and environments in which that take place" (NORBERG-HODGE, 1996, p.23).

In many countries organising is underway. Powerful coalitions are being built that represent the interests of those who are being victimised by the global economy (CAVANAGH and BROAD, 1996; HALL, 1995). Evidence that activism and struggle do have an impact is seen in the announcement by Nike Inc. Chairman Phil Knight that "...In the face of persistent criticism over foreign labour practices, his company (would) do more to monitor labour practices at its contract manufacturing plants in Asia" (ECONOMIC UPDATES, 1996, p.1).

Social analyst NOAM CHOMSKY (1992) noted that if it is assumed that there is no hope, then it is guaranteed that there will be no hope. If it is assumed that there are opportunities to change things, there is a chance of contributing to make a better world. That is the choice. But if the belief is relinquished that a difference can be made, then the forces of [oppression and] greed will have won.

References

ASSOCIATED PRESS: "Gifford offers to pay workers". In: *Greeley (Colorado) Tribune*, 31 May 1996, p.11A.

BALLINGER, J.: "The new free-trade heel". In: *Harper's Magazine*, August 1992, pp. 46-47.

BARNET, J., and CAVANAGH, J.: *Global dreams: imperial corporations and the New World order.* New York, Simon and Schuster, 1994.

BAUM, B.: "Jordan expects Nike to 'do the right thing' in anti-sweatshop crusade". In: *Rocky Mountain News*, 7 June 1996, p.4B.

BERBEROGLU, B.: *The political economy of development: development theory and the prospect for change in the third world.* Albany, NY, SUNY Press, 1992.

BROOKES, B., and MADDEN, P.: *The globe-trotting sports shoe.* London, Christian Aid, 1995.

BROWNE, H., and SIMS, B.: *Runaway America: U.S. jobs and factories on the move.* Albuquerque, NM, Resource Center Press, 1993.

BYRNE, J.A.: "How high can CEO pay go?". In: *Business Week*, 22 April 1996, pp. 100-106.

CAVANAGH, J., and BROAD, R.: "Global reach: workers fight the multi-nationals". In: *The Nation*, 18 March 1996, pp.21-24.

CHOMSKY, N.: *Chronicles of dissent.* Monroe, ME, Common Courage Press, 1992.

CRAYPU, C., and NISSEN, B.: *Grand designs: the impact of corporate strategies on workers, unions, and communities.* Washington, D.C., ILR Press, 1993.

DEWIND, J., and KINLEY, D.H.III: *Aiding migration: the impact of international development assistance on Haiti.* Boulder, CO, Westview Press, 1988.

ECONOMIC UPDATES: The new Oregon Trail: Oregon economic updates. (*http://www.teleport.com/~garski/hi-tech.htm*) 21 August 1996, p.1.

ENLOE, C.: "The globetrotting sneaker". In: *Ms.*, March/April 1995, pp.10-15.

ESTES, R.: *Tyranny of the bottom line*: why corporations make good people do bad things. San Francisco, Berrett-Koehler Publishers, 1996.

FRANK, R.H., and COOK, P.J.: *The winner-take-all society*. New York, Free Press, 1995.

GORDON, D.M.: *Fat and mean: the corporate squeeze of working American and the myth of managerial 'downsizing'*. New York, Free Press, 1996.

GREENHOUSE, S.: "Lone crusader puts sweatshops back in public eye". In: *The Denver Post*, 23 June 1996, p.23A.

HALL, M.F.: *Poor people's social movement organizations: the goal is to win*. New York, Greenwood Publishing Group, 1995.

HARRISON, B.: *Lean and mean: the changing landscape of corporate power in the age of flexibility*. New York, Basic Books, 1994.

HOUCK, J.W., and WILLIAMS, O.F., (Eds.): *Is the good corporation dead? Social responsibility in a global economy*. Lanham, MD, Rowman and Littlefield Publishers, 1996.

INGI LABOR WORKING GROUP: "Unjust but doing it! Nike operations in Indonesia". In: *Inside Indonesia*, June 1991.

JOSEPH, J.D.: "Say no to the Nike mafia". In: *The Progressive Populist*, July 1996, p. 23.

KOPINAK, K.: Desert capitalism: *Maquiladoras in North America's western industrial corridor*. Tucson, University of Arizona Press, 1996.

KORTEN, D.C.: *When corporations rule the world*. San Francisco: Berrett-Koehler Publishers, 1995.

KRIEGER, D.: "Jordan not happy he was shoe-horned into controversy". In: *Rocky Mountain News*, 7 June 1996, p.2C.

KUTTNER, R.: "Happy labor day, Joe Six-Pack. Have some crumbs". In: *Business Week*, 9 September 1996, p.13.

MANDER, J.: "The dark side of globalization". In: *The Nation*, 15/22 July 1996, pp.9-10, 12-14.

MCFATE, K., LAWSON, R., and WILSON, W.J., (Eds.): *Poverty, inequality, and the future of social policy: western states in the New World order*. New York, Russell Sage, 1995.

NELSON, J.I.: *Post-industrial capitalism: exploring economic inequality in America*. Thousand Oaks, Sage, 1995.

NORBERG-HODGE, H.: "Break up the monoculture". In: *The Nation*, 15/22 July 1996, pp.20-23.

OMICINSKI, J.: "Gap between rich, poor much wider, U.N. says". In: *The Denver Post*, 18 July 1996, p.28A.

SALEM-FITZGERALD, D'J.: "House bill targets child labor". In: *The Denver Post*, 16 July 1996, p.5A.

SCHAEFFER, R.: *Understanding Globalization*. Lanham, MD: Rowman and Littlefield Publications, 1996.

SCHANDBERG, S.H.: "Six Cents an Hour". In: *Life*, June 1996, pp.38-46.

SKLAR, H.: "Upsized CEOs". *Z Magazine*, 9, June 1996, pp.32-35.

STROM, S.: "Kathie Lee's crisis uncovered sweatshop tangle". *The Denver Post*, 1 July 1996, p.2E.

SWEENEY, J.J.: *America needs a raise: fighting for economic security and social justice*. New York, Houghton Mifflin, 1996.

THE NATION: *"Incorporating the world"*. 15-22 July 1996, p.3.

THE WORLD BANK: *World development report 1995: workers in an integrating world*. New York, Oxford University Press, 1995.

THOMAS, K.: "Kathie Lee goes to Washington". In: *USA Today*, 15 July 1996a, p.1D.

THOMAS, K: "Gifford testifies". In: *USA Today*, 16 July 1996b, p.2D.

WHYE, C.: "The saga of Kathie, Nike, Spike and the rest of us". *The Denver Post*, 27 June 1996, p.7B.

WIRPSA, L.: "Where every Rawlings baseball is a foul ball". *National Catholic Reporter*, 28 December 1990, p.1.

WOLFF, E.: *Top Heavy: A study of increasing inequality of wealth in America*. New York, The Twentieth Century Fund, 1995.

Chapter 20

Structural Changes in the Sports Industry in Japan

Munehiko Harada

Introduction

In post-World War II years, Japan underwent sharp economic development and soon registered the highest trade profit in the world for the latter half of this century. Concomitant with material affluence in society, the Japanese are seeking enrichment in body and mind. Priority has shifted from basic subsistence needs and concerns to issues regarding quality of life, inclusive of leisure. Governmental planning also aims at developing a more spiritually as well as materially sound nation into the 21st century as initiatives are being implemented to reduce working hours while providing infrastructure for leisure and sport. Revamping a work-oriented society to one with a leisure orientation has meant rapid development and structural changes in Japan's sports industry. This contribution analyses the current state of trends in working hours and increasing leisure demands and provides an explanatory overview of the developmental process, highlighting some structural changes in sports business in Japan.

Changing Japanese Lifestyle

Actual annual working hours in Japan show a major difference before and after World War II. Immediately prior to the war, annual working hours in Japan averaged 2,950. A significant reduction in working hours occurred, however, following the introduction of the Labour Standards Law in 1947, which imposed an eight-hour-a-day, 48-hour-a-week work system. Between 1947 and 1950, people worked an average of 2,200 hours per year, a reduction (induced by post-war democratisation and legislative processes) of 700 hours from the previous annual working hours.

Subsequently, work hours continued to increase from the time of post-war recovery to the early stages of strong economic growth, with the highest post-war annual working hours of 2432 in 1960. Daily working hours saw little change during that period, but 18 days were added to the yearly work schedule. During the period 1960-1975, high levels of economic growth and the adverse affects of the first oil crisis combined to reverse the trend toward an increase in working hours, with annual working hours dropping to 2,064 by 1975. The next decade witnessed the second oil crisis, a short-term economic downturn caused by the increased international value of the yen, ensuing rapid economic growth and an upward trend in the annual total hours, which peaked at 2110 working hours in 1985 (the Japanese figures are an industry average taken from companies with 30 employees or more and excluding the agricultural, forestry, and marine industries). This level was maintained until 1988, when the Labour Standards Law was revised following calls from both within Japan and abroad for shortened working hours. The 1988 revision forged a reduced working hours policy (*Jitan Seisaku*), with a target of a 40-hour working week. The policy, promoted strongly by the government, was intended to reduce the working hours of each individual worker, to stimulate leisure-related consumption during the expanded non-work hours and to fuel domestic demand. Government plans called for a sudden reduction in annual working hours by 300 hours by 1992 (four years after the enactment of the policy) thus, bringing Japan into line with Europe and North America at 1,800 working hours per year. The plans stayed on the drawing table. Long-term poor economic conditions over the following years, however, led to a reduction in working hours, which fell to 1,909 hours per year in 1995.

Mature Economy and Impoverished Leisure

The strong development of the Japanese economy during the high growth years of the 1960s and 1970s was followed by a period of maturation starting from the 1980s and continuing into the 1990s. With the increased growth of the Japanese securities market by the latter half of the 1980s and the aggregate market value of the Tokyo Stock Exchange accounting for 44% of the world aggregate market value, Japan became, nominally, the richest country in the world. Material wealth was high and an unprecedented consumer boom pervaded the country. Rocketing economic growth encouraged widespread popular speculation and membership rights at expensive golf ranges and fine arts sold like wildfire as speculative ventures. It was a period when the aggregate value of land in Japan, which is only 1/25 the area of that of the United States, reached four times the worth of the aggregate value of the land of the U.S.A, or $16 trillion.

The period also exhibited striking changes in leisure consumption patterns of the Japanese. Leisure became a desired object and people competed to stay ahead of each other through consumption of leisure goods and activities. Generally, there was a pervasive ambience of extravagance with zealous shopping overseas for brand-name goods and purchases of overseas' hotels and resorts being standard practice. Affluent companies overflowing with money turned their attention away from their main lines of business and towards real estate and overseas investments. The four years from 1987 through 1990, when the Nikkei Average Stock Index sustained a rapid ascent, were termed the 'Abnormal Consumer Behaviour Period' when the "spirit of modern capitalism", based on highly theoretical principles of lifestyle and living, had become an all but obsolete phrase.

The strong bullish economy finally yielded to sluggish economic conditions in 1991 and the once extravagant Japanese were suddenly obliged to seek a simpler lifestyle. With regard to leisure, the trend to seek satisfaction as a proportion of money expended changed direction and attitudes emerged, whereby people sought for leisure time spent simply but meaningfully. Indicative of the change is the recent popularity of "auto camps", "outdoor sports", and "exercise walking", which mark a return to a simple lifestyle caused by the economic downturn. However, the search for simplicity has come about because of a decrease in income and is a reaction against abnormal consumer behaviour.

The actual composition of "impoverished leisure " has not actually changed very much. There are 17,000 'pachinko' parlours nation wide, for example, where people can have fun gambling as part of their daily routine. That number far exceeds the 1,800 libraries and 800 fine art and natural history museums in Japan. The leisure activity most enjoyed by workers is watching television and simply resting. Only 20% of Japanese males feel they lead an affluent lifestyle. The amount of land area in city parks per capita is a mere 2.3 square feet in Tokyo. This figure does not bear comparison with the 30 square feet afforded by parks in London or the 45.7 square feet allotted in Washington D.C. Additionally, most of the leisure activities that take place in large cities are dependent on the purchase of city-style leisure services provided by the leisure industry. The so-called bursting of the over-inflated economic bubble in the latter half of the 1980s, when material affluence had reached a peak, served to stimulate a re-appraisal of the meaning of wealth. Today in Japan, inner satisfaction as an important component of quality of life, outweighs striving for material wealth in the societal value system.

The Developing Sport Market

From the 1980's to the 1990's, the Japanese leisure market experienced accelerated growth. The decade was a "period of exponential growth" (HARADA, 1993a) with the sports market also continuously growing. In 1982, the market was at US$25 billion; by 1992, the growth achieved had reached US$60 billion. The favourable market conditions continued until 1992, since when the market has slowly declined. The Gross National Sports Product (GNSP) - the sum of the output and services generated by the sports industry - totalled US$56.7 billion in 1995, lower by 0.8% than the 1994 GNSP of US$57.2 billion. The annual growth percentile was slightly dented in 1992 in the aftermath of the 'bubble' economy. At that time, although steady growth was predicted to continue in pace with greater leisure-minded trends exhibited by the Japanese people, because of a return to a simple lifestyle, the GNSP reached US$60.1 billion in 1992 and commenced its decline in 1993.

Evolving Sports Business

Structural changes in the sports industry that have accompanied market scale expansion have been neither small nor insignificant until recently. The sports industry in Japan has encompassed 3 distinct business sectors: (i) the sports facilities industry; (ii) the sporting goods industry; and (iii) the sports service and media industry.

The sports facilities industry provides the consumer with a determined location and facility for sports and recreation which can be roughly divided according to the conditions of locations into an urban type for daily recreation and a resort type, which takes advantage of natural resources. The former type includes baseball diamonds, bowling alleys, golf ranges, swimming pools etc. and the latter includes ski resorts, camp sites, marinas and the like.

The sporting goods industry includes all equipment and gear used in sports and recreation, which can be subdivided into outdoor sports, competitive sports and health/fitness activities based on product usage. The sports service and media industry is occupied to a large extent large proportion by sports journalism, which is associated with sports viewing and written media. This includes newspapers and magazines as printed media, radio and TV as broadcast media, and videos and movies as image media. Consulting and skill instruction related to sports are also part of this industry, which has evolved with the development of Japan's economy from the mid-1970's on into the 1980's.

Emergence of New Compounded Sectors

1. The sports distribution industry

At present, the traditional sports industries are overlapping their interests while gradually changing the structure of their relationship (HARADA, 1993). Recently, two new compounded industries have emerged from the evolving sports industrial sectors. One of these is the sports distribution industry that was born of the sporting goods industry and sports service and media industry. One of the more notable trends here is the large-size manufacturer's break from the "manufacturing only" line of business. Worth mentioning are, for example, the manufacturer's absorption of wholesale services by directly operating dealerships and increased profits raised by shortening and widening distribution routes. In other words, the manufacturer is no longer limiting operations to the production of goods alone, but by being aggressively involved in wholesale and retail services, has launched the sports distribution industry. Also not to be forgotten is the increase in stores with retailers "going chain" and the expansion of the distribution industry as a result of development and promotion of name brand products. As a matter of fact, large volume retailers *Alpen* and *Victoria* have set up a distribution system by developing chain operations across the entire country, offering the consumer low priced and good quality name brand goods. What has been an important sales point is to go beyond merely providing high quality products, and bring in services that offer the consumer an avenue of communication.

2. Facility management industry

The other new compounded industry is the facility management industry born from the overlapping interest in managerial operations of the sports facility industry and the software of the sports service and media industry. Some typical examples of the business applications include fitness clubs, swimming schools and tennis schools. Fitness clubs have added the membership system to facilities enabling members to enjoy complete services. In both cases, market scale is expanding and further development is expected from the public as well as private sectors. For example, the number of fitness clubs has increased during the first half of the 1980's. The expansion of the fitness club industry has been influenced by increases in people's interest towards health, as well as the fitness and health boom associated with western countries. Also, due to surplus capital of the 1980's (during the 'bubble economy' period), there were circumstances in which Japanese companies were willing to risk money and enter into the health business striving to be at the forefront of the boom (HARADA, 1993b).

3. Ultimate sports industry: modern professional sports

There exists an area where all three sports industries and the newly created industries overlap one another. Here are found sports tourism and professional soccer (J League), which are expected to grow as sports businesses in the future. In regard to sports tourism, it has been reported in England for example that sports are incorporated in tourism to the extent of 56% (GLYPTIS and JACKSON, 1993). This would indicate the need for Japan as well to direct attention to the association of sport and tourism. Large-size sporting goods manufacturers in Japan have already begun to offer comprehensive sports services by arranging sites, facilities, means of transport and hotel accommodation as well as equipment rentals. Further development also is expected from major sports clubs and commission operators who will be functioning as travel agents within membership service systems to co-ordinate participation in the Honolulu Marathon or overseas golf tours.

In April 1993, professional soccer was launched in Japan with the official start of the J. League. With the first round of action over, statistics show overall attendance of some 1.5 million spectators with an average of 16,000 per game. Sales in J. League-related markets have reached a total of US$1.05 billion dollars.

The reason for the success of professional soccer in Japan is believed to lie in the following factors: (a) a management strategy different from that of professional baseball that keeps the sport out of company internal affairs and roots the club in the local area; (b) broadcast and licensing rights are entirely the property of the league; (c) signing of foreign players and a reformed consciousness of the game; and (d) penetration of a post modern consumer market mood (that bases consumption on dependency and symbolic value). When viewed from the structural perspective of the sports industry, the J. League is making headway as a new and influential sports business that effectively draws from of a mixture of the sporting goods, facility and space, and service and news sectors. Cautious voices have nonetheless been raised about a possible drop in popularity since the league has rapidly progressed. Furthermore, income is not yet sufficient to balance player contracts, estimated to average US10 million dollars per team thus, causing many clubs to be in the red in the inaugural season. Two opinions have been raised concerning this matter: (i) a belief that problems can be avoided as long as participating companies compensate the deficit as declared losses; and (ii) the fact that businesses can at anytime quit sponsoring a team depending on how the sport might proceed in the future.

Conclusion

Sports in Japan grew rapidly from the 1980's on into the 1990's. Though growth was slowed down with the demise of the 'bubble economy' in 1991, market scale continued and still continues to grow steadfastly. However, as seen in the example of the J. League, many cases can be cited of advertisements and commercials causing a "dependency effect", stirring consumerism and bewitching the consumer with the image and symbolic value of the sport. This kind of boom, typical of post-modern consumer markets, carries the risk of ending the J. League as a mere and simple fad (SAEKI, 1993). Nevertheless, as life styles change in Japan, people should be showing greater interest in lifetime sports activities and thus, sports business on the whole should see an increase in market scale.

References

GLYPTIS, S., and JACKSON, G.: *Sport and tourism.* Paper presented at the 3rd Leisure Studies Association International Conference, Loughborough University, England, 1993.

HARADA, M.: Basic theory of sports industry. In: *Sports Business,* 132(9), 1993a, pp.38-39.

HARADA, M.: *Towards a renaissance of leisure in Japan.* Paper presented at the 3rd Leisure Studies Association International Conference, Loughborough University, England, 1993b.

SAEKI, T.: Sports and current society (in Japanese). In: *Physical Education,* 10, 1993, pp.10-13.

Chapter 21

A Comparative Analysis of Policy Initiatives in Tobacco-sponsored Sport

Eric J. Solberg, March L. Krotee and Alan M. Blum

Introduction

Cigarette smoking has been directly related to more than 434,000 deaths each year in the United States, and more than 3 million deaths annually on a global scale (CENTERS FOR DISEASE CONTROL [CDC], 1994). Ironically, while tobacco use has been identified as the most preventable cause of death and disease, tobacco products remain the most advertised and promoted products of our epoch (BLUM, 1980). A primary means of promoting cigarettes and other tobacco products (both in terms of financial investment and visibility) has been through the brand-name sponsorship of sporting events, teams, and individual athletes. However, little research has broadened the understanding of the role and effectiveness of legislative efforts to restrict or eliminate tobacco advertising and promotion, including tobacco-sponsored sport.

Historical Dimensions of Tobacco and Sport

The connection between tobacco and sport is not new. In fact, its relationship can be traced to nearly a century ago when North Carolina's James Buchanan Duke built his great tobacco dynasty and baseball players' photographs first appeared on trading cards (BLUM, 1988; KROTEE, SOLBERG and BLUM, 1993). Such cards were not the bubble-gum trading " that we think of today, but rather, were contained in cigarette packages (the cards were used to keep the soft-pack "stiff" to protect its contents) (BLUM, 1995).

Many variables have played a role in the now synonymous ties between tobacco and sport. The very fact that tobacco use and sport are universal is just one variable in this connection. In North America, the relationship between tobacco and sport evolved primarily out of baseball (BLUM, 1988). Numerous brands of tobacco products (primarily cigarettes and cigars) have been named after sports themes. One brand of plug tobacco, *Bull Durham*, was advertised on outfield fences in the Southern baseball circuit; hence, the name "bullpen" was attached to the warm-up area behind the fence (BLUM, 1988).

So closely associated was a cigarette brand to the baseball team it sponsored that baseball fans identified their loyalty in such a way that invariably a New York Giant fan smoked Chesterfield, a Yankee fan Camel, and a Dodger fan Lucky Strike (BLUM, 1990). Baseball stars such as Lou Gehrig and Joe DiMaggio became synonymous with Camel cigarettes, as did Stan Musial, Ewell Blackwell, and Ted Williams with Chesterfield when their advertisements inundated score cards, programmes, and the mass media (BLUM, 1988).

Sport appears to have become a frequent motif in cigarette advertising in the early decades of this century - tennis, golf, swimming, running, baseball, football and skiing were frequently depicted as activities requiring a cigarette for enhanced performance and enjoyment. Such sport themes in cigarette advertising reached the public-at-large through print media (magazines and newspapers), billboards, and especially radio and television.

Methods

The study reported here investigated the enactment and enforcement of policies in four countries designed to restrict or eliminate tobacco advertising and promotion, including tobacco-sponsored sport (table 1). The methodology employed in the study is best described as ethnographic inquiry (MARSHALL and ROSSMAN, 1989) since it included inductively oriented strategies, employing naturalistic observation over time as the primary approach to data collection.

Table 1.
Legislative efforts to restrict tobacco advertising and promotion

Country	Total Ban	Restrictions on the use of mass media (television, radio, press, billboards)	Restrictions on the promotion of tobacco through sponsorship of sports and cultural events	Restrictions on the content, format or location of advertising
Australia				
Australian Capital Terr.		X	X	
South Australia			X	
Victoria		X	X	
Western Aust.	X	X	X	
Canada	X	X	X	
France	X	X	X	
United States		X		

Note: Legislation interpreted by World Health Organisation.

Adapted from ROEMER, (1993).

During a five-year period beginning in 1990, ethnographic strategies were applied to the comparative case studies of the four countries (United States, Canada, France, and Australia). These strategies included a combination of data collection techniques: i) historical methods (retrieval of data and archival analyses); ii) observation through film ethnography; and iii) visits and personal communication.

Historical data collection methods were employed to document specific examples of tobacco-sponsored sport prior to the enactment of policies, which were intended to restrict or ban tobacco-sponsored sport. Various sources of historical data were also analysed including public reports (newspapers, periodicals, trade journals), contemporary records (annual corporate reports, business and trade papers, newsletters), government documents (health reports, transcripts of hearings, published monographs), conference proceedings, as well as photographs, video and audio tapes.

Visits were made to each of the countries involved in the study. During the visits, efforts were made to attend tobacco-sponsored sports events and document tobacco promotion activities by means of direct observation, informal interviews and television. Televised events were also videotaped for research and educational purposes. When events could not be attended or videotaped, information and data was gained through personal communication with selected individuals in each country.

Results

1. United States

In the United States, a modest effort has been made to restrict tobacco advertising and promotion, the cornerstones for which are two significant pieces of federal legislation. In 1969, Congress passed the Public Health Cigarette Smoking Act, which prohibited cigarette advertising on television and radio (the Act became effective on January 2, 1971). The Comprehensive Smokeless Tobacco Health Education Act, enacted by Congress in 1986, further prohibited the advertising and promotion of smokeless ("spitting") tobacco brands on television and radio. A third but less significant measure, related to the content of cigarette advertisements, was enacted in 1982, when the Federal Cigarette Labeling and Advertising Act was amended to require cigarette advertisements to carry one of three rotating warning labels.

The dramatic increase in tobacco sponsorship of sport in the United States began to occur in 1971, the year in which cigarette advertisements were banned on television. It was then that R.J. Reynolds Tobacco Company teamed up with NASCAR (National Association for Stock Car Racing) and began one of the most durable relationships in sport marketing, the Winston Cup (named after R. J. Reynolds' top selling cigarette brand). In 1971 Philip Morris' Virginia Slims cigarette brand began sponsoring a women's tennis circuit (BLUM, 1985).

Similarly, 1973 witnessed the birth of the "Marlboro Cup," a nationally televised thoroughbred horse race (sponsored by Marlboro cigarettes). The Marlboro Cup was unusual because it marked the first time that a premier horse race was created from scratch as a commercially sponsored event, rather than as a relationship to an already well-established race (BLUM, 1988). Also during the 1970s, U.S. tobacco companies began their sponsorship of soccer. The world's most popular sport has long had financial ties with tobacco companies in several countries (BLUM, 1988). The international telecast of the World Cup, the premier, one-month long quadrennial tournament involving national teams from 32 countries, drew a television audience of 10 billion in 1982 and 12.5 billion in 1986. The event in 1982, held in Spain, was co-sponsored by Winston cigarettes (U.S. Tobacco Journal, 1982).

No other sport provides more television coverage of tobacco sponsorship programmes than motor sports (BLUM, 1985; BLUM, 1991). Since 1971, R.J. Reynolds' support of motor sports has grown from individual NASCAR (National Association for Stock Car Racing) events to sponsoring the entire NASCAR circuit of 31 televised races (called the Winston Cup Series).

Since 1975, Winston has teamed up to sponsor the NHRA (National Hot Rod Association) Winston Drag Racing Series of 19 nationally televised events (the company also sponsors a drag racing team/car with their Camel cigarettes ["Smokin' Joe"] theme). Television has extended NHRA Winston Drag Racing's reach to more than 230 million viewers annually in the United States (NHRA, 1992). The goal of total coverage for NHRA Winston Drag Racing events was achieved in 1986, and in 1988 included more than 140 hours of television coverage in the United States, through NBC, ESPN, and TNN (The Nashville Network) (NHRA, 1992).

Philip Morris' involvement in auto racing kept pace with that of R.J. Reynolds, also shortly after direct cigarette advertisements were banned from television. The company's primary support has been given to CART (Championship Auto Racing Team) Indy-car racing and Formula One auto racing through its Marlboro cigarette brand (GLOEDE, 1988). An example of the extent of the television exposure received by Marlboro in Indy-car racing during a single season is provided by JOYCE JULIUS and ASSOCIATES (1994): according to the company's *Sponsors Report* (which documents the amount of in-focus exposure auto racing sponsors receive), Philip Morris's Marlboro cigarette brand received more than 5 hours 39 minutes of national television exposure in 1993. A single auto race in 1989, the "Marlboro Grand Prix", calculated 5,933 visual and verbal mentions for Marlboro in a single 90 minute telecast of the event, accounting for more than 47 minutes of the total air-time (BLUM, 1991).

The virtual lack of enforcement of the Public Health Cigarette Smoking Act of 1969 and the Comprehensive Smokeless Tobacco Health Education Act of 1986 have led policy makers, public health advocates, researchers, and consumer and health advocacy groups to propose policy efforts designed to rectify the problem. New policy initiatives have been introduced in the United States Congress to close the "loopholes" in already enacted legislation.

Representatives Henry Waxman (D-California) and Mike Synar (D-Oklahoma), and Senator Edward Kennedy (D-Massachusetts) have introduced legislation during recent years. The one common element in each of these policy initiatives has been to restrict or prohibit tobacco-sponsorship of sport. None of the Bills passed their respective committees.

More recently, on August 10, 1995, President Bill Clinton unveiled a set of proposed regulations on cigarette and smokeless tobacco marketing. The U.S. Food and Drug Administration, an agency that has never before taken action on the tobacco issue developed the proposed regulations.

The proposed regulations would, among other things, "prohibit a sponsored event from being identified with a cigarette or smokeless tobacco brand name or any other brand identifying characteristic" (DEPARTMENT OF HEALTH and HUMAN SERVICES, 1995). However, the proposed regulations would permit any athletic, musical, artistic, or other social or cultural event to be sponsored in the name of the Tobacco Company, providing that the corporation, in whose name the sponsorship would undertake, had been established prior to January 1, 1995. This latter provision was intended to prevent manufacturers from circumventing this restriction by incorporating (separately) each brand that they manufacture for use in sponsorship. It was intended that the proposed regulations would become effective in 1997.

2. Canada

Prior to the enactment of federal legislation by the Canadian government to eliminate tobacco advertising and promotion, the tobacco industry agreed to a voluntary code of advertising in the late 1960s. The code included a ban on cigarette advertising on television, which became effective January 1, 1972.

Even before the voluntary withdrawal of cigarette advertising from television by the Canadian tobacco Industry, the ties between tobacco and sport had begun. For example, in 1969 the Canadian Olympic-training Regatta (training centre for windsurfing) was sponsored by cigarette manufacturer Rothmans Pall Mall Canada Limited (now Rothmans, Benson & Hedges Inc.). According to Michael Davies, then public relations officer for the Regatta training centre, "tobacco companies don't sponsor regattas because they think windsurfing is a marvelous thing... They want to sell cigarettes" (MANGIACASALE, 1985, p.440).

After the removal of cigarette advertising from Canadian television, Canada's three major tobacco companies (Imperial Tobacco Ltd., Rothmans-Benson and Hedges Inc. and RJR-MacDonald Inc.) increased their presence as sponsors of sport, including auto racing, equestrian (horse jumping), golf, skiing, and ice hockey. Of the three companies, Imperial Tobacco has maintained the lead as the primary tobacco-sponsor of sport in Canada (Imperial Tobacco Ltd. is owned by Imasco Ltd., and its primary cigarette brands are Player's, du Maurier, and Matinee).

Much like the tobacco and sport connection in the United States, televised tobacco-sponsored sport in Canada experienced an increase with the involvement in motor sports. In 1961, Imperial Tobacco's Player's cigarette brand began sponsoring auto racing, staging the first international race in Canada - the 'Player's 200' (PLAYER'S LTD., 1993). Player's involvement in motor sports was a major factor in the evolution of the sport in Canada, bringing the Formula One Grand Prix to the country for the first time in 1967. During the 1970s, the Player's Challenge for Formula Atlantic cars (a smaller version of the cars raced in Formula One races) allowed Canadian drivers to begin competing at higher levels of competition. In 1986, Player's cigarette brand began sponsoring a Canadian version of NASCAR racing (inviting the best drivers from the U.S. to compete) with the inaugural event called the 'Player's 500'. The single event grew to include a series of five televised events (the Player's Cup). Player's has since added powerboat racing to its list of sponsored motor sports.

The first apparently successful effort to break the connection between tobacco and sport in Canada evolved in 1984, after RJR-MacDonald had signed a five-year contract to sponsor the Canadian Ski Association national championships providing its Export 'A' cigarette brand extensive exposure on television (MANGIACASALE, 1985). The Canadian Non-Smokers' Rights Association paid for full-page advertisements in major Canadian newspapers with hard-hitting text that read, "... should the Canadian Ski Association get in bed with the tobacco industry". The anti-smoking advertisements, along with some behind-the-scenes lobbying, influenced the Canadian federal government to announce a policy that ended tobacco industry sponsorship of federally funded sport (a policy that required only Executive action and not formal legislation). The contract between RJR-MacDonald and the Canadian Ski Association was permitted to run its course, but a compromise prohibited the Export 'A' cigarette brand from appearing at all national events.

Canada is most recognised for its enactment in 1988 of Bill C-51 (the Tobacco Products Control Act), which sought to ban all tobacco advertising and promotion in Canada, including sponsorship of sport by tobacco brand names. The federal legislation, which was phased in over a period of three years (most of its provisions were effective January 1, 1989), including several restrictions on tobacco product advertising and promotion, e.g. the prohibition of the use of a tobacco brand name "that promotes a cultural or sporting activity or event" (TOBACCO PRODUCTS CONTROL ACT, 1988). Sub-section 1 of Section 6 of the Act states that "the full name of a manufacturer or importer of tobacco products ... may be used ... in a representation to the public that promotes a cultural or sporting activity or event" (TOBACCO PRODUCTS CONTROL ACT, 1988). In other words, tobacco manufacturers were still allowed to sponsor sporting events using the full names of the corporations or manufacturers.

Additionally, the Act exempted "the retransmission of radio or television broadcasts originating outside Canada" (TOBACCO PRODUCTS CONTROL ACT, 1988). Thus, satellite, cable, or pay-per-view broadcasts of sporting events sponsored by tobacco brand names originating outside Canada's borders were not restricted under the Act. This exemption may have led Imperial Tobacco to increase its presence in Indy-car racing in the United States, whereby they were able to sponsor a team with the Player's cigarette brand name with no restrictions, realising that the television broadcasts originating from the U.S. would reach Canadian audiences.

While the passage of the Tobacco Products Control Act was championed by health, medical, and consumer organisations in Canada (and other countries) as a successful legislative effort to ban tobacco advertising and promotion, the ability of the tobacco industry to circumvent many provisions in the law soon became apparent. For example, in order to end-run the provision prohibiting tobacco-sponsored sport, tobacco companies established corporations with names matching tobacco brands sold in Canada (SWORD, 1992). Imperial Tobacco, which sponsored motor sports with its cigarette brand Player's, formed a new corporation named Player's Ltd. in order to continue sponsoring motor sports events. Similarly, because the Tobacco Products Control Act also prohibited tobacco advertising on billboards, the newly formed Player's Ltd. was able to promote its motor sports connection in this medium. In a similar vein, du Maurier cigarette-sponsored equestrian events were sponsored by du Maurier Ltd., another new corporation formed by Imperial Tobacco.

The ultimate reaction by the tobacco industry to the Tobacco Products Control Act came not in the form of new ways to circumvent the law, but rather through court battles. Imperial Tobacco Ltd. and RJR-MacDonald Inc. launched a court challenge in 1989 when they sued the government, arguing that the Act infringed the freedom of expression guaranteed by the 1981 Charter of Rights and Freedoms - a freedom that previous court decisions have extended to commercial speech. In September 1995, the Canadian Supreme Court ruled that the Tobacco Products Control Act violated the tobacco industry's constitutional right to free speech (MCKENNA, 1995). This ruling means that tobacco companies in

Canada are free to resume all forms of advertising and promotion (in their original form), including sponsorship of sport.

3. France

Beginning in 1976, French legislation placed restrictions on the advertising and promotion of tobacco products. Tobacco advertising was prohibited from television and radio. Billboard advertisements were restricted to "tombstone" format, in which only the name of the product, the package and the lettering could be shown (ROEMER, 1993). Sponsorship of sport and sports events by the tobacco industry was prohibited, with the exception of motor sports.

Such restrictions were easily circumvented by tobacco companies as they began using their tobacco brand names in advertisements for other products such as lighters, matches, clothes, and travel services (BITTOUN, 1985). The ban on tobacco advertising on television was easily circumvented through increased tobacco sponsorship of motor sports, which was exempt from the 1976 legislation.

As a result of the tobacco industry's ability to end-run the legislation, in 1991 the French Parliament repealed the 1976 law and enacted a new statute (the "Loi Evin"), banning all advertising of tobacco products, including

> ... indirect advertising of tobacco ... advertising for an agency, service, activity, product or article other than tobacco or a tobacco product, when that advertising, on account of its logo, presentation, use of trade mark, symbol, or any other distinctive design, is suggestive of tobacco or a tobacco product
>
> (ROEMER, 1993).

The new law, effective January 1, 1993, also banned tobacco-sponsored sport and sports events, including motor sports, which had previously been granted exemption from the 1976 French legislation.

In July 1992, six months before the new French legislation would be effective, a court in Quimper, ruled that the televised images (broadcast in France) of cigarette advertisements at Formula One Grand Prix auto races were illegal in accordance with the 1976 French law banning tobacco advertisements from television (SOLBERG and BLUM, 1993). The court ruled that the 1993 French Grand Prix would not be permitted to appear on French television, regardless of where the event was held. The Williams-Renault Formula One team, which at that time was sponsored by R.J. Reynolds' Camel cigarettes, was the main focus of the ruling. The court also demanded that the British-based Williams team pay a fine the equivalent of $5.6m. while the French engine manufacturer Renault was fined $765,000 for displaying the Camel logo at the Japanese and Australian Grand Prix. The court also warned TFI, the French television channel, which holds the exclusive right to the coverage of the French Grand Prix, that the Television Company would be fined $2,000 for each televised image of a tobacco brand logo.

In the wake of that decision, combined with the new legislation in France, the Federation Internationale du Sport Auto (FISA), the world-wide sanctioning organisation for Formula One racing, announced it would cancel the 1993 French Grand Prix, one of 16 annual FISA races. However, after a collaborative lobbying effort by the tobacco industry, automobile manufacturers, and racing associations in France, the French Senate passed an amendment that allowed the French Grand Prix to take place and be televised in France. Jean-Marie Ballestre, chairman of the French Federation of Automobile Sports and former chairman of FISA, claimed that the new French law banning all cigarette advertising would bring an end to auto racing in France, arguing that this would result in a loss of 500 million francs (US $100 million) to the French economy each year (BLUM and SOLBERG, 1993). In order to compensate for any possible financial loss of tobacco sponsorship, the Parliamentary amendment included a tax increase of 1 centime per cigarette (approximately US 4 cents per pack of 20 cigarettes) to be dedicated to sport.

Despite the courts well-intentioned efforts to enforce the law, nothing has prevented the broadcasts, via cable and satellite television, of tobacco-sponsored sports events originating outside of France. A visit to France in October 1994 revealed that Eurosport television broadcasts, originating from the United Kingdom, continue to broadcast tobacco-sponsored sports events from around the world, including motor sports, rugby, soccer, cricket, and others.

4. Australia

Legislative efforts in Australia, designed to restrict or eliminate tobacco advertising and promotion, are more difficult to follow in that the legislation has been left to individual states rather than set at the federal level. However, federal legislation was passed in 1976 prohibiting cigarette advertising on television and radio. This legislation was soon followed by an increase in tobacco sponsorship of televised sport (AUSTRALIA COUNCIL ON SMOKING and HEALTH, 1993).

The first major legislative attempt to restrict cigarette advertising and tobacco sponsorship of sport came in 1982 with the introduction of the Tobacco Products Advertising BW in Western Australia. The Bill was defeated in the Legislative Council.

The increased presence of televised tobacco-sponsored sport in Australia after the 1976 legislation prohibiting cigarette advertising on television and radio resulted in action by health groups to press for legislation designed specifically to end the tobacco-sport connection. In 1987, the Victorian Tobacco Act was passed, prohibiting tobacco sponsorship of sporting and cultural events (VICTORIAN HEALTH PROMOTION FOUNDATION, 1987). The Act also established the Victoria Health Promotion Foundation to provide replacement funding to sport and arts groups affected by the loss of funding from tobacco companies. However, the legislation also included a provision whereby the government could grant exemptions to certain sport or arts events or functions.

In 1988, a Bill similar to the Victorian Act was passed in South Australia (AUSTRALIAN COUNCIL ON SMOKING and HEALTH, 1993). The South Australia Act allows only a finite number of specific exemptions to the general prohibition of sport sponsorship by tobacco companies. These exemptions included the Australia Grand Prix (Formula One race) and international cricket matches.

In Western Australia, the Tobacco Control Act was passed in 1990 to restrict tobacco advertising and prohibit tobacco sponsorship of sport and arts. The Act also established the Western Australia Health Promotion Foundation to replace tobacco sponsorship dollars lost by certain groups. A similar law (The Tobacco Advertising Prohibition Act) was passed in 1991 in New South Wales, but a health promotion foundation was not part of the Act.

Finally, in 1992, the Federal Government passed the Tobacco Advertising Prohibition Act. The Act mandated an end to tobacco sponsorship of sport by December 31 1995, except for cricket, which was to end with the conclusion of the 1995-96 season.

The fact that exceptions to the various forms of state and federal legislation have been granted for certain tobacco-sponsored sport has enabled tobacco companies to maintain a presence in the world of sport and, more importantly, keep their brand names before the public via television. Most recently, the Australian Grand Prix, the Australian sports event with the largest worldwide television audience, was granted an exemption by the government for the 1996 race to take place in Melbourne, Australia.

The recent World Cup rugby matches, broadcast on worldwide television from Great Britain, prove that exemptions are not needed in order for tobacco companies to continue their sponsorship of Australia's national team. While Australian law may have prevented the tobacco industry from supporting the team in Australia, the Australian cigarette brand Winfield sponsored the team as it competed and won the 1995 World Cup in the United Kingdom. Millions of viewers from around the world watched the victorious Australian team, and the coach for Australia's "Winfield Kangaroos", who spoke on international television wearing his Winfield team cap.

A summary of findings is provided in table 2 to compare the major policy initiatives in tobacco-sponsored sport across countries. The dates indicate the year in which the policy(ies) became effective.

Table 2.

Summary of findings

	United States	Canada	France	Australia
Federal legislation prohibiting tobacco advertising on television	1971 (1) 1986 (2)	--	1976 (3)	1976
Tobacco industry voluntary ban of tobacco advertising from television	--	1972 (4)	--	--
Beginning of major involvement in sport sponsorship by tobacco companies	1971	1961	1968	1969
Federal legislation prohibiting tobacco sponsorship of sport	--	1989	1993	1996 (5)

Notes: (1) The tobacco industry agreed to legislation in the United States prohibiting cigarette advertising on television and radio. (2) Legislation banning smokeless tobacco from television and radio was enacted in 1986 in the United States. (3) The 1976 legislation in France prohibited tobacco advertising on television and radio, restricted billboard advertising to "tombstone" format, and prohibited tobacco-sponsored sport and sports events with the exception of motor sports. (4) In 1967, the tobacco industry agreed to a voluntary code of advertising, which included a ban on cigarette advertising on television. The code became effective in 1972. (5) Federal legislation in Australia to prohibit tobacco sponsorship of sport became effective in 1996 (passed in 1992). However, the states of Victoria, South Australia, Western Australia, and New South Wales had passed state legislation to restrict or prohibit tobacco sponsorship of sport in 1987, 1988, 1990 and 1991 respectively.

Conclusions

In spite of the best intention of health organisations to undermine and cease the association between tobacco and sports, one overwhelming conclusion is clear: namely the failure to predict the circumvention of the legislation passed to end tobacco sponsorship of sport. Tobacco Company involvement as major sport sponsors emerged in each country at approximately the same time legislation was passed prohibiting tobacco advertising on television. The tobacco industry's market research from throughout the world had shown that a sophisticated and effective form of advertising existed and was capable of replacing overt cigarette advertisements that were banned from television: sport sponsorship.

Despite legislative efforts to restrict or eliminate tobacco advertising and promotion from certain media, tobacco companies have been able to adapt and resurface with new ways to promote their brand names. It was as a result of legislation prohibiting tobacco advertising from television that tobacco companies were led to invest heavily in sport sponsorship, thereby maintaining a presence on television. Arguably, in terms of the number of total brand name impressions, tobacco's presence on television is greater than ever before!

Even when what appears to be the most stringent legislative efforts prohibiting tobacco sponsored sport, the tobacco industry has been able to circumvent such legislation, or has been granted exemptions for some of the most prominent sports events, often with large world-wide television audiences, such as Formula One auto races like the Australian Grand Prix.

As individual countries work to enact legislation to ban tobacco advertising and promotion, including tobacco sponsorship of sport, television broadcasts, because of new technology, circumvent the globe through satellite, cable, pay-per-view, and interactive television. The result is that tobacco companies, doubtless largely intentionally, but also with extraordinary good timing with advances in electronic tele-casting, have maintained their presence in sport and thus, have kept their brand names on television and before the public.

The world's number one selling cigarette brand is Marlboro, which is also one of the most prominent brands associated with sport throughout the world. The red and white colours and logos have become so identifiable in many sports, that the word Marlboro may not even have to be present in order for a sports fan to understand that red and white means Marlboro. The colours red and white together cannot be banned from a race-car, sideline, team cap, helmet, or uniform.

The efforts of educational institutions, health agencies and medical organisations that have united to push for the enactment of legislation designed to ban tobacco advertising and promotion have been well-intentioned, but have failed to cross the economic barriers and engage the business world on this issue. Sport and sport sponsorship is business, and should be studied more closely and systematically in order to discover sound solutions to the problem of tobacco sponsorship of sport.

References

AUSTRALIAN COUNCIL ON SMOKING AND HEALTH: *Ashes to Dust*, 10(2), 1993, pp.16-17.

BITTOUN, R.: Smoking in France: a dismal picture. In: *New York State Journal of Medicine*, 85, 1985, pp.407-408.

BLUM, A.: Medicine vs. Madison Avenue. Fighting smoke with smoke. In: *Journal of the American Medical Association*, 243(8), 1980, pp.739-740.

BLUM, A.: Deadly pushers: how sports sells tobacco. In: *The Miami Herald*, 25 August 1985, pp. E1, E-5.

BLUM, A.: Tobacco industry sponsorship of sports - a growing dependency. In: *Surgeon General's Interagency Committee on Smoking and Health*. Proceedings, Department of Health and Human Services, 1988.

BLUM, A.: Tobacco industry sponsorship of sports. In: HEALTH DEPARTMENT OF WESTERN AUSTRALIA, *Tobacco and Health: The Global War*. Perth, Western Australia, 1990, pp.882-884.

BLUM, A.: The Marlboro Grand Prix: circumvention of the television ad ban on tobacco advertising. In: *New England Journal of Medicine*, 324, 1991, pp.913-916.

BLUM, A.: Cigarette cards-irony and propaganda. In: *Tobacco Control*, 4(2), 1995, p.117.

BLUM, A., and SOLBERG, E.J.: Re-start your engines. In: *Tobacco Control.* 2(2), 1993, pp.100-101.

CENTERS FOR DISEASE CONTROL: Cigarette smoking among adults - United States, 1993. In: DEPARTMENT OF HEALTH AND HUMAN SERVICES, CENTERS FOR DISEASE CONTROL, *Morbidity and Mortality Weekly Report.* 43(50), 1994, pp.925-930.

DEPARTMENT OF HEALTH AND HUMAN SERVICES, FOOD AND DRUG ADMINISTRATION: *Regulations Restricting the Sale and Distribution of Cigarettes and Smokeless Tobacco Products to Protect Children and Adolescents* [proposed rule]. DHHS Docket No. 95N-0253. Washington, DC: U.S. Government Printing Office, 11 August 1995.

GLOEDE, B.: Top five smokes in sports. In: *Sports Inc.* 8 February 1988, p.26.

JOYCE JULIUS AND ASSOCIATES: *Marlboro Leads CART Series.* Ann Arbour, MI, 1994.

KROTEE, M.L., SOLBERG, E.J., and BLUM, A.: *Clouding issues in the transnationalization of sport in the global marketplace.* Paper presented at the meeting of the American Association of Health. Physical Education, Recreation, and Dance (AAHPERD). Washington, DC, 1993.

MANGIACASALE, A.: The Canadian Non-Smokers' Rights Association: shaming the establishment. In: *New York State Journal of Medicine*, 85, 1985, pp.439-441.

MARSHALL, C., and ROSSMAN, G.: *Designing Qualitative Research.* London, Sage, 1989.

MCKENNA, B.: Tobacco ad ban struck down: Supreme Court ruling affects radio, TV promotions, warnings on packages. In: *The Globe and Mail*, 22 September 1995, pp. A1, A11.

PLAYER'S LTD.: *Player's Ltd. Cup: a tradition of excellence.* Canada, Player's Ltd., 1993.

ROEMER, R.: *Legislative action to combat the world tobacco epidemic.* (2nd ed.). Geneva, World Health Organisation, 1993.

SOLBERG, E.J. and BLUM, A.: Vive la France! In: *Tobacco Control,* 2(1), 1993, pp.10-11.

SWORD, P.: Ban tobacco sponsored events, city council told. In: *Halifax Chronicle-Herald,* 24 September 1992, p.A1.

TOBACCO PRODUCTS CONTROL ACT: *Chapter 201.* Ottawa, Canada, Queen's Printer for Canada, 28 June 1988.

VICTORIAN HEALTH PROMOTION FOUNDATION: *At last there's a way to replace tobacco sponsorship without harming sport or the arts.* Carlton South, Victoria, 1987.

Chapter 22

Sport and Tourism - How Symbiotic is their Relation?

Joy Standeven

Introduction

Every four years, cities throughout the world spend millions in their attempt to win the privilege of hosting the Olympic Games. One major reason for such investment is the anticipation of attracting thousands of visitors (competitors, officials, media personnel and spectators) who will generate huge revenues to benefit the city and the region in the short-term, and create prestige and momentum for ongoing developments for years to come. HOWARD (1996) reported an Atlanta hotel's sales manager stating "... We regard the Olympics as a springboard to give Atlanta the exposure we need in the global market place" (p.36).

The sport-tourism relationship has come to be viewed as a significant component of business and economics. This is reflected in the extent to which tourist entrepreneurs have used sport in recent years as a special interest sector to increase tourism and to boost company or destination profits. Sports events world-wide have been seen as a force for economic (re)generation, and alongside these the activity and adventure holiday market is seen to be expanding on a global scale. In the UK alone, the market value of activity holidays has increased by some 35% since 1990, to reach an estimated \$3.9bn in 1995 (MINTEL, 1995). Examples are used here to illustrate the economic benefits that can accrue from the sport and tourism relation. However, this simply demonstrates how tourism has benefited from its relation with sport. A much less attested relation concerns the reciprocal issues of the extent to which sport has benefited from becoming an increasingly popular sector of tourism and whether tourism can be harnessed to the cause of sports development at all levels of continuum involvement - foundation, participation, performance and excellence.

The argument presented suggests that whilst the inter-relatedness of sport and tourism can create new opportunities for economic benefit, the potential for sports development has remained largely dormant. The opportunity and responsibility for government and official agencies to use holidays as a way of bringing people into sport and sustaining their interest to which GLYPTIS (1991) drew attention is only now becoming evident. Yet with activity holidays as an increasingly popular component of the overall holiday market, there is growth potential for sports development in the community. Clearly, there are implications for policy integration and management action if the sport/tourism relationship is to become more symbiotic.

Major sports events have become an international business with the potential for economic success or failure. Globetrotting sports tourists, participants and spectators alike, are drawn increasingly to international venues. In order to examine the interdependence of sport and tourism, the examples used in this chapter have been drawn from a number of countries around the world, thus providing an international rather than a comparative perspective.

Sport-tourism as an Economic Force

The Olympic Games are considered to be the pinnacle of the sports tourism business, with the Games of the XXVI Olympiad claimed to have been the world's largest sporting event. World and European Cup Football run second and third respectively in terms of big business, but events such as the Hong Kong Rugby 7s, World Championship Bowls and Le Tour cycle race also offer great opportunities for generating tourist activity.

Atlanta, the capital of the state of Georgia and host to the 1996 Olympic Games, is the eighth largest metropolitan area in the US with a population of some 3.4 million people. Over 10,700 athletes from 197 countries were expected to participate in 26 sports at the XXVI Olympiad (STEVENS, 1996). According to the Atlanta Committee for the Olympic Games (ACOG), the total economic impact of the Games on the state of Georgia's economy was estimated at US$5.1 billion (EICHORN, 1995). A year before the Games began, more than US$300 million in retail sales of Olympic-themed merchandise were recorded - that is more than the total sales figure for merchandise from the Los Angeles Games in 1984 (CANDLISH, 1996). Two million visitors were expected to attend the Games in Atlanta and generate $531.6m. in lodging and amusements. Other spending estimates included: $428.8m new construction projects; $398.2m real estate; $380.7m eating and drinking; $358.2m. in retail trade; $328m. in transportation and $206m. in food products (EICHORN, 1995). It is claimed 11 million tickets were sold. ACOG also expected visitor spending to reach US$2.7 billion (WANG and IRWIN, 1993). Against this huge income, it was further estimated that the cost of the construction of sporting facilities would be $599m. out of a total cost of $1bn. Thus, identifying an enormous profit potential.

Euro96 tournament revenues were expected to be large and the Football Association (UK) thought it worthwhile to spend $1.25m) on the bid process (WHEAT, 1996). The British Tourist Authority anticipated 250,000 overseas tourists would arrive specifically for the championship matches, spending $180m. mainly on accommodation and entertainment (OSBOURNE, 1996). Ticket sales were expected to total $82.5m. and sponsorship deals around $75m. From taxes raised on ticket sales, merchandising, hospitality, betting duty, salaries and corporate and commercial profits, the UK government was expected to net around $96m. (BALDWIN, 1996). These figures demonstrate the economic benefits at stake in the most prestigious sporting events. Yet less well known events also promise attractive profits.

Hong Kong is the 12th largest market in the world and tourism is its second largest earner of foreign exchange. In 1992, tourism earned revenue equivalent to $1050 per head of population, and for every 15 cents spent on marketing overseas by the Hong Kong Tourist Association (HKTA), $18.75 was received in tourism receipts (WELLS, 1996). Amongst its aims, the Hong Kong Sports Development Board (HKSDB) wanted to create new and imaginative events to "show-off" Hong Kong (WELLS, 1996). This wish fitted particularly well with HKTA's ambitions "... so it was appropriate and possibly politically sensible for HKTA to co-ordinate the development of an events strategy" (WELLS, 1996, p.2). One major event "driven" by the HKTA, the International Dragon Boat races, attract teams from many countries and from this event an international federation has developed: an example of sports development generated by tourism.

The world famous Hong Kong's Rugby Sevens are now in their 21st year with matches screened to more than 90 countries world-wide. The new national stadium seats 40,000 people and with only 8,000 tickets available within Hong Kong, there has been an opportunity for the HKTA to work with overseas promoters and trips from the UK in particular are arranged (WELLS, 1996). At the 2Oth anniversary event (1996), 97,000 paying fans spent on average $60 per head over three days and drank more than 2 million pints of beer, 5,800 jugs of Pimms and 2,520 litres of wine; 1,850 workers were employed to dispense beer and other drinks, including 300 roving vendors. Based on Hong Kong's experience there can be little doubt of the potential for economic benefit arising from the deliberately developed partnership between sport and tourism particularly where a portfolio of events is promoted.

A traditional holiday resort situated on the south coast of England, with one of the highest proportions of elderly residents in the UK, has itself developed an events' strategy using the principle of a portfolio. Worthing, like many other British resorts, suffered a serious decline in its visitor numbers as package holidays to guaranteed sunshine destinations abroad became cheaper. Its decision to attract sporting events, and bowls in particular, as a niche marketing strategy has been highly successful. In 1992, it staged the World Bowls Championship, a world class event which attracted over 200,000 visitors to the town. Almost one in ten visitors that year (8%) came to Worthing specifically for the World Championships and a further 12% were bowls-related visitors. For an outlay of $109,500, the local economy benefited by an estimated $16.5m. with television coverage transmitted to more than 29 countries. Beach Hurst Park, the National Centre for bowls, has four championship greens laid out in a close square formation ideal for hosting World class events. In order to adopt a more youthful and contemporary image to its market, Worthing has also focused on windsurfing.

In the summer of 1994, sporting history was made when the Tour de France, the cycle race claimed to be the world's largest annual sporting event, included two-day stages in the UK. On the first day alone (6th July 1994) with the stage from Dover to Brighton, the number of spectators was estimated to have been between 1.2 and 1.3 million. There were 180 competitors with a 3,500 strong back-up team of helpers, officials and media travelling in 1,500 support vehicles. On the basis of survey work undertaken during the event, it was estimated that 200,000 spectators were drawn to Brighton, of which 75% were visitors to the district. One third had come to Brighton for the first time. Le Tour attracted visitors from a wide catchment area: 80% were from Britain, 20% from abroad, and three out of four came specifically to see the race and 41% travelled over 100 miles. Almost half of the visitors (46%) stayed at least one night, and of these more than one third stayed for 5 nights or more. A business survey carried out in conjunction with Le Tour found that more than two thirds (69%) of businesses in catering, accommodation and retail felt the event had been of general benefit. The economic impact of Le Tour arose from visitor arrivals, the length of stay and accommodation used, related tourism activity including use of facilities and attractions, and expenditure in general.

These examples have shown that large (and comparatively small) sporting events can transform the image of their host city, create a niche market for tourism and produce economic benefits.

The Increase in Adventure and Activity Holidays

At a time when cheaper package holidays are suffering a downturn and tour operators are seeking ways of attracting greater interest, the adventure and activity holiday market is expanding. The UK travel operator 'Explore Worldwide', which specialises in active adventure holidays and has agents in eight other countries, is experiencing around 20% growth year on year, and the adventure holiday market as a whole is increasing by around 10% (TERRY, 1996). Top-of-the-range specialist adventure holidays were booked by an estimated 30,000 people in 1994 in the UK alone (ELLIOTT, 1994) and LEISURE CONSULTANTS (1992) estimated that around 1.5 million sports holidays were taken abroad by Britons.

Karkoram Experience (KE) Adventure travel, an operator at the leading edge of sports and adventure holidays, claim a marked increase every year in the number of people rejecting the popular notion that a holiday consists of a sedentary visit to a crowded resort, choosing instead the adventure option. Trekking, climbing and mountain biking in Asia and South America are among its specialist excursions. Mountain biking across the highest road passes in the world includes a descent from the Khardung La (5380m.) in northern India's Himalayan ranges. To celebrate Pakistan's Golden Jubilee in 1997, the company ran a special two-week holiday that took in the Shandur Festival where polo is played at the world's highest polo ground 4000 m above sea level. This event marks the annual rivalry between the two famous polo teams from Gilgit and Chitral and also includes competition from top international teams.

In the domestic UK activity holiday market, MINTEL (1995) estimated that altogether 12.7m. trips were taken worth $3.9bn. and accounting for 22% of total domestic holidays. These holidays MINTEL defined as concentrating on sport and recreation where the activity was the main purpose of the holiday. On average, two thirds of all activity holidays last for 4+ nights, as long stays are often necessary to learn or improve the skills involved. Around 3,000 sites were estimated to service the domestic UK market, with 60% of sales being repeat business. The most popular type of activity holiday was walking with 3.92m trips and a market value estimated at $920m. Swimming involved fewer trips (2.24m.) but had the same market value as walking (MINTEL, 1995). Activity holidays are comparatively expensive. On average, they cost $300 during 1994 compared with an average $234 for any UK holiday, resulting in a biased profile of activity holiday takers who are drawn disproportionately from the higher socio-economic groups, the 15-34 age range and attracting proportionately more male participants than there are males in the population as a whole.

The growing interest in sporting holidays is now being exploited by such established companies as Kuoni, one of the world's largest travel operators formed in Switzerland in 1906. This high profile commercial operator is utilising niche marketing and demonstrating its confidence in the attraction of sporting holidays as a way to sell more packages. In one of its recently published brochures, *Kuoni Sporting Holidays*, it states:

... Kuoni Travel, in association with our friends at Travel Centre Bowling Holidays, have carefully chosen four exciting holidays which span the world and offer you the opportunity to experience the very best that each country has to offer. Each tour has been carefully planned to offer just the right balance of sightseeing, bowling and free time...

(KUONI, 1996, p.2).

Each of the four tours allows several days bowling with matches against local clubs at the beginning and end of each holiday giving participants a real opportunity to develop their bowling skills.

Whilst four out of ten (38%) of MINTEL's U.K. representative sample had taken some form of activity holiday in 1995, 65% claimed to have an interest in taking such a holiday. This indicates the potential for future growth both in the sports holiday market itself (MINTEL, 1995) and, in addition, it identifies a latent market for sports development in the community.

Sport-tourism as a Catalyst for Sports Development

Generally speaking, tourism has been both the initiator of, and the beneficiary from, the sport tourism relation. It is considerably more difficult to point to examples where tourism has been the catalyst for sports development. The questions are whether the sport-tourism relation can transform non-regular or non-sports participants into people with active leisure lifestyles and whether tourism can be exploited as a means of developing of sport. In a forthcoming text (DE KNOP and STANDEVEN), seven ways in which tourism can be the source for sports development have been identified:

• sports development as a result of tourism to natural environments

• sports development as a result of tourism to artificial facilities

• sports development from facilities built to generate tourism

• sports development from special programmes

- sports development from the presence of qualified instructors

- sports development from hosting major events

- sports development from the presence of elite performers

Skiing, which involves tourism to natural environments, with total participant numbers worldwide estimated to exceed 85 million, illustrates the first way in which tourism has played a critically important role in the development of sport (DE KNOP and STANDEVEN, forthcoming).

The desire to practise skiing between holidays or to obtain a feel for the techniques before the first holiday has led to the construction of artificial slopes, and ambitious projects designed to simulate snow villages, where sports can be practised year round from tourism to artificial facilities. This is the second source of sports development from tourism.

An example of facilities built deliberately to attract tourism includes indoor water leisure complexes found in several European cities and coastal resorts. *Tropicana*, in the city of Rotterdam, the Netherlands, is one example. GRATTON and TAYLOR (1990) found such pools generated a new demand and created a broader interest in swimming. Similarly, at 'Seagala' in Miyazaki Kyushu, Japan, a massive artificially created beach resort with a sliding sun-roof provides an opportunity for swimming development year round for those who cannot take a holiday.

Travel operators have recognised that sports development holidays have an appeal across a wide range of sports, so special programmes with coaching and playing opportunities built into them, such as Kuoni's Bowling Holidays to South Africa, the USA, Asia and New Zealand have been developed.

In a number of sports, development occurs as a result of athletes travelling to destinations to be coached by highly qualified instructors. For example, Richard Brain, at one time the teaching professional at a Country Club in Oklahoma, while residing in Singapore, taught golf to a range of students, many of whom travelled from throughout Asia for their lessons (STODDART, 1994).

Sports development as one of the three reasons for seeking to host major events, has resulted in the Sports Council in the UK setting up a Major Events Support Group (MESG) to assist with UK bids for international sporting events (MALONEY, 1996). One of Brighton's stated aims in its bid to attract Le Tour to the town was cycling development in the Borough. A programme concentrating on a school's cycling package and community cycling days was initiated. The school's programme included cycling proficiency and safety, cycle maintenance, the health benefits of cycling as well as projects that related cycling to geography, physics, art and French lessons with educational packages and promotional videos used as part of the curriculum. Community cycling days were held in a local park and as a result of sponsorship, the local cycling track was refurbished and a national championships held there a week after Le Tour. Most recently Brighton hosted the BMX World Championships.

The All England Lawn Tennis Championships held at Wimbledon provide an example of sports development occurring from the presence of elite performers. The Lawn Tennis Association (UK), in conjunction with local tennis centres nation-wide, runs a free coaching programme called 'Love Tennis' intended to increase awareness of the game and project it, via the media, as fun to play. As part of this programme, on the middle Saturday of the Wimbledon championships, elite players teach and coach more than 300 local children (beginners to more proficient players) in Wimbledon Park. Nationally, in 1995, the 'Love Tennis' programme introduced 22,000 new players to the game for an investment of $187,500 (LTA, 1996).

Factors inhibiting Tourism as the Catalyst for Sports Development

A number of inhibitors can be identified including:

- failure to take a holiday so precluding the opportunity to become a sports tourist

- lack of adequate resources (time and money) to engage in sports development

- the fragmented nature of the industry and opportunities

As far as participants are concerned, European research published in 1987 showed that almost half (44%) of the total EC population took no holiday trips in 1985, with 21% habitually staying at home, though there was wide diversity in the holiday-taking habits of individual countries (CEC, 1987). The same piece of research concluded that socio-occupational status and the level of a family's income were the major barriers that precluded holiday-taking.

In the 1990s, world-wide recession had a significant impact on holiday-taking behaviour which led to consumers favouring cheaper packaged trips and an increasing number of Europeans who took no holiday or failed to take their full holiday entitlement (WOODS, 1993). In 1991 for instance, only two thirds (64%) of the UK population took a holiday and spent 16% of their total expenditure on leisure-based items on it. Holidays accounted for a quarter of all leisure expenditure in the UK amounting to almost $15 per week (WOODS, 1993).

Researching leisure participation in the UK, KAY and JACKSON (1991) found that of 19 constraints that stopped people doing what they wanted in their leisure time, two were most frequently reported: financial constraints were cited by 56%; and lack of time by 45%. Analysis showed that whilst high levels of constraint were experienced by lower socio-economic groups, shortages of time and money were identified as major constraints by people whose financial situations and time commitments differed markedly from each other. Their research led to the conclusion that there is no inevitable link between people perceiving constraints and actually doing less leisure activities, since people can find ways of overcoming constraints. SHAW, BONEN and MCCABE (1991) came to some similar conclusions when they examined constraints affecting people's participation in physically active leisure in Canada. Reported constraints did not necessarily act as real constraints, but social structural factors such as age, income, occupational status and gender were linked and were found to be related to leisure constraints.

The relationship between work and leisure is complex and there is little evidence of the 'leisure society' anticipated by a previous generation. Although working time can be seen to be increasing rather than declining in many westernised societies (TERRY, 1996), research on Canadians asked respondents what they would do if non-work time and leisure increased over the next five to ten years (REID and MANNELL, 1993). Seven out of ten said they would engage in travel (69.9%), (incidentally, the same percentage who, in the UK, agreed that taking an annual holiday was important (VEARES, 1993), and over half of the Canadians (56.4%) wanted to participate in more recreational activities and sport (REID and MANNELL, 1993).

Diversity within the leisure industry, tourism as predominantly a commercial profit-making enterprise, and sport split between public social policy and the private sector, help to explain the administrative complexity found when the sport-tourism relation is examined. In 1991, GLYPTIS called for "...sport and tourist authorities (in the U.K.) to talk to one another, and to forge real working partnerships to establish coherent policies, programmes and provisions" (p.81).

The fragmentation of sport and tourism impacts at all levels: duplication occurs in some aspects, gaps are evident in others and comparatively few examples can be cited of successfully integrated and strategic management. Even at the most prestigious and costly level of the sport-tourism relation, there are failures, witness Atlanta. The 1996 Games have been widely criticised. Samaranch, the IOC President, was reportedly critical of the "appalling accreditation system at the airport, of the dysfunctional transport and of the length of the athlete's parade at the opening ceremony" (MILLER, 1996, p.25). Athletes, officials and media personnel likewise identified failures of organisation in Atlanta. The under-performance in organisation ability did not produce the IOC President's accustomed accolade of the "greatest Games". Yet successful partnerships between different agencies, as well as between business communities and sport and tourism, are obtainable, as this contribution has sought to demonstrate.

Fragmented organisation inevitably leads to fragmented marketing, which, from the consumers' point of view, inhibits access. The development of integrated packages and their delivery to aspirants is essential. For sports development to arise from tourism, host communities also need to be seen more widely than simply as a resource input into tourism, which has long been their traditional role according to SIMMONS (1993). He elaborates commenting "... we should also be asking what priority should be given to the host community needs from tourism vis à vis tourist needs" (SIMMONS, 1993, p.664). In other words, where sports facilities and sports events are developed as 'tourist products', it is important to recognise that destination communities, too, "...have their own independent set of needs, desires and wants..." (SIMMONS, 1993, p.664), which in some instances may oppose development.

Government Roles, Policy Integration and Management Action

Given the possibility of around 60% of individuals overcoming the constraints of time and money, what role should governments and official agencies play in seeking to use holidays as a catalyst for sports development? Further, what are the implications for policy integration and management action if the sport/tourism relationship is to become more symbiotic?

World recession has led to government downsizing on an almost global scale and to privatisation of even essential services such as transport and health. In this situation, it is not surprising to find both sport and tourism as relatively low priorities on many government agendas. Yet it is governments that frame the context in which the sports and tourism sectors operate: they establish financial priorities; influence disposable incomes; manipulate exchange rates; and control the roles of different providers (WELCH, 1988). Governments, and national, regional and local agencies can have a pivotal role in generating and facilitating sport and tourism links.

With the increasing popularity of activity holidays, the expressed wish to increase sporting participation (by many consumers and by governments seeking to reduce the costs of public health), and the real possibility for individuals to overcome perceived constraints to participation, a latent market for sports development in the community can be identified. The implications for policy integration include the need for policy makers (local, regional and national) to become more closely involved and recognise the links, issuing guidelines to enable sport and tourism activities to work more closely together. Policy makers need to develop a joint strategic approach and establish infrastructures that facilitate linkages between operators in the different sectors. If direct funding is impractical or undesirable, governments and official agencies at least need to create a favourable fiscal environment that encourages both tourism and sporting activities. Legislation must be in place to regulate safety and guarantee quality of experience for visitors and the local community alike. Providers should be encouraged to consider the needs of both the local and tourism market in the design and promotion of their facilities. Examples of "best practice" need to be identified and knowledge shared, in particular, examples where tourism is genuinely helping to provide or sustain local community sport initiatives.

Management action requires partnerships to be forged between operators in all sectors, building portfolios of events and combining these with accommodation and activity packages. Sports and tourist activities need to be managed in a way that creates ease of movement between different venues, activities, destinations and levels so making it easy for people to do what they want to do. Links between the tourism industry and local residents need to be increased in order that sports opportunities may add to the quality of visitors' experiences and increase the appeal of destinations at the same time as encouraging increased sports participation by both residents and visitors. Well-designed promotional initiatives are needed to better inform all potential participants of the opportunities to develop their sporting interests on holiday and at home. Community sports and recreation officers should endeavour to manage the introduction of sports tourists to sports clubs and facilitate the transition to an active leisure lifestyle at 'home'.

Conclusion

There are signs of an increasing symbiotic relation between sport and tourism in many countries, but there is still a long way to go to achieve an evenly balanced benefit, particularly for tourism to act as a catalyst for sports development in the community. Links between sport and tourism need to be given official recognition, and collaboration encouraged at all levels from individual business enterprises through to government agencies, if the sport-tourism relation is to deliver its full economic and sports development potential in the globalised world.

References

BALDWIN, R.: *Memorandum submitted to the National Heritage Committee.* London, Touche Ross and Co., 1996 (unpublished).

BALDWIN, R.: (1996). *Euro 96 - estimated tax payable.* Private communication, 25 July 1996.

CANDLISH, L.: Selling the Olympics. In: *High Life.* London, British Airways, July, 1996, pp.78-82.

COMMISSION OF THE EUROPEAN COMMUNITIES: *Europeans and their holidays.* Luxembourg, Office for Official Publication of the European Community, 1987.

DE KNOP, P., and STANDEVEN, J.: *Sport and tourism: international perspectives.* Champaign, IL, Human Kinetics Publishers Inc. (in press).

EICHORN, R.: Atlanta calling. In: *New Zealand Sport Monthly*, 41, October 1995, p.23.

ELLIOTT, H.: You're never too old for an adventure. In: *The Times*, November 10, 1994, p.35.

GLYPTIS, S.: Sport and tourism. In: COOPER, C.P., (Ed.), *Progress in Tourism and Hospitality Management*, 3, 1991, pp.165-183.

GRATTON, C., and TAYLOR, P.: Leisure vs. conventional pools. In: *Leisure Management*, 1, 1990, pp.42-44.

HOWARD, B.: (1996). Georgia's best. In: *Leisure Management*, 16(7), 1996, pp.35-37.

KAY, T., and JACKSON, G.: Leisure despite constraint: the impact of leisure constraints on leisure participation. In: *Journal of Leisure Research*, 23(4), 1991, pp.301-313.

LAWN TENNIS ASSOCIATION: *Personal communication*, 25 July 1996.

LEISURE CONSULTANTS: *Activity holidays: the growth market in tourism.* Suffolk, UK, Leisure Consultants, 1992.

MALONEY, A.: Attracting major events. In: THE SPORTS COUNCIL, *Sport*, 5, Spring, 1996, p.19.

MILLER, D.: Olympic spirit survives Atlanta. In: *The Times*, August 5, 1996, p.25.

MINTEL MARKETING INTELLIGENCE: *Activity holidays in the UK.* London, Mintel International Group Ltd., 1995.

OSBOURNE, A.: Euro96 - shooting for net profits. In: *Investors Chronicle*, 14 June 1996, pp.21-22.

REID, D.G., and MANNELL, R.C.: Future possibilities: the changing patterns of work and leisure. In: VEAL, A.J., JONSON, P., and CUSHMAN, G., (Eds.), *Leisure and tourism: social and environmental change.* Papers from the World Leisure and Recreation Assoc. Congress, Sydney, Australia 16-19 July 1991, Sydney, Australia, University of Technology, Centre for Leisure and Tourism Studies, 1993.

SHAW, S.M., BONEN, A., and MCCABE, J.F.: Do more constraints mean less leisure? Examining the relationship between constraints and participation. In: *Journal of Leisure Research*, 4, 1991, pp.286-300.

STEVENS, T.: Olympic gains. In: *Leisure Management*, 16(7), 1996, pp.34-37.

STODDART, B.: Golf international: considerations of sport in the global marketplace. In: WILCOX, R., (Ed.), *Sport in the global village.* Morgantown, WV, Fitness Information Technology, 1994, pp.21-34.

TERRY, L.: Holidayers seek thrills. In: *Leisure Management*, 16(6), June 1996, pp.14.

USHER, R.: Some don't like it hot. In: *Time*, September 2, 1996, pp.46-49.

VEARES, L.: Holidays. In: THE HENLEY CENTRE FOR FORECASTING, *Leisure Futures*, 4, London, 1993, p.96.

WANG, P., and IRWIN, R.L.: An assessment of economic impact techniques for small sporting events. In: *Sport Marketing Quarterly*, 11(3), 1993, pp.33-37.

WELCH, D.: Politics and leisure in Britain. In: *World Leisure and Recreation*, 30(2), 1988, pp.26-28.

WEST COUNTRY TOURIST BOARD AND SPORTS COUNCIL (SOUTH WEST): *Tourism and sport*. Exeter, Devon and Crewkerne, Somerset, West Country Tourist Board and Sports Council (South West), 1992.

WHEAT, S.: Profile - Glen Kirton. In: *Leisure Management*, 16(4), 1996, pp.20-22.

WOODS, R.: Europe on holiday. In: THE HENLEY CENTRE FOR FORECASTING, *Leisure Futures*, 1, London, 1993, p.7.

Chapter 23

IOC Trans-nationalism and the Nationalist Agenda of the Parti Quebecois: Politics, Ideology and Nationalism in an Olympic Games Bid

Michael Letters

Introduction

Despite the International Olympic Committee's (IOC) universal humanistic philosophy of placing sport "at the service of the harmonious development of man," (IOC, 1992), the institutionalised position of the polity and its symbols in the Olympics suggests that the promotion of competition between states is primal. The International Olympic Committee (IOC) embraces a pragmatic attitude towards nationalism, one which facilitates its operations as a Trans-national Organisation by allowing nationalism to enhance the international importance of the Games (TAYLOR, 1986). This acceptance of nationalism is, however, conditional. Since the Olympics provide a world-wide forum for governments to celebrate their national identity and to achieve a measure of international recognition, the IOC is careful to ensure that expressions of nationalism do not damage the Games' reputation, but rather, promulgate their significance. To manage the tensions created by nationalism, the IOC endorses expressions of "acceptable nationalism," such as national teams, flags and anthems, which define the struggle between nationalities but do not challenge the Committee's authority or its philosophical rhetoric. Conversely, overtly national political decisions, such as the boycotting of an Olympic Games, are condemned because they conflict with the interests of the IOC and ignore the Olympics' internationalist ideology (HOBERMAN, 1995). The politics of nationalism in the Olympic Movement are not restricted merely to the superimposition of meanings on the contest between athletes at the Games. In countries where national groups are not represented by a separate Olympic team, such as the Catalonians in Spain or the Quebecois in Canada, attempts to host an Olympic Games provide an avenue to highlight contested identities particularly when the proposed

Host City is located within a nationalist region. While the staging of the Olympic Games provides a unique opportunity for international exposure for nationalist and independence movements, their political involvement also challenges the expectation that nationalism will automatically acquiesce to IOC trans-nationalism.

The unsuccessful bid of Quebec City, Canada, to host the 2002 Winter Olympics serves as an illustrative nexus for the conflict of ideologies between the IOC and Quebec's provincial nationalist political party, the Parti Quebecois. The Parti Quebecois' incorporation of Quebec City's bid into its nationalist discourse can be evaluated as a case of' "unacceptable nationalism" within the Olympic Movement. The linking of the bid with the Parti Quebecois programme of Quebec sovereignty was not in itself "unacceptable", but the Parti Quebecois' insistence of the primacy of nationalistic political objectives over the IOC's trans-national goals challenged the discretionary authority of the IOC. The Quebec City case study not only highlights the nationalism that is attached to Games' bids, but also illustrates their contested meaning as national and international festivals. Thus, where there is a significant nationalistic aspect to a city bidding for, or hosting, the Games, the event becomes a conduit for the establishment of power relationships between local and national political forces and the trans-national authority of the IOC.

The IOC as a Trans-national Organisation

International sport and politics are structured around the fundamental unit of the sovereign state. Political interactions between states are organised either bi-laterally, or through their membership to various International Organisations, such as the United Nations. This assumes that all states which conform to this system, by the recognition of their sovereignty, have equal rights to certain instruments that regulate inter-state relations, such as international law or representation at the United Nations (ARCHER, 1992). International sport is conducted on a similar premise, with the globalised nature of sport increasingly requiring the acceptance of the regulatory role of International Sports Federations and bodies like the IOC to organise the world's major multi-sport events. This represents the forces of globalisation or the "intensification of global inter-connectedness," (JARVIE and MAGUIRE, 1994, p.230), which dilutes the sovereignty of states as their borders become more and more permeable to the operations of inter-governmental bodies, Trans-national Organisations and multi-national corporations. Without the base of territory to anchor their authority, organisations like the IOC sustain their powerful position through the monopoly control of certain international practices. If nations wish to participate in the Olympics, they are required to conduct themselves in the manner prescribed by the IOC, which implicitly involves the subjugation of the sovereign state's power to the IOC's trans-national practices.

Unlike International Organisations that are composed of member states, (e.g. the United Nations or the European Union), the IOC operates as a non-governmental Trans-national Organisation, where access to states, rather than their membership, is central to its operations. Typically, Trans-national Organisations comprise groups, associations or individuals that do not usually represent governments, though they may have interactions with various levels of government (ARCHER, 1992). Huntington (1991) outlines the general characteristics of Trans-national Organisations as: (i) comprising a relatively large and hierarchical organisation with a centrally directed bureaucracy; (ii) performing a relatively limited range of functions; and (iii) performing its functions across more international boundaries and, where possible, in relative disregard for those boundaries. The International Red Cross is an example of organisations that conform to Huntington's model. The IOC clearly meets the criteria of a Trans-national Organisation. The network of the National Olympic Committees (NOCs) and Olympic Games Organising Committees are regulated by the IOC (MACINTOSH and HAWES, 1992), and in particular by the IOC's Executive and President. The limited range of functions that the IOC undertakes, are directed towards the organisation of the Olympic Games and the promotion of the philosophy of Olympism. The IOC's capacity to operate across international boundaries is illustrated, beyond the staging of the Games themselves, by its related activities such as the administration of the Olympic Solidarity programme and its economic relationships with major multi-national corporations.

HUNTINGTON (1991) points out that one of the key features that differentiates Trans-national Organisations like the IOC from International Organisations is that "international organisations require accord amongst nations; the trans-national organisation requires access to nations" (p.215). In an organisational sense, the IOC gains access to a state by the activities of a recognised NOC operating within its territory, whose functions are directed towards the advancement of the IOC's goals in the country and to a lesser extent, in the region. In the latter, advancement of the Olympic Movement can be achieved through the NOC's participation in its respective regional association of NOCs, such as the European Association of National Olympic Committees. The communication between the IOC and the network of NOCs, as well as the increasing interaction between NOCs themselves through organisations subsidiary to the IOC, like the Association of National Olympic Committees (ANOC), facilitates the Olympic Movement's operations across national boundaries. Ideally, NOCs are completely independent from the influence of governments, but the importance of the Olympics as an expression of national identity and the financial costs associated with competing at the Games have led to significant political involvement in the affairs of many NOCs.

Because of its exclusive authority to grant the right to compete at, or host, the Olympic Games, the IOC is in a position of relative power compared with many states. Unlike most other Trans-national Organisations, the IOC is enthusiastically petitioned by national governments offering access to their territory. This is usually in the form of applying to the IOC for the recognition of a nation's NOC or through the competition between cities to host future Olympic Games. The international recognition that is afforded by the media coverage of the Olympics provides an excellent arena for new or small states to display their nationalism and the national symbols. The IOC's exclusive authority to admit or expel NOCs from the Olympic Movement places it in a position of power that is rarely experienced by Trans-national Organisations. As the case of South African involvement in the Olympic Movement demonstrated, the IOC through its self-conferred authority and trans-national operations, can dictate the terms by which nations are admitted, or re-admitted after expulsion, as well as influence their domestic and external political affairs. The international prestige and exposure resulting from competing at the Olympic Games thus stimulates governments to grant the IOC access to its territory on favourable terms, particularly where other means of international prestige and recognition are less available.

For states seeking re-admission to the international community (such as Cambodia after the political turmoil of the Khmer Rouge regime and the subsequent civil war) or new states forging a new national image (as with the constituent states of the former Yugoslavia and the Soviet Union), recognition of the state's NOC and its right to send athletes to the Olympics are seen as a project of national significance, with national political leaders often prominent in discussions with the IOC President over their inclusion. This reflects, in part, the relatively powerless position small states, new states and states that do not generate large television rights for the Olympics have to influence the IOC and their necessity to mobilise the best political resources to secure its patronage. The capacity to confer access to the international media present at an Olympic Games also prompts applications for NOC recognition from autonomous or semi-autonomous regions within existing states as a means to validating what they perceive as a separate national identity. The unsuccessful efforts of the Palestinian NOC and the Catalan NOC to gain recognition from the IOC not only reflect the desire of groups to obtain recognition through inclusion in the Olympic Movement, but also the IOC's politically based decisions to recognise the legitimacy of the existing NOC based on the territory of an existing state. These elements of national identity and state legitimacy inevitably involve the IOC in political decisions concerning the legitimacy and authority of governments, as only one NOC can be recognised within a country (TAYLOR, 1986). From a Trans-national Organisation's perspective, the IOC endorses new NOCs, or recognises more representative NOCs, because such recognition re-establishes the IOC's access to a region. This is important for the maintenance of the IOC's power, since its influence and rhetoric are based on its unique ability to bring together representatives of nearly all the world's states under the intense media coverage of the Olympic Games. Conversely, more established nations within the Olympic Movement, such as the United States, can challenge the position of the IOC by adopting strong ideological or nationalistic positions regarding participation. The boycotts that such national policies can instigate can directly impact on the IOC's importance by reducing the "meaning" or "validity" of the Games through the absence of certain nations. Because of the unacceptability of these nationalistic expressions, the IOC has legislated against such actions in the *Olympic Charter*.

Under the Presidency of Juan Antonio Samaranch, the IOC has capitalised on the Olympic Movement's "neutrality" and the exposure nations receive at the Olympics, to establish relations with states that other organisations have found difficult to emulate. In addition to the access granted through NOCs, Samaranch as augmented the lOC's access to states by formulating direct contacts with governments (TAYLOR, 1986) and through the strategic appointment of new IOC members. The nationalities of the 11 new members elected at the IOC's 104th Congress highlight an agenda to expand the IOC's influence within the international community by establishing links with states with whom other states have found diplomatic relations difficult. Included in those elected were Antun Vrdoljak (Croatia), Reynaldo Gonzalez Lopez (Cuba) and Toni Khouri (Libya). The election of Sam Ramsamy (South Africa), Vera Caslavaska (Czech Republic) and Patrick Hickey (Ireland) also suggests that the IOC seeks greater access to states in the face of changing political circumstances. In comparison, other Trans-national Organisations, such as *Amnesty International*, have a greater difficulty gaining access to states because of the potential damage their scrutiny can cause to a state's reputation. Thus, the duality of nationalism and the provision of access to the Olympic Games form the dynamic relationship that sustains the IOC's position of power and influence in the international community. While nations desire access to the Olympic Games to express their national identity, the IOC relies on that desire for the power to maintain its position and insist on the suppression of nationalism in preference of its internationalism. The expression of nationalism and the assertion of the state do, however, pose problems for the Olympic Movement, since the power of nationalism is sufficient to jeopardise the trans-national power of the IOC if it is not harnessed and "controlled" within the context of celebrating Olympism. Samaranch's statement that "sport must have good relations with governments and in return we ask that governments respect us" (THE TIMES, 1983), poignantly illustrates the trade-off for governments of the international exposure at the Olympic Games and the expression of "acceptable nationalism" in return for not impeding the IOC's trans-national operations and authority.

The IOC's Trans-national Power and Bidding to Host the Olympics

While the discretion of the IOC to regulate the competing nations at the Olympic Games confers upon the Committee significant political influence, the applications of cities to host future Olympic Games represents the assertion of the IOC's trans-national power in its most potent form. When cities formulate a bid to host the Olympic Games, the nations within which those cities are located are exposed to a relationship where potential host nations must comply scrupulously with IOC policies, directives and ideology. For the 2002 Winter Olympic Games bids, this involved hundreds of pages of manuals and technical specifications regarding the construction of the Olympic Village; the facilities for the written, photographic and broadcast media; the recommendations of the various winter sports federations; as well as guidelines from the IOC concerning the methods and protocols of lobbying its members for votes. In addition there are the contractual agreements of *The Bid City Agreement* and *The Host City Contract*, which stipulate the rights and responsibilities of the city, the NOC and the Host Nation. These contracts also legally inscribe the position and authority of the IOC and its directives to the bidding and/or hosting city. Failure to follow the IOC's guidelines can result in the squandering of millions of dollars of public and private money in the staging of unsuccessful Olympic bids. In the case of the Quebec City bid, the budget was $12 million (Canadian). HILL (1992) related the importance of signing the contracts before the Host City is announced as a means of preserving the IOC's authority:

> ... The IOC's firmness is that it has found that cities
> have ignored aspects of the contract once the Games
> had been awarded, or interpreted it in ways
> unacceptable to the IOC, and that the purpose has been
> to ensure that the IOC's interpretation will prevail
>
> (p.68).

Nevertheless, bidding nations must also provide access to the IOC and its members through the personal visits of IOC members and the review of the IOC's Site Evaluation Committee. This Committee visits all the sites bidding for the right to host a particular Summer or Winter Olympics and compiles a report on all the bids that it then submits to the rest of the IOC membership. All aspects of a bid from the facilities, financial plan, health care facilities, logistics as well as the city's overall appeal are evaluated.

To make a bid to host an Olympics most attractive to the IOC, it must be constructed to best service the IOC by contributing to the development of the Olympics' international prestige. Rod McGeoch, the Director of the successful Sydney 2000 bid, articulated the relationship between the bid, the IOC members and the Olympics ideology in commercial terms, concluding:

> ... there's a lot to be said for rising above the ruck and standing for worthy principles. If you have a quality product, you've got to stand for something more than just making a sale or turning a dollar... the IOC members, our customers, were charged with the responsibility of upholding the ideals and traditions of the Olympic Charter. I knew the image that I wanted our bid to have would somehow have to be linked to those ideals
> (MCGREGOR and KORPORAL, p.67, p.72).

For bids to be successful, they must embrace the internationalism of the Olympic Movement over the nationalism of the state, as well as provide the IOC by their location, their image, or their financial plan, with a proposal, which will perpetuate the IOC's influence. Since the IOC has a monopoly over only one cultural and economic product, the Olympic Games, the staging of an Olympic festival that is deemed internationally successful is the key to ensuring the continuation of the IOC's prestige. For a city to win the right to stage the Games, a high level of IOC access and assessment of the country's national affairs is necessary. This requires cities to provide specific responses to questions regarding the country's political institutions, current political debates, economic resources, immigration procedures, weather, heath-care facilities, diplomatic relations and economic performance as measured by statistics like Gross Domestic Product, inflation, unemployment and per capita income. These facts are used to help the IOC members evaluate the capacity of a nation to host the Games and the context within which they might be staged.

Although the internationalist rhetoric is essential in the success of any Olympic bid, the reality is that they are based on the potential economic benefits and nationalistic sentiments that can result from hosting the Games. The profit recorded from the staging of the Los Angeles Olympics revolutionised the demand for cities to host the Games after the billion dollar (Canadian) loss of the 1976 Montreal Olympics. The $110 million (Canadian) profit at Calgary and the $85 million (US) profit of the 1994 Lillehammer Games served to emphasise that the Olympics, even the smaller Winter Olympics, could be self-funding. The additional benefits of economic stimulation and the celebration of the Host Nation's identity need not result in financial losses from governments. The power of nationalism within a national enterprise, such as hosting the Olympics, results in adherence to the authority of the IOC decreasing as the Games approach. While bidding cities must convince IOC members that their city is the best venue for the Games, the closer that the Host City comes to the staging the Olympics, the greater its power becomes with respect to the IOC because of the difficulty in the IOC's relocation of the Games to an alternative city. Having 'crossed the Rubicon' by selecting a Host City and allowing its preparations to proceed, the trans-national power of the IOC is reduced with respect to the bidding country as facility construction, event management and the political significance of the Games re-define the enterprise as a national project. In the case of Canada's hosting of the 1976 Summer Olympics, the assertion of national policies over international ones resulted in Canada's refusal to admit the Taiwanese Olympic team to the country if it sought to compete as the Republic of China, since Canada recognised the Communist regime of Mainland China. This political action was taken despite the Canadian Government's previous assurances that all athletes and officials representing recognised NOCs would be admitted to compete at the Games (MACINTOSH and HAWES, 1994).

In order to maximise its position of power, the IOC requires bids to conform to its stringent technical guidelines and ideological framework so as to best perpetuate its influence during the phases of preparations where its exercisable power is diminished. For the bidding cities, they must also comply with the IOC's legal requirements and ideological demands in order to be selected as the host of the Games. A bid must project the image of a proud, yet subservient host, despite the millions of tax dollars that contribute to the construction of facilities with an uncertain return and the thousands of unpaid hours of volunteer labour, which are provided to the Olympic movement by citizens of the Host Nation. With the cities from 15 different nations expressing interest in hosting the 2004 Olympic Games, the IOC's capacity to demand the compliance of nations will continue. Bidding cities, which are themselves involved in a contest between nations for their selection as the Host City, must suppress the obvious economic and nationalistic self-interest by accommodating the internationalism of the Olympics and the authority of the IOC. Frank Sartor, the Lord Mayor of Sydney during that city's successful Olympic bid, described the actions of lobbyists as "prostituting" themselves to obtain the votes of IOC members (BOOTH and TATZ, 1994). The transient, though powerful, influence of the IOC during Olympic bids was also illustrated in the actions of the Chinese government during Beijing's bid for the 2000 Olympics. Attempting to create an international image that catered to the ideology of the IOC, the Chinese government's actions were reported in the following manner:

> China's recent actions contrast with its behaviour during its bid to host the Olympic Games in 2000. Shortly before the decision was made last month on the site of the Games, China released several prominent dissidents including Wei Yingsheng, and allowed others to go abroad. After losing the bid to Sydney, however, China has proceeded swiftly in trying pending cases against dissidents, as well as uncovering new ones
>
> (WALL STREET JOURNAL, 1993).

The bidding process, which involves an inherently national project, must moderate the nationalistic motivations for bidding for the Games until such time as the bid is selected, or is unsuccessful. At the same time, the review by the IOC and the competition between cities has strong elements of nationalism, since it is seen as a review of the entire nation's capacity (politically, economically and ideologically) to host the world's most prominent sporting festival. This type of assessment can impact on feelings of national pride amongst the citizens of bidding nations because of the insight that it provides individuals about the reputation of their country internationally. While winning the right to host the Games allows cities and nations progressively greater national power within this international festival, the relationship between nationalism and Olympic bids remains contentious. As will be illustrated by the Quebec 2002 case and the involvement of the Parti Quebecois, the role of nationalism must be compared and referenced to the city's role as the vehicle of the IOC to stage the Olympic Games. Nationalism and nationalist politics must thus be structured within the limits acceptable to the IOC; otherwise the perceptions of arrogance towards the IOC's trans-national authority can result in decreasing the chances of selection.

The Parti Quebecois and the Politicisation of the Quebec City 2000 Winter Olympics Bid

The re-election of Quebec's nationalist political party, the Parti Quebecois, in September 1994 redirected Canadian political interests and energies towards the contesting of a new referendum on Quebec's separation from Canada. The close result in the October 1995 referendum on Quebec sovereignty, where 49.4% of Quebec voters supported the independence proposal of province's nationalist parties (which was just 26,750 votes short of a majority), demonstrates the potency of nationalism and identity politics in the province that is home to seven million French-speaking Canadians. The narrow defeat of the sovereignty campaign in Quebec has stimulated nationalist leaders not to "accept the verdict" in the words of Canadian Prime Minister Jean Chretien, but rather to embrace the sentiments of Quebec nationalist Lucien Bouchard to "not stop until we have our nation" (WILSON-SMITH, 1995, p. 14).

While the future of Quebec and the Canadian remains in the balance until the contesting of another sovereignty referendum in the next term of Quebec's parliament, support for Quebec sovereignty was appreciably lower during the Parti Quebecois election campaign in August 1994 and in the first months of the Parti Quebecois government. Faced with an electorate which polls indicated only around one-third of voters supported creating a sovereign Quebec, Jacques Parrieau, then leader of the Parti Quebecois, employed a political strategy designed to galvanise support for sovereignty and to polarise voters who held loyalty to both Quebec and Canada. This political strategy was designed to "derail the federal machine" (THE GAZETTE, 1994, p.B.7) by adopting obstructionist or confrontational positions on a range of issues that involved political interactions between the provincial government and the federal government of Canada. The issues, which were often emotive and politically sensitive, demonstrated the Parti Quebecois' capacity to use a range of governmental functions to widen the cleft between the federal and provincial governments and present the Quebec state as the best representative of the Quebec nation.

As part of the programme to develop support for the Parti Quebecois' sovereignty platform, Parizeau politicised Quebec City's bid to host the 2002 Winter Olympics. Parizeau commented that should Quebec achieve independence after winning the right to host the Games, he would insist that the Canadian government uphold its commitment of $208 million (Canadian) out of the Games' total budget of $740 million (Canadian). While the comment was designed to use the symbolism and national sentimentality of the Olympic Games to elicit conflict with the federal government of Canada, it also drew the Quebec City bid and the provincial government's nationalist ideology into conflict with the IOC's trans-national practices and internationalist philosophy. The conflict in ideology present in the nationalist political discourse surrounding the Quebec 2002 bid highlights the Parti Quebecois' actions a case of "unacceptable nationalism" within the Olympic Movement. Parizeau's motivation for commenting on the financial commitments of the Canadian federal Government for a possible Quebec City Olympics was to solicit a response from federal political figures that would provide a forum for the contesting of federalist and nationalist ideologies, while simultaneously using the federal response as an example of Ottawa's continuing bad faith in promises to Quebec. Federal politicians were, for the most part, measured in their responses to issues, which were hypothetical, yet potentially emotive.

In a more important sense, Parizeau's comments regarding the Quebec City bid, and possible staging of the Winter Olympics in 2002 by an independent Quebec, was a metaphor for the dictation of a nationalist political agenda to Canada's federal government. Indeed, the contribution of over $200 million to a Quebec Olympics because of previously existing agreements was consistent with the Parti Quebecois' assumptions throughout the sovereignty campaign regarding Canadian responses to Quebec independence. For example, _The Draft Bill on the Sovereignty of Quebec_, which was passed in Quebec's National Assembly in 1994, and on the contents of which, voters opted to remain in Canada or to become sovereign, provided for Quebec citizens to keep their Canadian citizenship and for the Canadian dollar to remain the legal tender. The insistence of the Quebec sovereigntists that Canada could not stop it using its dollar or allowing its residents to be dual citizens focused on two potent symbols of the Canadian nation to demonstrate the incapacity of the federal government to challenge the basic assumptions of the Quebec independence programme. While federalist political leaders contested the validity of these assumptions throughout the sovereignty campaign, the fact remained that throughout the debate on Quebec sovereignty, nationalist politicians set and maintained the political agenda in the struggle for the loyalty of the voters of Quebec. In this context, Freeman and Grady (1995) described the Parti Quebecois assumptions about the Quebec City bid as the 'coup de grace' of the "PQ Shopping List" (p.25).

Issues such as the Quebec City bid and the maintenance of the Trans-Canada Highway became peripheral in the debate as the sovereigntists' plans for the institution of an independent Quebec and the political mechanisms for achieving their goals were revealed. For the Parti Quebecois, the Quebec 2002 Bid was not an issue within itself, but rather, a tool to be used in confronting the federal government on multiple fronts in the early phase of the sovereignty debate. Indeed, the use of the funding arrangements of the Quebec 2002 bid ran counter to the Parti Quebecois' own philosophy regarding the fiscal rationality for sovereignty, which insisted that "choosing sovereignty means opting out of a federal system that is inefficient, costly and paralysing but, primarily it means deciding to be fully responsible for our own actions" (PARTI QUEBECOIS, 1994, p1).

Unlike many of the other issues concerning Quebec-Ottawa relations, the incorporation of the Quebec 2002 bid into the nationalist issues of the Parti Quebecois had a significant impact on the bid's progress during the last nine months of lobbying. When compared with the IOC's internationalism and its desire to promulgate its trans-national operations, the programme of the Parti Quebecois presented a challenge to the IOC because of its focus on specific nationalist political goals rather than the government's subservience to the IOC's internationalist rhetoric. At least initially, the application of the IOC 's ideology was seen as having the same relationship to the Parti Quebecois' ideology as did that of Canadian federalism. Incorrectly, the Parti Quebecois assumed that, as with the federal government of Canada, it could dictate the terms of future relations with the IOC. As with its projected relations with Canada after independence, the Parti Quebecois assumed that the IOC would perform certain tasks (such as recognising a Quebec NOC) because of the apparent necessity to adapt to the change to an independent Quebec. As the interaction between the bid and the IOC revealed, the relationship was not a struggle for the "hearts and minds" of Quebec voters, but rather, for those of voting IOC members, who unlike voters in Quebec, were offered numerous viable alternatives.

The Quebec 2002 Bid, Nationalism and the IOC's Trans-national Response

The actions of the Parti Quebecois leadership in establishing a clear link between the Quebec 2002 bid and its political campaign enhanced the problems for the bid in its presentation of its assets to the IOC members. The bid had the fundamental political basis of its financial guarantees and its assumptions concerning its political system radically altered just nine months before the IOC's final decision. The bid's introduction into the ideological conflict between the Parti Quebecois and the Canadian Federal government made it increasingly difficult for it to maintain a position that reflected the bid's and the city's responsiveness to the demands of the IOC. Instead, it became a conduit for the expression of the nationalist goals of the Parti Quebecois while trying to promote itself as an apolitical undertaking accepting the supreme authority of the IOC.

At the 104th session of the IOC in Budapest in June 1995, the voting members chose Salt Lake City, Utah, USA, to host the 2002 Winter Olympics in the first round of voting. The Quebec City bid came last of the four finalist cities, receiving just seven of the ninety-two votes. There were several factors for the Quebec City's poor performance, including the bid's problems in creating a site for the men's downhill events, the quality of the competing cities and the difficulties of changing political circumstances. The issue of sovereignty was not alone responsible for the bid's failure, but the disruption it caused to the bid's political environment made it difficult for Quebec 2002 to project a consistent image to the IOC that focused on the certainty of the bid's technical aspects.

Given the practice of IOC members being guarded about their true impressions of bids and their voting preferences, it is difficult to ascertain to what extent Quebec sovereignty was an issue of concern for IOC members. Throughout the bid, reports existed that IOC members had enquired about the sovereignty issue, but Jean Grenier, Executive Vice President of Quebec 2002, characterised these enquiries as just expressions of interest, not a concern (JOURNAL DE QUEBEC, 1994). Throughout these interactions, the bid reinforced to IOC members that the political process would be conducted in a thoroughly democratic and peaceful manner and that sovereignty was not likely before 2002 (THE GAZETTE, 1995). The IOC's own *Evaluation Committee* supported this conclusion, stating that "secession is a very remote possibility before 2002" (THE GLOBE AND MAIL, 1995, p.C6). The inaccuracy of this evaluation was made self-evident by the political affairs in Quebec during 1995. Samaranch's reaction to the myriad of possibilities resulting from the Quebec sovereignty debate was to take a statesmanlike approach, saying that the sovereignty issue "is a Canadian affair, we respect that. It is yours to solve" (THE GLOBE AND MAIL, 1994, p.7).

The conflicting political and ideological relationship between the Quebec 2002 bid and the nationalism represented by the political agenda of the Parti Quebecois was highlighted by the controversy surrounding comments made by Richard Pound, IOC member in Canada and a member of the IOC Executive Board. Responsible for the IOC's negotiations with broadcast corporations for the television rights to the Summer and Winter Olympics, Pound is one of the more respected, and influential, members of the IOC. Although the Quebec City bid insisted that IOC members were not worried about the referendum, Pound suggested that the IOC members may simply have been too polite to say so, with what he described as the "political iffiness" of the sovereignty referendum presenting a major obstacle to be overcome by the bid. Commenting on the attitudes of IOC members, Pound intimated that "Salt Lake might be a lot duller than Quebec, but you know that in 2002 Salt Lake and Utah will still be part of the United States" (THE GAZETTE, 1995, p.B4). Parti Quebecois Minister for Municipal Affairs, Guy Chevrette, responded by citing Pound's comments as being a politicisation of the bid for the benefit of the federalist campaign in Quebec. Chevrette's remark that "a Canadian would say something like this is an indication of the spirit of English Canada" (THE GAZETTE,

1995, p. A8) illustrated the political efforts of the Parti Quebecois to prove bad faith on the part of federal (i.e. English-speaking) Canada through the bid. Ironically, Parizeau, the leader of the Parti Quebecois government, attacked the political content of Pound's comments, eulogising that "... That kind of politics doesn't correspond to the Olympic Spirit" and suggesting that the comments were motivated by the need for the 'blessings of the federal government" (THE GAZETTE, 1995, p.A8) should he aspire to the IOC Presidency after Samaranch's retirement.

These comments illustrate the Quebec City bid as a contested ideological entity between the nationalist, federalist and internationalist interests. Parizeau sought to redefine the internationalism of the bid to include the possibility or inevitability of Quebec independence. The symbols of national identity in the bid were used by Parizeau to damage the image of Canada, which was defended by the Canadian federal government. By comparison, Pound's international perspective was interpreted as being motivated by federalist allegiances, since he had highlighted potentially negative consequences of the Quebec sovereignty campaign. Indeed, Parizeau was not willing to admit that his political use of the Quebec bid was not in the "Olympic Spirit", but instead, contested the right of federalists to use the bid of a city in Quebec for the political objective of promoting Canada. As stated previously, this represents the continuing struggle in Quebec politics for the identities of the province's residents as Canadian or Quebecois. The leadership of the Parti Quebecois was also unwilling to concede that the political programme for the creation of an independent Quebec significantly impacted on the bid's chances of success. To accept that the Parti Quebecois politics did not integrate well with the IOC's trans-nationalism was to accept that certain governmental or cultural practices were beyond the influence of the sovereigntist party. Similarly, the Parti Quebecois' political vision was one in which the federal government, International Organisations and economic trading blocs would automatically accept its independence. This political position remained fiercely debated during the sovereignty campaign, with federalists claiming that the image of an independent Quebec presented by the Parti Quebecois and Bloc Quebecois[1] was not an accurate appraisal of the reaction of other institutions and governments. The Parti Quebecois contended, however, that an independent Quebec would continue to host the Olympics in the same way that it would continue to enjoy the existing benefits of NAFTA or NATO membership, apparently because these organisations believed that the inclusion of Quebec would be in their best interests.

Unlike the Canadian government that would be faced with the inevitability of rationalising a new relationship with an independent Quebec, the IOC had the capacity to utilise high quality and low risk alternatives, in the form of the other bids competing for the 2002 Games. Carol Anne Letheran, Canada's other IOC member, commented that debates like the sovereignty one in Quebec gave IOC members "an excuse which you don't want to provide" (THE GAZETTE, 1995, p.A8) for not voting for the bid. In fact, the resistance of the IOC to the Parti Quebecois' political influence, led Quebec's sovereigntists to realise that if they wanted Quebec City to stay a viable bid, they would have to moderate their behaviour to better accommodate the trans-national authority of the IOC. The first action in this reconciliation of the Parti Quebecois' confrontationalist political ideology with the trans-national expectations of the IOC was Parizeau's clarification of his comment regarding the financial commitments for the Games. With the financial arrangements of the bid uncertain, the bid stood little chance on winning and even faced the possibility of being eliminated in the IOC's initial review of bids, which reduced the bidding cities to just four finalists. Prior to this preliminary selection by members of the IOC, Parizeau wrote to the IOC informing the Committee that irrespective of the future political status of Quebec, the government of Quebec would guarantee to meet any deficit resulting from staging the Games (LE NOUVELLISTE, 1995, p.25). The Quebec government's guarantee to meet the federal government's commitment's should Quebec become independent (in the form of providing assurances to cover the Games' possible deficit), while softening the initial position adopted by Parizeau, still assumed that the IOC would be interested in the Quebec City proposal, despite the uncertainty and potential economic ramifications of political change.

The second episode that resulted in the Parti Quebecois being diverted from its hard nationalist line with the IOC was with respect to Parizeau's comments about Pound. Parizeau was obliged to write a letter of apology to Pound, which stated in part that he "was sorry that certain words that were used were excessive and that you were shocked by them...Those statements in no way reflect the position of my government" (THE

GLOBE AND MAIL, 1995, p.A4). Thus, the Parti Quebecois had to moderate it efforts to establish a stronger nationalist affiliation with the bid, since its statements about Pound were not interpreted by the IOC as an issue of provincial-federal identities, but as an attack on the integrity of one of its members.

The contested meanings of the Quebec City bid were also apparent in the final days of lobbying before the IOC. Both Shiela Copps, the Deputy Prime Minister of Canada, and Jacques Parizeau, the Premier of Quebec, who were bitter opponents in the political contest for the future of Quebec, were used by the bid in its lobbying. Although Parizeau stated that "we are all going in the same direction" (LE SOLEIL, 1995, p.A3), the realities of the political stakes and motivations of Quebec and Canada's political leaders were quite different. The federal political presence ensured that the Quebec City bid was viewed as a Canadian project, rather than exclusively a Quebecois one. The presence of Jacques Parizeau, while asserting the separate national identity of the Quebecois through the representation of the Parti Quebecois, also expressed that a Quebec City Games would be a Quebecois festival, irrespective of whether it was staged within the borders of Canada or an independent Quebec. Thus, until the final stages of the bid, the political ideologies and national identities represented by Canadian and Quebec nationalism, were required to co-exist, somewhat uncomfortably, in the way the Quebec City portrayed itself.

The Parti Quebecois' relationship towards the IOC remained presumptive, despite being moderated in some sense by Parizeau's climb-downs concerning the funding of the Games and his opinions regarding the motivations of Pound. The assumptions inherent in the practical aspects of an independent Quebec staging the Games would further erode the IOC's discretionary power. The IOC would, for example, have to recognise a separate NOC for Quebec, since only cities sponsored by a recognised NOC can host the Olympics. Unlike the IOC's recognition of other newly formed NOCs, such as from the former Yugoslavia or Soviet Union, the power to be recognised would not be on the IOC's terms, but rather, on Quebec's, since Quebec would already have the power of being the Host City of the Games. This represented a challenge to the IOC's trans-national operations by altering the potential power relationship between bidding cities or new NOCs and the IOC. According the Trans-national Organisations' model, this would also reduce the level of access the IOC could gain to the new state because of its weakened position of authority. If the IOC selected Quebec City to host the 2002 Winter Olympics, it would have done so without the knowledge of the political context within which the Games might be staged. While all parties associated with the bid reiterated the process of determining Quebec's political future would be done only in a peaceful and democratic manner, the Quebec City bid essentially asked the IOC to turn over control of the Games to a country of unknown political structures and economic strength. With the possibility that the Parti Quebecois could further incorporate nationalism in the Olympic Movement as the government of an independent Quebec, the potential remained for more damage to the IOC's prestige by additionally diminishing the role of internationalism in the Olympics. The unique festival that the Olympic Games represent and which the IOC manages would be tarnished by their use as a vehicle for other political or economic interests outside those, which sustain the IOC's international influence.

The nationalist ideology of the Parti Quebecois and the prospect of a changing political and economic environment is one that the IOC was not compelled to accept, since viable alternatives existed. Why would the IOC embroil itself in the a debate over cultural ownership of the Games between the Canadian and Quebec NOCs (since Quebec City would have bid for and won the Games as a Canadian city), when the possibility existed to select another city within North America where political stability is guaranteed and television revenues enlarged? For the Parti Quebecois, the bid embraced more than the efforts of the city to host the Games, it was a vehicle for the expression of an identity that was different from the Canadian identity and whose nationalist sentiments were represented by the Parti Quebecois. The IOC would have only selected Quebec City, as it would only select any city, in the belief that it best served the purposes of the IOC by contributing to its financial status, international prestige, trans-national power or a combination of all three.

Conclusion

The politicisation of the Quebec City bid to host the 2002 Winter Olympics highlights the dynamic power relationships that exist between the IOC and national political forces. With its international philosophy and trans-national operations, the IOC seeks to regulate the expression of nationalism in the Olympics by harnessing its potentially divisive sentiments to perpetuate the Games' international significance. The "acceptability" of nationalism is, however, restricted to those forms of national identification which do not challenge the centrality of the Olympics' internationalist rhetoric or the IOC's authority. When compared with the Parti Quebecois' politicisation of the Quebec 2002 bid, the assertion of the primacy of sovereigntist interests over those of Canada or the IOC created an issue through which the access to power of the various entities could be evaluated. The Quebec 2002 bid became an expression of "unacceptable" nationalism because the political involvement in the bid was not structured within the framework of maintaining the IOC as an influential Trans-national Organisation. With its trans-national operations facilitating the choice of the viable alternative of Salt Lake City, the IOC's position of power was challenged by the Parti Quebecois, but not threatened. The capacity for an Olympic bid to absorb multiple contested ideologies, such as those represented by the political forces of Quebec nationalism, Canadian federalism and IOC internationalism, was also demonstrated in the politics of the Quebec City bid. While the politics of Quebec's future were contested, in part, through the Quebec 2002 bid, the interrelationship of politics, identity and ideology encapsulated in the bid has significant comparative value. In a global political environment that is increasingly confronted with the redefining of political identities on the basis nationalism, the Quebec City case provides a window into how nationalism and trans-nationalism may interact within the Olympic Movement. The challenge for the IOC remains to continue to suppress the significance of the nation in the Olympic Movement, when the pursuit to a new state is the over-riding political objective of many governments, political parties and individuals.

Note

1. The *Bloc Quebecois* is the Quebec sovereigntist party, which holds seats and operates in the federal parliament of Canada. While partnered with the *Parti Quebecois* in the pursuit of Quebec sovereignty, the *Bloc Quebecois* and the *Parti Action Democratique* were not involved in any of the political interactions concerning the Quebec 2002 bid.

References

ARCHER, C.: *International organisations*. Second Edition, Routledge, London, 1992.

BOOTH, D., and TATZ, C.: Swimming with the big boys?: the politics of the Sydney 2000 bid. In: *Sporting Traditions: the Journal of the Australian Society for Sports History*, 11(1), November 1994, p.12.

FREEMAN, A., and GRADY, P.: Dividing the house: planning for a Canada without Quebec. *Harper Perennial*, Toronto, 1995.

HILL, C.: *Olympic politics*. Manchester University Press, Manchester, 1992.

HOBERMAN, J.: Towards a theory of Olympic internationalism. In: *Journal of Sport History*, 22(1), Spring , 1995, pp.1-37.

HUNTINGTON, S.: Transnational Organisations in World Politics. In LITTLE, R., and SMITH, M., (Eds.), *Perspectives on world politics*. Second Edition, Routledge, London, 1991, pp.212-215.

INTERNATIONAL OLYMPIC COMMITTEE: *Olympic Charter*. Lausanne, IOC.

INTERNATIONAL OLYMPIC COMMITTEE: *Manual for cities bidding to host the XIX Olympic Winter Games - 2002*. Lausanne, IOC.

JARVIE, G., and MAGUIRE, J.: Sport and leisure in social thought. Routledge, London, 1994. TAYLOR, T.: Politics of the Olympic spirit. In: ALLISON, L., (Ed.), *The politics of sport*. Manchester University Press, Manchester, 1986.

JOURNAL DE QUEBEC: 29 August 1994, p.7.

LE NOUVELLISTE: 19 January 1995, p.25.

LE SOLEIL: 16 June 1995, p.A3.

MACINTOSH D., and HAWES, M.: The IOC and the world of interdependence. In: *Olympika*, 1, 1992, p.35.

MACINTOSH, D., and HAWES, M.: *Sport and Canadian diplomacy.* Kingston, McGill-Queen's Press, 1994.

MCGEOCH, R., and KORPORAL, G.: *The bid: Australia's greatest marketing coup.* Melbourne, Mandarin, 1994.

TAYLOR, T.: Sport and international relations: a case of mutual neglect. In: ALLINSON, L., (Ed.), *The politics of sport.* Manchester University Press, Manchester, 1986, p.33.

PARTI QUEBECOIS: *A challenging project for Quebec: summary of the PQ 'S program.* Parti Quebecois, Montreal, 1994.

THE GAZETTE: Montreal, 5 October 1994, p.B7.

THE GAZETTE: Montreal, 19 January 1995, p.B4.

THE GAZETTE: Montreal, 21 January 1995, p.A8.

THE GAZETTE: Montreal, 24 January 1995, p.D9.

THE GLOBE AND MAIL: 21 March 1995, p.A4.

THE GLOBE AND MAIL: 25 January 1995, p.C6.

THE TIMES: 30 March 1983.

THE WALL STREET JOURNAL: 27 October 1993.

WILSON-SMITH, A.: A house divided. In: *Maclean's*, 108(45), 6 November 1995, p.14.

Chapter 24

Purging Parasites: Canadian Olympic Association Initiatives and Protection of the Olympic Words, Emblems and Rings

Scott G. Martyn

Introduction

Within the modern Olympic Movement "... marketing has become an increasingly important issue...the revenues derived from television, sponsorship and general fund-raising help to provide the Movement with its financial independence" (IOC MARKETING DEPARTMENT, 1994a, p.2). In today's world of Olympic commercialism, the exploitation of Olympic symbols is an important matter. By the same token, the International Olympic Committee (IOC), National Olympic Committees (NOCs) and the Organising Committees of the Olympic Games (OCOGs) pursue initiatives that seek to protect such symbols from unlawful use by those who have not paid for the privilege. The origin and evolution of insignia protection are an area of historical research that has been given little attention to date. Given what is at stake in today's world, that is, literally millions of dollars generated by the Olympic five ring symbol alone, it is appropriate to revisit the cases that have challenged the IOC's and NOC's collective authority over use of Olympic words, emblem and rings.

With regard to Olympic matters in Canada, the Canadian Olympic Association (COA) has identified and acted upon numerous misuses of the Olympic words and emblems. Prior to the 1988 Winter Games in Calgary, the COA tracked down some 300 individuals, small businesses and large corporations, filing fifty-two lawsuits in the energetic attempt to protect the Olympic words, emblems and rings (QUINN, 1987). The COA has maintained the position that unauthorised use of the Olympic insignia has been illegal since 1981 when the Supreme Court of Canada recognised its exclusive right to all these insignia, granting it exclusivity under the Canadian Trademarks Act.

The intention here is to shed some light on the origin and evolution concerning the protection of the Olympic insignia and, more significantly, the present day efforts of the COA to protect those insignia from unlawful use. The Olympic Trust (the COA's arm) has been vigorous in its protection of the Olympic insignia, stating that "one of our greatest sources of revenue is licensing companies to call themselves the 'Official Olympic Company' or 'Official Olympic Supplier' in a particular category..." and if they did not protect their "official marks", they "... would be cutting... (their) own throats" (POSTHUMA, 1991, p.1).

Historical Review

Amidst the celebratory atmosphere of what was supposedly the fifth anniversary of the Union des Sport Athletiques, Pierre de Coubertin announced his resolution to bring about a revival of the Olympic Games. However, despite the applause of the French and foreign dignatories, according to Coubertin, no one in attendance really understood the meaning of his announcement. In his memoirs, COUBERTIN (1989) recalled that it was a period that lacked total comprehension of what was about to start, citing an American lady, who, after congratulating him on his achievement commented that she had "already watched Olympic Games...in San Francisco (and that)...Caesar was there" (p.6).

On 16 June 1894, in the inspiring main amphitheatre of the Sorbonne, Coubertin began to create the desired atmosphere that would ensure the revival's success (GUTTMANN, 1992). Delegates sat, mesmerised by the events that unfolded. The walls of the amphitheatre had been "graced" with Puvis de Chavannes' striking mural, *Sacred Copse*, while the ancient *Hymn to Apollo*, discovered in the ruins of Delphi and set to music by Gabriel Fauré, echoed forth. It was in this atmosphere that Coubertin knew no one could express the will to vote against the revival of the Olympic Games. Coubertin was right! On 23 June 1894, during the last session, the delegates voted unanimously to support a revival of the Olympic Games (DE COUBERTIN, 1989).

Two years later, in Athens, Greece's King George at the opening ceremony of the 1st Olympiad of the modern era, officially proclaimed the revival of the Olympic Games to all who had gathered. Cannons were fired and pigeons were released as choirs sang a cantata by the Greek composer Samara. The idea had become reality, but the most familiar symbols of the Olympic movement, such as the Olympic five rings and the motto 'Citius, Altius, Fortius' were still to come.

The 1896 Olympic Games were funded by stamps (22%), ticket sales, commemorative medals (11%), programme advertising and private donations (67%) (IOC MARKETING DEPARTMENT, 1994b, p.1). Kodak became one of the first companies to capitalise on an association with the Olympic Movement when it advertised its products in the official souvenir results book of the Athens Games. The Games, however, might have never been realised without the generosity of George Averoff, a wealthy Greek, who provided the money necessary for the restoration of the ancient stadium originally constructed by Herodes Atticus during the reign of Hadrian.

The commercial exploitation of the Olympic Games began soon after, as local entrepreneurial interests in the host nations began to capitalise on the emergent Olympic enthusiasm. The Games of the 2nd Olympiad were held in conjunction with the Paris Universal Exhibition, and the third Olympiad in 1904 with the St. Louis Exhibition, after it was generally agreed that the Games might add lustre to already gigantic celebrations. Though the 1906 intercalary Games in Athens avoided this association, they were staged to appease Greek frustrations over IOC refusal to accept Greece as the permanent site of the Olympic Games (GUTTMANN, 1992). The Fourth Olympiad, despite misgivings by Coubertin, continued the relationship between commercial interests and the Olympic Games by linking them with the Franco-British Exhibition inaugurated in London on 26 November 1906.

By this time, the IOC had become aware that the title "Olympic Games" had been freely utilised by the International Sports Federations (IFs) for their respective competitions. This abuse prompted Coubertin to request that efforts be undertaken to persuade the IFs to avoid all further use of the title in the future (IOC, 1910). The success of the Games of the fifth Olympiad in Stockholm two years later once again prompted greater attention by the IOC to the protection of the title "Olympic Games." Members at the 1913 IOC General Session meeting in Lausanne were told to verify that the title was not used in their prospective countries and, if discovered, immediately protest. One such abuse between organisers of an athletic meeting in Chicago, who had decided to call them *American Olympic Games*, was noted. In this instance, the organisers, responding to protests from American IOC members, decided not to use the title. The IOC, recognising the growing necessity to protect the title, established the following guidelines; the title *Olympic Games* could only be used in connection with the IOC's Olympic Games and the intermediate Athens Games taking place between the Games of the third and fourth Olympiad (IOC, 1913).

Determined to make the IOC's 20th anniversary of the Modern Olympic Movement celebrated at the Sorbonne monumental, Coubertin greeted delegates with the first public appearance of the Olympic flag. The Games of the seventh Olympiad on 14 August 1920 were the first in which athletes took the Olympic oath beneath the new Olympic flag with its five interlocking rings. These Games also included the first introduction of the Olympic motto *Citius, Altius, Fortius* (Faster, Higher, Stronger) (DE COUBERTIN, 1989), a phrase suggested by French cleric, Pere Henri Didon.

The IOC continued its reactive policy of identification and protest to protect the growing number of Olympic symbols. At the 1921 IOC General Session Meeting in Lausanne, Elias Y. Juncosa from Barcelona informed the delegates that the title *Olympiad Catalan* had been changed to *Jeux Catalans* (IOC, 1921). One year later at the Paris Session, Charles H. Sherrill, IOC member to the United States, requested the IOC officially to forbid the use of the words *Olympics* and *Olympiad*. Prompted by Sherrill's request, Coubertin conceded with regret that this was legally impossible; the IOC could only discourage their use (IOC, 1922).

A circular letter was then sent out to all NOCs and International Sport Federations (IFs) explaining the necessity of maintaining strict adherence to the IOC resolution, drawing attention to the designation *Olympics* as only quadrennial competition and to the term *Olympiad* technically applying to an interval of four calendar years, and not being used to designate any other competition (IOC, 1992). Information regarding the Olympic emblem was also distributed to all NOC's as a proactive measure in the hope of stopping its misuse. France and Hungary reported to the 1923 IOC General Session in Rome that they had already acquired legal protection of the emblem in their respective countries (IOC, 1923).

In 1925, the IOC elected Henri de Baillet-Latour President when the founder of the Modern Olympic Movement, Pierre de Coubertin, retired. The title of Honorary Life President of the Olympic Games was bestowed on Coubertin that same year in Prague. Unfortunately, 1925 also saw misuse of the word *Olympic* grow rapidly because of its considerable utility for promoting national prestige and local commercial growth GRUNEAU and CANTELON, 1995). Baillet-Latour, at both the 1925 General Session in Lisbon   and   the   Executive   Committee Meetings in Paris, reported that six new cases of abuse had been identified, including Olympic Games for Women and The Worker's Olympic Games (IOC, 1926). The IOC informed members from these organisations that the word *Olympic* was IOC property and that its use was forbidden. This contradicts Coubertin's admission at the 1922 Paris IOC General Session, where he stated that the IOC could only discourage the use of the words *Olympics* and *Olympiad*.

Continued reactive intervention by IOC members has been necessary throughout the world. On occasions, the IOC was successful in convincing a government that it had legitimate claim to the Olympic insignia as was the case with the Greek government, which accepted that the Olympic emblem and names are the property of the IOC (IOC, 1928). However, the conflicts have shown few signs of subsiding. Even with the advantage of precedent-setting cases such as the Helms Bakery Company vs. the United States Olympic Committee (USOC), the IOC has been unsuccessful in stemming the tide of Olympic exploitation (MARTYN, 1995). The symbolic connection within the public mind that exists between a commercial product and the Olympics for those exploiters is simply due to the lure of the almighty dollar.

Today, the Olympic movement is primarily financed through the sale of television rights (48%), sponsorship (34%), licensing (4%), ticket sales (10%) and coins and stamps (4%) (IOC MARKETING DEPARTMENT, 1994b), all of which are directly impacted by the unlawful use of Olympic insignia. The importance of the monies generated through sponsorship and commercialism to the Olympic Movement is illustrated in IOC Executive Board member, Richard W. Pound's assertion that sponsorship support and commercialisation have facilitated the growth of sport "... as an international phenomenon over the last 100 years" (IOC MARKETING DEPARTMENT, 1994b, p.2). The one over-riding fact is that Olympic sponsorship and commercialism is not as new to the Olympic Movement as some have contended.

The Canadian Olympic Association

The Canadian Olympic Association was founded in 1907 as a Committee of the Amateur Athletic Union of Canada (AAU of C). During its first twenty years of operation a number of structural changes occurred; however, its main duties remained the selection and promotion of the Olympic team and associated fund raising necessary to send these teams to the Olympic Games. COA independence came on 5 January 1950, after then COA President A. Sidney Dawes, a graduate of McGill University of Montreal, enlisted the support of IOC President Johannes Sigfrid Edström, and Vice-President Avery Brundage. The newly acquired independence paved the way for a new era in the administration of Canada's participation in the Olympic Games (WENN, 1990).

In September 1968, the COA chose Montreal as its candidate to bid to host the Summer Games. At the IOC 60th Session in May, 1970, Montreal secured the coveted 1976 Summer Games on the second ballot with a 42-28-1 majority over Moscow and Los Angeles respectively (GUTTMANN, 1992). Montreal's successful bid for the 1976 Summer Games acted as a catalyst for the COA's energetic attempts at protecting Olympic insignia. The COA, however, had not been operating in a vacuum: its members were well aware of the IOC's position regarding the protection of Olympic insignia. In a letter addressed to Otto Mayer dated August 27, 1949, President Dawes, responding to a circular concerning the protection of the Olympic words and rings, indicated that he was unaware of any abuse of these IOC marks in Canada. In September 1970, the COA in its official publication *Record* published an open letter to the members of the IOC, NOCs and IFs from Avery Brundage, President of the IOC:

It has come to our attention that organizations of various
kinds in different countries have recently arranged
competitions for school children or handicapped persons,
or for charitable purposes and have given to these
meetings the title "Olympics" in one form or another.

Some National Olympic Committees and Federations
have given their support, as they were perhaps organised
for highly commendable reasons.

We wish to remind you that the use of the word
"Olympic" or any of its derivations in connection with
sporting events should be restricted to the Olympic
Games, for obvious reasons. As a matter of fact, in some
countries this is the law and there are penalties for its
violation. In most instances, the promoters, when this has
been called to their attention, have refrained and used
another name to avoid confusion

(COA, 1970).

Understanding the international forum in which the Games would be
held, the Parliament of Canada assented to an Act respecting the 1976
Summer Olympic Games on 27 July 1973. This effort, however, would
have met serious opposition had it not been for the extensive
amendments to the *Olympic (1976) Act of the Parliament of Canada*
specifically relating *to Trade Marks and Symbols.* This newly amended
Act has been categorised as making the *Olympic Corporation* (i.e. the
Organising Committee) omnipotent when discussing Olympic trademark
and symbol protection within Canada. The Act, however, limited the
Olympic Corporation's power by defining its term: 13 June 1975 through
1 January 1977. This restriction left many within the COA concerned
about its ability to protect all of the Olympic insignia from unlawful use.
Yet another serious concern, was the definition of *Olympic Corporation*
assigned within the Act, leaving ownership of all Olympic-related
insignia in question. The COA sought help from Toronto lawyer Kenneth
McKay. Under the direction of the COA, McKay began to explore
avenues of trade-mark protection for the COA's *Official Marks.* Utilising
the Canadian *Trade-Marks Act,* McKay initiated formal procedures to
register the COA trade mark as a public authority under sub-paragraph

(iii) of s.9(1)(n). Unfortunately, the acting Registrar of Trade Marks refused the application on the grounds that the applicant did not qualify as a public authority. To qualify, the Registrar argued that a) there must be a duty to the public, b) there must be a significant degree of governmental control, and c) any profit earned must be for the benefit of the public and not for private benefit. (HUGHES, 1995). The applicant, McKay, appealed on behalf of the COA and sought to examine an official of the Trade Marks Office for discovery, but the appeal was rebuffed.

In November 1981, the COA's Federal Court appeal was allowed, thus, identifying it as a public authority within the contemplation of subparagraph (iii) of s.9(1)(n) of the Trade Marks Act. The judge's ruling recognised that:

> ... The appellant [COA] is a public authority within the contemplation of subpara. (iii) of s.9(1)(n) of the Trade Marks Act. The appellant (COA) is a non-profit organisation, which pursues objects of a public nature. The Canadian community wants those objects pursued. The appellant is, in fact, the only entity exercising the power to pursue those objects and is accepted by the community as exercising that power as of right
>
> (HENDERSON, 1981, p.53).

This victory was short lived as the Registrar of Trade Marks appealed. The sole issue in the appeal was whether or not the COA was to be considered a "public authority" entitled to be accorded the right to have its mark given public notice in accordance with subparagraph (iii) of s.9(1)(n) of the Trade-Marks Act. The Court upheld its original decision, finding that there was a sufficient degree of control exercised by the government over the activities of the COA to establish its public character as a "public authority".

Since the Federal Court decision recognising the COA's exclusive right to all Olympic insignia, the Olympic Trust has had the legal clout to restrict their use within the borders of Canada. Just having the exclusive rights to use these symbols is not enough to preserve exclusivity under Canadian Law. An organisation must demonstrate that it is actively protecting others from using them unlawfully (POSHTHUMA, 1991). In this regard, the COA has been vigorous in identifying and acting on misuses of the Olympic emblems and words. In a few cases, it has been so overzealous in protecting its symbols that it has led to negative publicity on a national level.

One such case was in October 1987, the COA and the XV Olympic Winter Games Organising Committee (OCO) filed an injunction against *Maclean's* magazine in an attempt to stop it from publishing a special issue devoted to the Games. They also sought $1 million in damages from the publication (LEWIS, 1997a). Eighteen days after filing the application for an injunction, the COA, along with the OCO, unconditionally withdrew its motion (LEWIS, 1997b). An official statement, however, retained the hard-line stance concerning the protection of the Olympic insignia: "... [the COA and OCO] will continue to have recourse for damages as a result of any unauthorized use of their official Olympic marks" (LEWIS, 1997b, p.51).

Not all cases have been so unwarranted and ill advised. In an action to enforce its rights over the "official marks" Calgary 1988 and the five interlocking rings, the COA applied for an interlocutory injunction to restrain Donkirk International Inc. from using the composite mark consisting of the expression *Calgary 1988*, three interlocking circles and two interlocking horse shoes (HENDERSON, 1988). Federal Court Judge J. Teitelbaum was so convinced of the COA's position that he made the following statement:

> ... I am satisfied that the registration of the defendant's (Donkirk International Inc.) trade mark was calculated to deceive or misled the public into believing that defendant's wares were wares produced by licensed manufacturers of plaintiff (COA). The defendant's mark so nearly resembles that of plaintiff's, unless one looks very carefully at the design, one would tend to believe the two horseshoes were two rings interlocked with the three other rings.
>
> I am fully satisfied that the plaintiff has shown by the evidence submitted a strong 'prima facie' case ... and that defendant's mark so nearly resembles, the two marks of

plaintiff, that it is not necessary for plaintiff, a public authority, to show irreparable harm nor that the balance of convenience is in its favour
(HENDERSON, 1988, pp.311-312).

The application for the interlocutory injunction by the COA over Donkirk International Inc. was granted.

Concluding Comments

The COA through its fundraising arm, the *Olympic Trust*, continues to pursue cases in which its marks and symbols are unlawfully infringed upon, and whose misuse would adversely affect its ability to generate revenues for the Canadian Olympic Movement. Without vigorous efforts to protect such symbols, the COA contends it "would be cutting (its) own throats" POSTHUMA, 1991, 1). Yet others exclaim the COA has been over zealous in its protectionist attitude. Iain Angus, MP for the riding of Thunder Bay-Atikokan, asked the House of Commons, "... What benefit could be derived to the Olympic Games, the organising committee or to Canada by threatening the Olympic Drywall Company or the Olympic Drilling Company?" (QUINN, 1987, p.61). The former federal Sport Minister Otto Jelinek has been quoted as saying: "... I think everyone will agree that they [the COA) went a little overboard" (POSTHUMA, 1991, p.61). Nevertheless, to those who have felt the wrath of the COA's lawyers like George Pantazopoulos, owner of *Ottawa's Olympian Dining Lounge*, the answer is simple: "... They come from Calgary, they call themselves Calgarians. Well, I come from Olympia, so I told them I was calling my place the Olympian and they could go to hell" POSTHUMA, 1991, p.61).

Today the COA has registered the rights to more than 200 words and symbols, capitalising on its identity as a public authority within the contemplation of subparagraph (iii) of s.9(1)(n) of the Trade Marks Act. The most obvious of these are the many forms of the word *Olympic* and the five interlocking rings, which enjoy extremely high public awareness. Because of this, commercialism has continued to grow and in so doing elevated the importance of Olympic insignia protection. To those sceptics who ask whether the commercialisation of the Olympic Games has gone too far, Andrew Young, Chair of the Atlanta Olympic Games Organising

Committee, adopted the view that "the commercialisation of sport is the democratisation of sport" (IOC MARKETING DEPARTMENT, 1994a, p.49).

As the Centennial Olympic Games in Atlanta approached, similar problems over Olympic symbol protection arose. This time, they concerned the Atlanta Committee for the Olympic Games (ACOG). One such example concerned Dave & Buster's Inc., when it advertised its local entertainment complex on a billboard featuring the slogan *Olympic-sized fun*. The company said it was innocently referring to "local pride" for the upcoming Olympic Games. The ACOG citing its trademark rights to "all things Olympic", advised Dave & Buster's to take down the sign immediately. "... We changed it, and none of us use the '0' word anymore..." said a spokesperson for Dave & Buster's "... not even in conversation" (FRANK, 1995).

According to the ACOG, the very survival of the Olympic Movement in the United States hinges on its ability to protect the Olympic words and symbols (THE ATLANTA CONSTITUTION, 1995). "... Sure, sometimes this doesn't make for the best PR..." says Darby Coker, a spokesperson for the ACOG, "... But the law doesn't discriminate between big or small, rich or poor. Those rights are the most important way we have of raising funds". Make no mistake, marketing has become an important issue for all within the Olympic Movement, and they will continue to "crack down hard on companies or individuals who might be impinging on Olympic trademarks" (FRANK, 1995).

Looking ahead to future Olympics, the Olympic Movement will need to continue to respond to those who would use the Olympic symbols without paying for the privilege. The symbolic connection between a commercial product and the Olympics, for those who would exploit them, is simply the lure of the almighty dollar.

References

CANADIAN OLYMPIC ASSOCIATION: Open letter. In: *Record*, 1(3), September 1970.

CANADIAN OLYMPIC ASSOCIATION: Olympic '76 - no finer legacy for our youth. In: *Record*, 3(1), March 1972, p.5.

DE COUBERTIN, P.: *Olympic Memoirs*. Trans. G. DE NAVACELLE, Lausanne, Comité International Olympique, 1989.

FRANK, R.: Olympic staffers crack down on users of games' name. In: *The Wall Street Journal*, 23 March 1995.

GRUNEAU, R., and CANTELON, H.: Capitalism, commercialism and the Olympics. In: BARNEY, R.K., *Issues in modern Olympic history: an anthology*. London, Centre for Olympic Studies, 1995, pp.206-216.

GUTTMANN, A.: *The Olympics: a History of the modern games*. Urbana-Chicago, University of Illinois Press, 1992.

HENDERSON, G.F., (Ed.): Canadian Olympic Association v. Registrar of trademarks. In: *Canadian Patent Reporter*, 59, 1981, pp.53-55.

HENDERSON, G.F., (Ed.): Canadian Olympic Association v. Donkirk International Inc. In: *Canadian Patent Reporter*, 1988, pp.299-312.

HUGHES, R.J., (Ed.): *Robic-Leger Canadian Trade-marks Act Annotated*. 1, 1995.

INTERNATIONAL OLYMPIC COMMITTEE: *General session minutes volume I 1894-1919*. Lausanne, IOC, 1910.

INTERNATIONAL OLYMPIC COMMITTEE: *General session minutes volume I 1894-1919*. Lausanne, IOC, 1913.

INTERNATIONAL OLYMPIC COMMITTEE: *General session minutes volume III 1920-1947*. Lausanne, IOC, 1921.

INTERNATIONAL OLYMPIC COMMITTEE: *General session minutes volume III 1920-1947*. Paris, IOC, 1922.

INTERNATIONAL OLYMPIC COMMITTEE: *General session minutes volume II 1920-1947*. Rome, IOC, 1923.

INTERNATIONAL OLYMPIC COMMITTEE: *General session minutes volume II 1920-1947.* Lisbonne, IOC, 1926.

INTERNATIONAL OLYMPIC EXECUTIVE COMMITTEE: *Minutes volume I 1921-1948.* Amsterdam, 1928.

INTERNATIONAL OLYMPIC COMMITTEE MARKETING DEPARTMENT: *1994 Olympic marketing fact file.* Lausanne, Switzerland, IOC, 1994a.

INTERNATIONAL OLYMPIC COMMITTEE MARKETING DEPARTMENT: 100 years of the Olympic Movement/100 years of Olympic marketing. In: *Marketing Matters*, 5, 1994b.

LEWIS, R., (Ed.): An Olympic struggle. In: *Maclean's*, 9 November 1987a, p.4.

LEWIS, R., (Ed.): Injunction withdrawn. In: *Maclean's*, 23 November 1987b, p.51.

MARTYN, S.G.: *Making dough, the Helms Bakery Company vs. the United States Olympic Committee on the issue of commercializing Olympic symbols, 1932 to 1953.* London, University of Western Ontario, 1995.

POSTHUMA, H., (Ed.): Olympic words and symbols: who do they belong to? In: *Olympinfo*, November 1991, pp.1-2.

QUINN, H.: Ceasing and desisting. In: *Maclean's*, 7 December 1987, p.61.

THE ATLANTA CONSTITUTION: *Individuals can't use symbols.* Editorial, 7 April 1995.

WENN, S.R.: A call to arms: a Sidney Dawes campaign for C.O.A. independence. In: *Canadian Journal of History of Sport*, XXI (29), December 1990, pp.33-46.

Chapter 25

An Analysis of Governmental Involvement in the Bids for the Summer 2000 Olympic Games

Daniel Kerry

Introduction

Prior to the summer Olympic Games of 1984 in Los Angeles, the hosting and running of an Olympic Games could be a considerably costly and risky business for the city and country involved. The murder of Israeli athletes in Munich in 1972, losses accrued by Montreal in 1976 and the boycott of the Moscow Games in 1980 had severely dented the glamour associated with hosting an Olympic Games. Los Angeles became the only viable bid for the 1984 Games and thus, placed the organising committee in a position of strength relative to the IOC. Peter Ueberroth, in charge of the L.A. bid, masterminded a re-allocation of revenues derived from hosting the Games and revamped the system of Olympic sponsorship. The result was a huge profit for Los Angeles and a successful Games despite the boycott by eastern bloc nations. Subsequently, there has been resurgence in interest in hosting the world's largest sporting event, with the bidding system and the Games themselves offering potential host cities economic gain and the respective governments, a useful political tool.

The bidding to host the Summer 2000 Olympiad was the most protracted in Olympic history. The candidate cities, Manchester, Beijing, Berlin, Istanbul, Brasilia (withdrawn) and Sydney, as well as the respective governments invested considerable resources into their bids despite the knowledge there could only be one winner. The rationale for such investment of time, money and political will within the sphere of Olympic bidding is examined here.

The Manchester 2000 Olympic Bid

On Wednesday 26th February 1992, then Prime Minister, John Major, and the Conservative Government pledged the sum of £55 million in support of Manchester's bid to stage the summer Olympic Games in the year 2000. By the time the bid was presented in Monaco 23 September 1993, this amount had increased to £75 million. This investment represented the single largest injection of money in the history of British sport by the central government. It also represented a considerable shift in policy from Mr Major's predecessor, Margaret Thatcher.

British cities had bid consecutively twice before for the Summer Olympic Games of 1992 (Birmingham) and 1996 (Manchester). The sum total of endorsement for the Birmingham and Manchester bids was in essence the bare minimum required by the IOC (HILL, 1992). Manchester remained well supported by its original sponsors for the 1996 bid and gained new investors. Robert Scott, the bid leader, was left with the task of trying to achieve what he had originally set out to do in the 1996 bid - that was to gain more credible government support. With Mrs Thatcher's resignation as Prime Minister and leader of the Conservative Party on 22 November 1990 and the election of John Major in her place, Scott's chances improved. Importantly, from Manchester's point of view, Major was seen to be a greater sports enthusiast than any of his predecessors. The initial £55 million backing of the Manchester 2000 bid was, therefore, breaking new ground. The British Government was actively supporting a British sporting campaign for which funds would be directly allocated. Mr Major had quite firmly associated with the bid, and would continue to do so. The importance of this fact was not lost on Robert Scott speaking outside 10 Downing Street alongside John Major after the news was broken:

> This is the first tranche, which will get us through the bidding process and to the vote in September 1993. If we win I'm quite sure there will be more, (Government money). We are at square one, on the starting line. Now it's the Government and Manchester against Beijing and their government and Sydney and the Australian government. It's a fair fight. It makes all the difference. We are on a level playing field now.
> (THE GUARDIAN, 1993a, p.1 and p.18)

John Major's own personal commitment was extensive. After the announcement outside 10 Downing Street, Major made further personal appearances in support of the Manchester bid, including a visit to the Barcelona Olympic Games and in a two day meeting with the IOC in Lausanne. His arrival in Monaco from Kuala Lumpur, after a tour of Australia and Asia, for the vote on 23 September 1993 and his impassioned personal speech at the final presentations of the bids to the IOC, were indicative of the seriousness of the government's commitment. Major also ensured that the rest of his government was fully involved in the effort. Michael Heseltine and later Michael Howard as Secretaries of State for the Environment co-operated closely with the bid team and Manchester City Council to ensure that the technical elements of the bid complied with the stipulations of the IOC. The official bid document included a personal letter of endorsement from the Prime Minister, plus an Environmental Charter prepared by Secretary of State, Howard. Members of the foreign office were also instructed to give any assistance necessary to the bid team, opening channels to international politicians and IOC members. As a result of such investment of government time and money, every detail of the 2000 project was checked by civil servants at the Department of the Environment. Why then did the Major Government, and John Major so personally, identify with the Manchester 2000 bid, whilst his predecessors had not?

At the time that John Major pledged £55 million in central government funds to the Manchester 2000 bid, Britain was facing its longest and deepest recession since the 1930's. With damaging statistics being published daily, the Government's reputation and the Prime Minister's personal popularity were rapidly diminishing. This scenario would have been bad enough at any point of a political party's time in office, but the whole situation was compounded by the prospect of a General Election. Within this context, the injection of central government funds into Manchester's bid can be viewed from a different perspective. The announcement of the Government's support of the Manchester Olympic bid by John Major on 26 February 1992 was carried on the front and back pages of every national newspaper. It represented a glimmer of good news amongst the dour tidings of the recession, something to divert attention, albeit temporarily, away from national problems. In terms of the General Election, therefore, it was a well-timed media event. The imminence of the General Election, announced only 13 days later on 11

March, made it virtually impossible for the Opposition to protest at a commitment of £55 million of taxpayers' money for fear of offending local and sporting sensibilities. At a personal level, John Major stood to gain much political deference from so closely associating with such a seemingly worthwhile cause, a view echoed in some sections of the national press (THE GUARDIAN, 1993c). John Major took an intentionally high profile in backing Manchester's bid, partly because he can sensed the political kudos and the Government almost certainly recognised that the geographical area, in which they were investing so much money, not only needed regeneration but also contained at least 10 marginal seats (THE GUARDAN, 1993a).

The Manchester 2000 bid presented the British government with another opportunity for potential pay back on its investment of time and money. One edict of the International Olympic Charter is that the hosting of an Olympic Games will provide the opportunity for urban regeneration of the Host City and the surrounding area, and possibly of the nation involved. In their bid document to the I.O.C., prospective cities must, therefore, make clear how hosting the Games will socially and economically benefit their particular city. The Government was fully aware of this fact, the bid providing the perfect vehicle for a programme of regeneration, which some had felt long overdue in Manchester. This potential for regeneration was cited, as the second objective of the environmental charter contained in the bid document. It was to prove a key element of the Manchester bid and Government strategy.

Manchester had long been established as one of Britain's premier cities, but the structural and economic changes that had affected much of the British economy over the last 40 years had also had their impact on Manchester and the North West regional economies. Unemployment in the area reflected the problems in the local economy, with Manchester as a city having an unemployment rate of 18%, with a rate in some districts, such as in the community surrounding the Eastlands' re-development site, (where the majority of events were to be held), of between 20 and 30% (THE FINANCIAL TIMES, 1993a). East Manchester was once the manufacturing heartland of the city but since the Second World War, it had been in decline. After the recession of the 1980s, traditional industries such as engineering and textiles had had little opportunity to revive. Urban regeneration for this area was needed on a large scale. The economic returns derived for Barcelona from the 1992 Olympic Games provided the spur. The government, under the guise of an Olympic bid, provided the initial momentum for this private sector investment. The bid provided a means for the government to start the ball rolling, reaping the rewards of private sector investment in an area that needed regeneration. The importance of this was that the Government was taking credit for what represented a small share of the actual investment in the area. Private investment into the bid, forthcoming after the introduction of government funds, actually totalled £200 million (THE FINANCIAL TIMES, 1993a, p.III). Effectively, the Government was getting a bargain.

What did Manchester, and the government actually secure for the efforts? On the Eastlands' site, where there once existed a derelict coalmine, gasworks and abandoned railway sidings, contractors cleared the site in preparation for a 65,000 capacity main stadium (originally the site for the 80,000-seater Olympic stadium). This proposed stadium had its design approved and £40 million of private sector funding was anticipated (THE FINANCIAL TIMES, 1993a, p.IV). One mile away, a 20,000 capacity indoor arena, one of the largest in Europe, was emerging beside Victoria station with work expected to be completed by the end of 1995. Also on the Eastlands' site, construction of 3,500 capacity velodrome (designated as the National Cycling Centre), which hosted the World Cycling Championships in 1996. Its unique design facilitates the capability of staging basketball, volleyball and badminton events. Riding on the back of these developments, as an indirect consequence of the bid, was the construction of a second airport terminal and rail link, a new concert hall and a new tram system. Manchester, as a consequence of the bid, has been left with a sporting, recreational and cultural legacy.

These facilities amounted to a considerable start to urban regeneration of East Manchester, an area that had suffered serious economic blight with the de-industrialisation of the 1980s. The 1996 Manchester bid had shown some evidence of providing some economic pay-off for Manchester hence, a more 'up-beat' 2000 bid represented a significant opportunity for urban regeneration of an area that the Government would have to redress sooner or later. The bid would ensure a catalyst of investment, creating a momentum of private sector support that would have been difficult to achieve without such a unifying force.

The British Government, therefore, was finding a new rationale for its intervention in sport, as a tool for redressing urban decay. The bid was not only a catalyst for tangible regeneration in the form of buildings and infrastructure. It created an air of optimism for business to come together and promote economic recovery in the area. Bearing in mind the recession that was embracing the UK, this was excellent news for the North West Region and for the government. A study conducted by accountant, Mr. Tim Johnston, specialising in urban regeneration and partnership between public and private sectors, emphasised the point that the "... international image of Manchester and north west England was improved during the 1996 bid. It has been enhanced by the 2000 bid, which is seen as even stronger and more exciting" (THE FINANCIAL TIMES, 1993b, p.11). Johnston estimated that about £200 million of expenditure, supporting 480 jobs would be created in the region as a result of the capital investment in new facilities, such as the velodrome and arena. Here would be enormous pay back for the government's investment in the bid.

In summary, it is evident that for the first time, sport in Britain was being vigorously and overtly used in promoting a sports populist image for the incumbent Prime Minister, John Major. The timing and scale of Government involvement was also used to maximum political advantage in an endeavour to generate public support in a forthcoming General Election in a geographical area containing ten marginal seats. Nevertheless, urban regeneration in the widest possible sense was the overriding justification for Government involvement. Sport was providing a 'social utility' function that has been particularly evident in the actions of successive British governments since the 1950s. The emphasis, however, now seems to be shifting to an all embracing 'urban regeneration' policy rather than one of purely 'social control'.

The Beijing Olympic Bid

In February 1991, the China Olympic Committee agreed to submit a bid to host the 27th Olympic Games in the year 2000. The Beijing municipal government and the State Physical Culture and Sports Commission jointly set up the Beijing 2000 Olympic Games Bidding Committee (BOBICO), which presented the city's application to the IOC in

December 1991. This was to be a Chinese Government funded and organised bid, fully in line with the 'central planning' characteristic of a communist regime. Wu Shaozu, China's Sports Minister, was made Executive President of BOBICO, and Chen Xitong, Mayor of Beijing and influential member of the Political Bureau of China's Communist Party Central Committee, the President. China was making its 2000 Olympic bid a central policy initiative. It became the most overtly political bid in sporting history. A point emphasised across wide sections of the broadsheet press for Beijing's bid was seen to be

> ... entirely different in concept from any other since the Olympic movement dared to take a risk with communism in 1974 when awarding the Games of 1980 to Moscow. Beijing has the models and the plans, but the motivation is entirely political
>
> (THE GUARDIAN, 1993d, p.23).

The primary philosophy behind the bid was that by holding the Olympic Games 2000 in China, the Government would, hopefully, have obtained a vehicle by which it could gain a great deal of international recognition. This would of course be international recognition of the positive variety, for the major obstacle that China faced in its bid for the Games was its human rights record. Chen Xitong, the mayor of Beijing and the man who ordered troops into Tiannamen Square, openly recalled the nationalistic reasons underpinning China's bid to British journalist, John Rodda:

> Giving the Games to China would be the most momentous decision the IOC has taken since Baron Pierre de Coubertin revived the movement. It would not only open the doors of China wider, bring the country more and more into contact with the West, but reduce the risk of confrontation ... If China is given the Games it will be a great chance not only for China but for the developing country as a whole
>
> (THE GUARDIAN, 1993d, p.23).

Nowhere in this discussion is the provision of a Games for the athletes, it was a decision motivated and run purely by politics. Repeated references to the opening of China to the world, a bid slogan of 'A More Open

China Awaits the Olympics 2000', were a constant drive to prove to the world that the Olympics would accelerate the process of change in China. The Beijing Review, a Chinese Government magazine published in English, constantly repeated these themes in its review of the Beijing bid:

Party General Secretary Jiang Zemin and Premier Li Peng announced on July 11 that Beijing's bid has been one of the symbols of China's deepening of reform and opening to the outside world. Beijing's bid for the Olympics shows political and social stability in China, and that the economy has developed and people's living standard improved" (BEIJING REVIEW, 1992, p. 4).

To enhance this image of political and economic reform, the Chinese Government was also seen to undertake some further propagandist measures. The release of a number of political dissidents, (among them Wei Jingsheng, leader of the pro-democracy demonstrations in Tiannamen Square), only eight days before the vote in Monaco, was seen by Western critics as an attempt at boosting Beijing's Olympic ambitions. A spate of world athletic records by Chinese female athletes was also seen as a further, and naïve, attempt to bolster the Beijing bid. The scale, nature and timing of these bids brought scepticism that these were drug-induced performances and seen as further evidence that China was not morally up to staging the Games. The Chinese administration then sought to counter this criticism claiming that revolutionary training techniques and diets of fresh turtle blood and a native fungus had been the source of success. What these measures did emphasise was that the Chinese Government was prepared to undertake any steps to enhance its chances of success at the IOC vote.

Much emphasis was also placed by the Chinese Government on the economic merits that both China and the West would gain from a Sino Olympic Games. The adoption of a 'private enterprise style economy' as part of the social and economic reforms of China was a major 'card' for the Beijing bid, one which was constantly played. Chen Xitong stated:

If we compare ourselves with the developed world we have only managed to feed and clothe our people, for although we are described as the third economic

power in the world we are in per-capita terms and living
standards very far behind many countries. The Games
would help take people off subsistence level
(THE GUARDIAN, 1993d, p. 23).

The deal for the West was particularly enticing, offering huge market
potential, which would supply Chinese needs and ease unemployment in
the West (THE GUARDIAN, 1993d, p. 23).

Indicative of the Chinese Government's drive for the Games was its
inclusion of preparatory Olympic projects in the National and Beijing 10-
Year Programme (1991-2000) and the Eighth 5-Year Plan (1991-95) for
national and economic social development (BEIJING REVIEW, 1993a,
p. 16).

Urban regeneration and environmental issues formed an important part of
the Beijing bid, and subsequently parts of the aforementioned plans. A
six-lane expressway from urban Beijing to the Capital Airport was to be
built, and upon its completion, the Capital Airport was to be expanded to
handle 15 million passengers. Expansion of the Beijing subway to the
planned Olympic village, an extended expressway from Beijing to
Tiannamen and Tanggu New Harbour and an extension and improvement
in the third and fourth ring roads planned for 2000 were only a few of the
projects aimed at improving infrastructure. Environmental improvements
were to include a 900km. long natural gas pipeline from Shaanxi to
Beijing. This was specifically aimed at reducing the levels of air
pollution from the burning of coal at power stations. It was rumoured that
local authorities ordered homes to douse their coal stoves to cut the smog
levels during the IOC inspection visit of Beijing. An 8-year re-
afforestation scheme was also established, with a goal of 40% vegetation
cover in the Beijing municipality, with 40sq.m. of vegetation per capita!
(BEIJING REVIEW, 1993b, p.17). The list of improvements planned
was seemingly endless, and all were, whether directly or indirectly,
related to the Olympic bid. All this was to be controlled and financed by
the central government. The infrastructural changes needed to hold the
Games were of an immense order, but few analysts doubted that the
Chinese Government with its unquestioned authority, wealth and public
mobilisation skills could finish the work on time. The Olympic bid was
overtly being used as a means of achieving the end gains of political

recognition, social and economic reform, and urban/environmental regeneration.

The Berlin Olympic Bid

The original idea of hosting the Olympic Games in Berlin was first conceived in the mid-1980s, and was publicly proposed by President Reagan as a way of uniting a city split by the Cold War and a means of uniting East and West. Then, East German leader, Eric Honecker, rejected the idea, but it was revived after the communists were swept from power and the opening of the Berlin Wall on 9 November 1989. The bid's philosophy was that the 2000 Games would give the city and country a world class stage to celebrate a unified and rebuilt Germany set to play a leading role in the post-Cold War Europe of the new century. The bid would provide an added stimulus for the process of economic unification of Germany.

The bid did have the backing of the German central government. Chancellor Helmut Kohl commented that the Games in Berlin would help heal the world-wide divisions caused by the Cold War, referring to Berlin as a symbol of the division of Europe over many years and which as a city could, therefore, be best "suited to breathe life into the Olympic spirit of peaceful competition and international understanding" (DIE WELT, 1993). However, government support ended with this personal backing. There was to be no central funds for the bid and private investment was set to provide all the necessary financial support. This, however, would not pose a problem to the Berlin bid team as finance was provided by a veritable who's who consortium of German big business, led by Daimler Benz, which pledged a $621 million loan guarantee to cover any losses made by the Games.

If private investment was in a position to provide the financial cover for the German bid, the German Government was not, at least that was the view of Finance Minister, Theo Waigel: "... With so many extra costs and burdens in the east and in Berlin, the government cannot spend additional billions on the Olympic Games" (THE GUARDIAN, 1993b, p. 6). This opinion was widely supported across large sections of the public, with opinion polls indicating that two-thirds of the German public were opposed to the bid (THE GUARDIAN, 1993b, p.6). Many held the view that money would be better spent on reconstructing the rundown eastern half of the city and creating jobs and houses. Further dissenting voices came from the Green Party, rejecting the Games possible association with the 1936 Olympics, as well as objecting on cost and environmental grounds. The intention to use the original stadium that staged the Nazis' 1936 Berlin Games, the Reichssportfeld, was the centre of considerable outrage. Many opponents of the bid believed that if the Games were brought to Berlin, it would provide a focal point for the resurgence of the neo-Nazi movement. This view was particularly poignant in that during the 20 months preceding the final IOC vote, 26 people had been killed in rightist attacks, almost half of them foreigners. Sports personalities Boris Becker and Katrina Witt added their voices to this particular concern. Manifestation of anti-Olympic sentiment came to a head in the form of a NOlympics' campaign. This was organised by Berlin's violent, left wing 'Autonomen' movement, which firebombed city department stores backing the Games, smashed windows of banks, and sent a video to IOC members featuring a masked man preparing to hurl a stone saying: "We will be waiting for you". In the city's Prenzlauer Berg district, NOlympics activists painted a three-storey high wall mural, which showed a dead and bleeding Berlin Olympia Bear being roasted on a spit.

Chancellor Kohl was, therefore, in an awkward position. The prospect of the Games presented an ideal opportunity to enhance the process of social and economic unification of Germany. It would make political sense to pursue such a policy, with the possibility of so much private investment into an Olympic Games, boosting large areas of Berlin and the former East German economy. However, this policy would add to the further alienation of the citizens of the former West Germany, who felt that they had already paid a large price in taxes for the process of unification with the East. National finances were generally perceived not to be in a position to support a multi-billion dollar event such as the Olympic Games. This ground-swell of public anti-Olympic sentiment, combined with the threats from neo-nazi's and the left wing 'NOlympics' campaign, was probably the reason for the luke-warm reception that the German Government gave the Berlin bid. It would not make political sense to financially support an event that was not wanted by two-thirds of the German electorate. Vocal support would have gone some way to appeasing the third of the electorate that was keen for the Games to come to Berlin, especially as Berlin would not require central public funds, as significant private investment would provide the backing. Within this context of German politics in sport, we have seen a juggling act in trying to maintain popular support for the bid. On the one hand, Chancellor Kohl was personally supporting the bid, as its success could provide an economic investment in the protracted process of economic unification with former East Germany. A successful bid and subsequent Games would also provide political symbolism of a unified and rebuilt Germany set to play a leading role in the new Europe and the world beyond. On the other hand, the lack of central funding may be viewed as an attempt to keep that sector of the electorate concerned over the cost they were paying for unification satisfied in the knowledge that taxpayers money would not be needed for the bid or Games.

The Istanbul Olympic Bid

The chance of the outsider, Istanbul, of securing any hope of hosting the 2000 Olympic Games rested on Turkey's predominantly Muslim population and devoutly secular constitution prompting an 'Islamic bloc' vote within the IOC. Traditionally, regional solidarity has played an influential role in the early stages of an IOC vote but this has become a decreasing phenomenon. Istanbul's catch phrase, "Let's meet where the continents meet", stemmed from its unique geographical position linking Europe with Asia. The bid officials made much of this, pointing to a first ever chance to simultaneously hold the Games on two continents, "emphasising the values of the Olympic movement as humanity crosses the threshold into the next millennium" (Anon).

Despite the impressive rhetoric, Istanbul never rose above 'long shot status'. Notwithstanding this, the Turkish Government played a full role in the bid. In April 1993, the Turkish parliament ratified a Bill, which identified and provided funding for the organisation of the Games. The income was to be derived from the sports and national lotteries, horse racing and an annual allocation from the consolidated budget. The parliament also passed a unique Olympic law providing the national IOC rights over the Olympic logo, important in a country with rudimentary trademark cover, and pledged to make up any shortfall in revenues stemming from the Games. The law also provided the national Olympic

Committee with the authority to go ahead with the bid even if the municipality or national governments had changed. In addition, the bid team was allowed free acquisition of state owned land for many of the proposed Olympic facilities. Mrs. Tansu Cillier, Turkey's first woman Prime Minister, also personally backed the bid, canvassing IOC members on their visits to Istanbul and making the trip to the IOC vote in Monaco, alongside the British and Australian Prime Ministers.

The Turkish Government expected a successful bid for the Games would precipitate massive redevelopment of Istanbul's infrastructure, and provide the incentive to progress political and economic reforms. Istanbul has a dire infrastructure problem, exacerbated by chronic traffic delays and pollution. Bid proposals included the increased supply of natural gas to help combat air pollution, a plan to transfer traffic to new ring roads and increase the capacity and variety of mass transit facilities. With the completion of the subway system under construction, the residential areas would become tied to work centres in the city, reducing traffic congestion. These initiatives, combined with the planned sporting facilities, would leave a legacy of infrastructure that has been commonly viewed as desperately overdue in Istanbul.

A major obstacle to the Turkish bid was the problem of Turkey's image. Years of military rule and a non-progressive economy had taken their toll. Turkey's ability to hold such a massive sporting extravaganza as the Olympics was questioned in many quarters. Opposition was also voiced by Human Rights organisations, with torture allegations and the on-going Kurdish 'Separatists' issue topping the list of concerns. The London-based organisation, Amnesty International, in its report of November 1992, claimed political killings were common, almost daily events in Turkey. Officials denied that torture was systematic and argued that individual cases were brought to courts. On the Kurdish issue, government officials claimed that Turkish troops were fighting the illegal Kurdistan Workers Party (PKK) in the south-east, where they had attacked villages. Since August 1984, some estimated 6000 people had been reported killed in PKK related violence. These issues, however, did not seem to weigh as heavy on the minds of the IOC and media as the 'image' problem already mentioned. Such was the extent of this antipathy that, in spite of a technically sound proposal, Istanbul would always remain an also-ran for the 2000 Olympics.

The Sydney Olympic Bid

Sydney's efforts to pursue the 2000 Olympic Games began in 1990 after Melbourne lost its bid to host the event in 1996. At that time, the New South Wales State government put up $7 million with the stipulation that the private sector would have to match it. The private sector was able to raise $9.8 million and Prime Minister Keating pledged $3.5 million of central government funds to the bid effort. Nick Greiner, who at the time was the Premier of New South Wales, raised $8 million in state funds from the state's horse racing proceeds, (betting tax), that normally went into state coffers. This effectively minimised the cost to the taxpayers.

In relative terms, Sydney's bid came as close to perfect as possible. The city's population of 3.5 million supports 140 ethnic groups, which guaranteed support from many members of the Olympic family. Additionally, it enjoyed a sports-mad population, near perfect climate, fine facilities and strong political backing. The IOC Enquiry Commission's technical report verified this, placing Sydney ahead of the other bidding cities on technical merit. Sydney's bid also projected the lowest, and some felt most realistic, revenues and spending for the 2000 Olympiad, with estimated income at $975 million, including $488 million from television rights, $207 million from local sponsorship and $139 million from tickets. The organisers estimated that the Games would cost $960 million to host thus, making a theoretical surplus of $15 million. In pursuing the bid, Sydney was the only city to win unconditional approval from all 25 international federations for the sports involved in the Games. Sydney also minimised the one negative variable that critics viewed could upset the staging of an Australian Games: union upheaval. Michael Easson, Secretary of the Labour Council of New South Wales, promised in writing that there would be no labour disputes to prevent the Olympic facilities in the Homebush region of Sydney, (where the athletes housing would be), from being completed on time and within budget.

Additional central government funding was made available to the bid team in 1991, when Sydney became established as a front-runner in the race. A federal government loan of $207 million was made available and the state of New South Wales provided an extra $17.25 million for expenses and agreed to underwrite any shortfall. Paul Keating, as the bid progressed, became more personally involved in the bid process, culminating in his appearance and speech in the final presentations to the IOC in Monaco on 23 September 1993.

Justification for Government and state investment was that the bid and the Games would provide a means of boosting the country's building and tourist industries. This rationale for government expenditure in Olympic bids is in line with the general economic and urban regeneration rationale prevalent in all the Olympic bids. Economic, and hence, political gain can be derived from the hosting (and bidding for) the Olympic Games. The Sydney bid also provided the opportunity for political benefit on a personal level for Australian Prime Minister Paul Keating. Keating during this period, and subsequently, made repeated calls for Australia to become a Republic, independent of Great Britain, and to remove the Queen as Head of State. This issue had divided the country. In some quarters, it was regarded as a diversionary issue to remove public attention from the present Australian government's handling of the recession, and as a means of ensuring Paul Keating would go down in the annals of Australian history. A successful bid, supported by the Australian government and Keating personally, would be a powerful symbolic gesture of Australia as an independent country in its own right. Keating, in his address to the IOC at Monaco, made clear his view of what effect hosting the Games would have: "... There couldn't be a greater indication to the world that Australia is a nation with its own identity, there in its own right. Australia must now become a Republic for the new millennium" (THE GUARDIAN, 1993e, p.1)

Conclusion

The submissions made to the International Olympic Committee by the cities of Beijing, Berlin, Istanbul, Sydney and Manchester to host the Games in the year 2000 all had considerable investment of central government funds and resources, with the anticipation of reaping some form of economic and political gain. Such gains come in the form of political kudos for the individual politicians concerned; international recognition and inward investment for the city/region/country; and significant potential for urban regeneration for the potential host city. It was this latter rationale that was the recurring theme in the bids for the

2000 Games. It was also a theme, which underpinned and pervaded bidding cities' hopes of hosting the 2004 Olympic Games.

References

BEIJING REVIEW: *Beijing's bid for the Olympics supported.* 20 July 1992, p.4.

BEIJING REVIEW: 1 March, 1993a, p.16.

BEIJING REVIEW: *China is capable of hosting the Olympic Games.* 17 March, 1993b, p.17.

DIE WELT: *Commentary.* 25 August 1993.

HILL, R: *Olympic Politics.* Manchester, Manchester University Press, 1992.

THE FINANCIAL TIMES: *Survey of Manchester and the Olympics* (1-3). 23 June 1993a, pp.III-IV.

THE FINANCIAL TIMES: *Defeated City counts its blessings.* 24 September 1993b, p.11.

THE GUARDIAN: *Major gives £55 million to Olympic bid.* 27 February 1993, p.1 and p.18.

THE GUARDIAN: *Berlin asks Gipper to pitch for Games.* 18 August 1993, p.6.

THE GUARDIAN: *China's final punch packs a heavy global warning.* 23 September 1993, p.23.

THE GUARDIAN: *Sydney wins right to stage Olympiad 2000.* 24 September 1993, p.1.

THE GUARDIAN: *'The City', centre of recovery.* 6 September 1993, Supplement pp.7-10.